THE JOURNALS OF
JOSEPH N. NICOLLET

—◆•■◆—

A Scientist on the Mississippi Headwaters
With Notes on Indian Life, 1836-37

TRANSLATED FROM THE FRENCH BY
André Fertey

EDITED BY
Martha Coleman Bray

MINNESOTA HISTORICAL SOCIETY · ST. PAUL

LIBRARY OF CONGRESS CATALOG CARD NUMBER: 70–632235
STANDARD BOOK NUMBER: 87351–062–3

The editor of this book was aided by research grants from the American Philosophical Society of Philadelphia and from the Minnesota Historical Society's McKnight Family Endowment research fund.

Translator's Preface

THE OPPORTUNITY to contribute in a small way to the publication of Joseph N. Nicollet's journals came to me in the form of an avalanche of photocopies. Although the often puzzling sheets had been sorted and arranged by the editor before they reached me, I regarded with some misgivings the imposing array of nineteenth-century French in Nicollet's longhand. Embarking with him upon one of history's most eventful waterways, my misgivings promptly turned into admiration. For this lonely Frenchman did not live in the days of the fountain pen, the ballpoint, or the tape recorder. He wrote the journals here printed in an unsteady canoe launched upon unpredictable waters, or assailed by mosquitoes in the cramped space of a tent by the dim glow of hesitant candlelight. His uncertain health often failed him. I concluded that Nicollet's material deserved all the care and insight I could give it.

Longhand manuscripts composed under such circumstances have their disadvantages. A man's writing can become small and neglectful, *pattes de mouche*, as the French say. But only on a very few trying occasions did Nicollet's hand become totally illegible. My closest allies in the deciphering process were the editor, Mrs. Martha Bray, who somehow managed to wade through many of the handicaps and who checked and often improved my English translation, Nicollet's magnificent map and report on the Upper Mississippi, and a magnifying glass, which became my constant companion.

Nicollet wrote a good, clear, formal French which presented no problem in itself. His handwriting, which is distinctive, was difficult to decipher at first, but it was astonishingly consistent and one could rely on the formation of individual letters wherever they were found. The principal problems of Nicollet's French were his old-fashioned spelling (such as *tems* for *temps*), his vocabulary, and his use of expressions now not common. For these, various nineteenth-century

v

dictionaries, especially the four volumes of the *Dictionnaire de la langue française* by E. Littré (1881 edition), generously lent me by a friend, proved invaluable in unlocking a few knotty puzzles.

These pounds of helpful information, however, were frequently not enough. One of the great trials in translating Nicollet was the virtually total lack of samples of his writing in English. Nicollet thought and wrote in French except in the most routine matters. In spite of his long stay in the United States, he was not really bilingual, and only two complete personal letters and a few, formal, routine notes are known to exist in English. His published report cannot be regarded as a reliable guide, for it, too, is a translation.

The photocopies, which originally constituted a notebook, often appeared to be out of sequence no matter how they were arranged, for Nicollet occasionally wrote on separate sheets loosely inserted. And Nicollet's style offered many translating problems. In the first place, it tended often to be redundant. It is odd that a man having so little time would express himself in so repetitive a way while jotting down field notes. Yet he probably did so for the sake of extreme clarity, and when one got right down to it, his style was difficult to condense. Although a sentence seemed to contain excessive words, Nicollet was a man of extraordinary precision, and there seemed always to be a reason for his apparently redundant way of expressing himself. Writing in haste and combining description with narrative, he frequently mixed past and present tense in bewildering succession. To this, however, the journals owe some of their vigor and immediacy, and it seemed best to retain Nicollet's changes of tense except where they became positively confusing. Nevertheless, the material here presented is not a literal translation of Nicollet's French. As Mrs. Bray has pointed out, Nicollet had a romantic turn of mind and often expressed himself in fanciful flights of language. To the best of my ability I have tried not only to convey into the English idiom exactly what Nicollet had to say, but I have also tried to reproduce the style, tone, and quality of his expression and feeling — perhaps one could say, the soul of the man on this journey.

In this task I have been greatly aided by others, especially by Mrs. Bray. For Nicollet led us into such esoteric domains as geology, fauna, vegetation, philosophy, and, hardest of all, Indian languages. While the substance of the journals caused little problem, botanical phrases and animal identifications were often puzzling — not to say insoluble without the help of those more familiar with the terrain than I. Mrs. Bray and I struggled together with many of the Indian words. Although these portions of the manuscript were the most difficult, I enormously enjoyed this aspect of the work. Since the phonetic Indian terms were different to a Frenchman, I spent much time compiling what became long Indian-language lists of words in the manuscript so they could be plainly read and spelled consistently. Even so, other sources of information—books, consultations, and visits to museums—were often necessary.

If handwritten manuscripts have their disadvantages, they also offer the opportunity of intimacy with the author. Although this translation was done from a photocopy, which however clear is not as clear as the original, it still contained the scratches, errors, and smudges which bring to life impulses, hesitations, wanderings of mind, and so many other things one misses in print. While they often presented a challenge to the translator in successfully reconstituting faded paragraphs, they also provided him with rewarding experiences.

I am grateful to the Minnesota Historical Society for the opportunity to translate Nicollet's journals and to Mrs. Bray for her help at every stage. I hope that I have done justice to Joseph Nicollet and that this book will open yet another door to the Mississippi's past at a time when its waters still ran pure.

ANDRÉ FERTEY

St. Paul, Minnesota
August 19, 1970

Editor's Preface

THE REPUTATION of Joseph N. Nicollet (1786-1843) as a scientist and geographer has rested for well over a century on his *Map of the Hydrographical Basin of the Upper Mississippi River*. It was printed in 1843 by the Senate (number 380 in the serial set of United States government documents) and again in 1845 by the House of Representatives (serial 464). Each printing was accompanied by a *Report Intended to Illustrate a Map of the Hydrographical Basin of the Upper Mississippi*, containing sixty-seven pages of text plus an explanation of methods, tables of geographical positions, distances, and various other historical and scientific data compiled by Nicollet. The Frenchman's last two expeditions to the region lying between the Mississippi and Missouri rivers were made in the summers of 1838 and 1839 under the authority of the United States War Department. Nicollet's report is addressed to Colonel John James Abert, chief of the Corps of Topographical Engineers, newly formed under the War Department.

The existence of the original plates used in printing the map, which are still in the possession of the Army Corps of Engineers, has made possible a modern reprint of this classic of American cartography. It was issued by the Minnesota Historical Society in 1965. The *Report*, however, is less well known. Densely packed with information, it continues to be rediscovered from time to time by scholars interested in the physical aspects of the country it describes, but to the general reader it presents a formidable challenge. Abert had returned the manuscript to Nicollet for reorganization, but he was too ill to finish the work, and the report as it stood was translated by a friend and published after the explorer's death in 1843.

Nicollet's official papers, nearly all of which were in French, were deposited with the Corps of Topographical Engineers, where they lay untouched until 1921, when the old War Department records were moved to new quarters and scholars were called in to identify the contents of a dusty box with iron handles which had a "very European look." The manuscripts here published for the first time are among those eventually transferred to the Library of Congress. These papers include correspondence; the St. Croix journal; a few scattered pages from what was apparently a personal notebook, the rest of which is lost; sketches for the map; collections of collateral material which Nicollet intended to use as reference for a great work on the history of the Mississippi Valley; and the important astronomical and meteorological notebooks, which reveal his methods of work and the chronology of his travels. The latter are of two kinds: the field notebooks and the more elaborate but less interesting calculations made at his leisure. The National Archives holds all of the full-scale Nicollet maps, published and unpublished, among them the manuscript map of the "Sources of the Mississippi," which the scientist made during his stay at Fort Snelling in 1836–37.

Two of the groups of documents published in this volume — the journal of a trip to the sources of the Mississippi and the Indian materials on separated sheets in no particular order — were at some time unaccountably dissociated from Nicollet's other papers and came eventually to rest in the Library of Congress among the papers of Henry Rowe Schoolcraft, who explored the sources of the Mississippi in 1832. There they were discovered only a few years ago by John Francis McDermott, research professor of history at Southern Illinois University, in the course of his own untiring investigation into the history of the Mississippi Valley.

The full extent of Nicollet's notes on the Indians cannot now be ascertained. According to Abert, they included material on the Choctaw and Osage as well as dictionaries and grammars of the Dakota and Ojibway languages. In 1840 Nicollet submitted to the American Philosophical Society a manuscript entitled *"Suite des notions sur la langue des Sioux,"* but shortly afterwards he requested that it be returned for revision, a request with which the society complied. Whether this paper contained more than the meager lists of Sioux vocabulary found among his official papers cannot be determined. A month after Nicollet's death, Abert wrote (November 4, 1843) that the scientist's "unfinished notes" had been given to one Dr. J. L. Martin to prepare for publication. The following April, Dr. Martin received payment from the government for this work, but the results of it have not come to light nor have the original notes which were sent to him — though the observations here published may have been among them.

I was led to Nicollet's papers by a desire to discover something about a man whose name evoked so much respect among historians but whose work was so little known even in Minnesota, the locality which had benefited most by it. As I read his agonizingly hurried and compressed *Report*, I sensed an intellect and a passion which is seldom found in routine government documents. Here was some volatile substance which could not be contained within such a constricted form.

Out of material which justifies a longer study of Nicollet's life and work in the United States I have selected for translation and publication these manuscripts dealing with his first visit to what is now Minnesota. The two journals comprise an almost complete record of this unofficial exploration. The Indian notes are of obvious value, providing observations of the Chippewa at a crucial period in their history. Together, the documents give us a view of a distinctive geographical region in an era that seems more distant from our own in its ways of life and thought than the passage of only a hundred years suggests. Also — and not less important — they reveal a man of extraordinary character and wide-ranging intellectual powers at the beginning of his American explorations, before he was assisted — and limited — by his appointment to government service. Since Nicollet did not live to present his own work as he would have liked it to appear, it is my hope that these manuscripts will speak across the years as nearly as possible within the context of his own experience and point of view. As I read the 1836 journal, I was rewarded by one of the few sentences Nicollet wrote in English. It is a reflection which inspired and gave direction to his life, and one which I often recalled as I tried to piece together this remarkably individual experience of the North American wilderness in the 1830s. On a scrap of paper Nicollet had written hastily, "He will triumph who understands how to conciliate and combine with the greatest skill the benefits of the past with the demands of the future."

In the introduction I have tried to set forth for the reader some of the little-known circumstances of Nicollet's life and to sketch the general framework of American geographical knowledge within which he worked in 1836–37. The substance of the Mississippi diary appears in Nicollet's *Report*, but a systematic correlation of the two accounts appeared to me to add little to an understanding of the narrative. When comparison seemed important, I have so indicated in a footnote, and when personal observations found in the astronomical notebooks of Nicollet added to the sense or color of the account, I have incorporated them into the text with appropriate designation.

The greatest editorial problem in relation to the diaries was the identification on modern maps of the geographical features mentioned by Nicollet. For most of this labor I am indebted to my husband, Edmund C. Bray, whose interest and patience were unflagging. For the Minnesota area, the best modern maps for this purpose are the *General Highway Maps of the Counties of Minnesota*, issued by the state department of highways. Only in northern Wisconsin did we have the added benefit of the United States Geological Survey maps. The lakes and forests of the upper Mississippi and St. Croix have changed relatively little in the more than one hundred and thirty years since Nicollet described them; much of the area is still inaccessible except by water. Modern damming and draining, however, have altered some natural features — rapids, islands, river courses, and even the size and shape of lakes. Also, according to weather records, the summer of 1836 was one of high water. Some lakes and streams described as large by Nicollet are therefore much smaller today, if they exist at all.

Where the modern name of a feature is known, it has been inserted in the text in brackets following the name as it appears in the journal. Those which either are not shown or are unnamed on modern maps or which might from Nicollet's description be any of several similar ones are labeled as unnamed or unidentified. Where the name in use has not changed, no notation appears.

Nicollet's attention to geographical names cannot be overemphasized. It constitutes one of the main reasons for present-day interest in his map. Occasionally, as he explained in his journal, Nicollet himself named a lake or stream in honor of a friend or a noted scientist. More often, he attempted to learn and preserve the Indian name for it. In recording these Indian words, however, the explorer set down widely varying spellings. This is apparent in a comparison of the journals, the unpublished map of the sources of the Mississippi in the National Archives, the astronomical notebooks, and the published map of 1843. Nicollet wrote as a heading in his astronomical note-book for his trip up the Mississippi that the names of places where he made observations "are given in this register as those which I adopt and which I intend to use on my map." Therefore, when such a name appears in his astronomical notebook, it has been given pref-erence in the text. For the convenience of those who are interested in the derivation of geographical names and those who wish to com-pare Nicollet's journal and notebooks with his maps, a table of names compiled from these sources has been supplied in an appendix.

With Nicollet's journal was found a table entitled "*Suite de table géographique des tributares du Mississippi*, etc." It included a list of mileages above the mouth of the Minnesota River. He used the more important of these in his *Report*, simply adding the distance from the Minnesota to the mouth of the Mississippi. An appendix shows Nicollet's mileages in comparison with those given by the United States War Department, Corps of Engineers, in *The Middle and Upper Mississippi River* (Washington, 1940). When distances are given in the journal itself, footnotes indicate the corresponding figure given by the Corps of Engineers. Distances appearing in the journal are substantially the same as those in Nicollet's published *Report*.

The Indian materials presented quite another editorial problem. Even to place the pages in logical and comprehensible sequence was a task requiring some months. The final arrangement of the chapters was determined by what appeared to be the order in which Nicollet composed them. A number of miscellaneous notes seemed to fall into no such order, and the most substantial of these have been placed in an appendix.

Ethnological studies written after Nicollet's time have been con-sulted, but they have not been used here to evaluate Nicollet's work, which is presented within the context of his time and background. Comments on Indian customs from contemporary sources are intro-duced only when Nicollet himself makes a comparison between his own observations and those of others. Incidents of intertribal war-fare referred to by Nicollet could not be further identified in every case. There were constant skirmishes, and contemporary sources give widely varying descriptions of them.

All Indian words have been italicized except those which, like manito and moccasin, are commonly accepted in current American usage. Personal and geographic names of distinctively Indian form not now in common use are italicized when they first occur but not thereafter. Nicollet's ear for Indian vocabulary was remarkably good, and many of the words he used are easily found in later sources on the Ojibway language. Others apparently did not make their way into standard dictionaries or were interpreted so differently as to make them unidentifiable. Specific comparisons have been made only when important discrepancies existed or when different interpretations seemed particularly revealing. Nicollet frequently used phonetic symbols but sometimes failed to include them with every repetition of a word. Whenever they were indicated once, they have been supplied in other occurrences of the same term. Nicollet's y and j often appeared identical. In Indian words the editor has transcribed them as seemed most logical.

Having been drawn into my study of Nicollet by the appeal of his comprehensive and imaginative view of geography, I soon found, as every student does, that the only approach to my subject lay through the relentless brambles and thickets of detail. I would soon have disappeared therein had I not received desperately needed help and advice from many people more patient, skillful, and knowledgeable in many areas of research than I. For the existence of this volume, I have first of all to thank Professor McDermott, who blazed the trail through the Nicollet papers in the Library of Congress, unearthed the other materials in the Schoolcraft collection, and generously shared his discoveries with me. I appreciate also the co-operation extended to me by the Library of Congress, which holds all of the original manuscripts here printed in translation. Although Nicollet's contribution to geology figures only briefly in these early expeditions, I would like to mention the special debt I owe to Dr. George W. White, research professor of geology, University of Illinois, Urbana, for aid which enabled me to evaluate Nicollet's work in this field.

Unfortunately all of the assistance I received in research which has contributed to my understanding of Nicollet's life and work cannot be appropriately acknowledged here. My thanks go especially, however, to Mrs. Frances Stadler of the Missouri Historical Society, St. Louis, for her cheerful answers to my many letters, and to Mrs. Mary Lee Spence, assistant editor of the John Charles Frémont papers, University of Illinois Press, who helped clear up a number of obscure points. Mrs. Karen Petersen, of St. Paul, who needs no introduction to scholars interested in the culture of the American Indian, was among those who encouraged me to recognize the value of Nicollet's contribution to this field. Others who willingly responded to my queries from time to time include Donald B. Lawrence and Thomas Morley of the Botany Department, James R. Beer of the Entomology Department, Walter E. Parham and Glenn B. Morey of the Geology Department, and Frederic C. Battell of the Forest Service Library—all of the University of Minnesota; and Bruce R. Erickson and Kevin Marx of the Science Museum of St. Paul.

In the labor of reordering Nicollet's papers, I was financially assisted by a grant from the American Philosophical Society which enabled me to have photocopies made for my own use. The work of editing and translating the documents for this volume was materially assisted by a grant from the Minnesota Historical Society's McKnight Family Endowment research funds in 1968.

To the copies of Nicollet's papers gathered by the manuscript department of the Minnesota Historical Society I returned again and again as I proceeded with my research, and Miss Lucile M. Kane, curator of manuscripts, was more than helpful in procuring for me copies of many additional documents. The translation of the St. Croix River journal was facilitated by a transcript of the original prepared by Mr. and Mrs. James Taylor Dunn during the course of research for Mr. Dunn's book, *The St. Croix: Midwest Border River.* I am grateful to Mr. Michael Brook, chief of reference in the Minnesota Historical Society's library, and to his staff for service beyond the call of duty and to Miss Betty Engebretson of the Minneapolis Athenaeum Library for her knowledgeable bibliographic assistance. Finally, to the careful and creative help of Mrs. Rhoda R. Gilman, the society's assistant managing editor, I owe the astonishing transformation of my manuscript into a book.

MARTHA COLEMAN BRAY

St. Paul, Minnesota
August 12, 1970.

Contents

Illustrations

THE JOURNALS OF
JOSEPH N. NICOLLET

Editor's Introduction

JOSEPH NICOLAS NICOLLET was born on July 29, 1786, in the French mountain village of Cluses in Savoy. The familiar story is that he was brought up by poor and perhaps illiterate parents, that when he was twelve years old he attracted the attention of a kindly priest who was drawn to him "by his graceful figure, the liveliness of his eyes and his intelligent manner."[1] It has recently been made clear, however, that as the fifth child of an innkeeper, who before the Revolution of 1789 was a skilled watchmaker, and as the godson of a schoolmaster, Joseph received adequate early instruction. At the age of eleven or twelve he was admitted, with one brother and a cousin, to a school for the training of future seminarians, a school whose enrollment was strictly limited to excellent scholars.[2]

Nicollet then pursued his studies in the Jesuit college in the medieval city of Chambéry. Gifted in mathematics and in that queen of eighteenth-century sciences, astronomy, he eventually became an astronomer at the Bureau of Longitudes in the Royal Observatory in Paris. Here he was a favored protégé of the aging director of the bureau, Pierre Simon Laplace, who had managed (not without considerable agility of principle) to maintain his prestige and many official

[1] Joseph F. Michaud, ed., *Biographie universelle*, Supplement, 75:373 (First Edition, Paris, 1811–57). This and all other quotations from French sources have been translated by the editor unless otherwise noted.

[2] F. Hette Casanova, great-grandniece of Joseph Nicollet, to the editor, May 25, 1969. The letter includes appropriate documentation from the records of the province of Savoy. For additional sources on Nicollet's European background, discussed in the following three paragraphs, see Martha Coleman Bray, "Joseph Nicolas Nicollet, Geographer," in John Francis McDermott, ed., *Frenchmen and French Ways in the Mississippi Valley*, 29–42 (Urbana, Ill., 1969). Other biographical accounts are: Henry H. Sibley, "Memoir of Jean [*sic*] N. Nicollet," in *Minnesota Historical Collections*, 1:146–156 (St. Paul, 1902); *Dictionary of American Biography*, 13:514 (New York, 1934); Newton H. Winchell, "Jean [*sic*] N. Nicollet," in *American Geologist*, 8:343–352 (December, 1891).

positions through the turmoil of French politics since the Revolution of 1789. Laplace's excellence in the field of celestial mechanics, however, was enough to dazzle any young mathematician. Nicollet's name is recognized in the last volume of Laplace's *Mécanique celeste*; his work — both as a member of an international team of scientists surveying for the great map of France which had been in progress since 1750 and as an observer of comets — was published by the Academy of Sciences in Paris. To his great disappointment, however, he failed to be elected a member of that illustrious body of savants. Perhaps it would have been only a matter of time before he achieved that goal had not the prevailing influences of his life carried him away from the political and social temper of the times. Younger scientists, pragmatic and experimental, cared nothing for Laplace's reputation, nor, indeed, for Nicollet's particular talents and his patrons.

Of gay, uncontentious, and sociable nature, a devout Catholic by upbringing and education, and a talented amateur violinist, Nicollet was at home in the Paris of the Bourbon restoration. Many scholarly, graceful, and intelligent articles on astronomy and biography appeared under his name in the *Encyclopédie moderne*, a publication which had a distinctly aristocratic and traditional point of view.[3] Nicollet's friends and patrons were among those men of wealth and leisure who, in a Paris of newly relaxed and tolerant mood, devoted themselves to essentially nonutilitarian studies such as archaeology, classics, philology, bibliography, and history.

Unfortunately, it was fashionable in some circles to assume that the new and much discussed (though little understood) theory of mathematical probability was a tool by which one could predict the vagaries of the stock market. Nicollet found this application of the theory very interesting and apparently made predictions a little too freely. The Revolution of 1830 which brought Louis Philippe to the throne was greeted with joy by many powerful members of the Academy of Sciences. It ruined Nicollet. The stock market collapsed overnight. Discredited and heartbroken, cut off with unrelenting finality from the rich who had been his friends, he sailed clandestinely from the port of Brest for America, arriving unheralded early in the year 1832.

[3] These articles reappeared in a new edition published after Nicollet's death. *Encyclopédie moderne: dictionnaire abrégé des sciences, des lettres, des arts* (New Edition, Paris, 1846–52). See, for example, vol. 10, column 218–234 (1847); vol. 14, column 657–674 (1848); vol. 19, column 576–588 (1849).

He was forty-six years old — by no means young in that day to begin a new career. His build was slight, suggestive of physical frailty, and he was without substantial personal resources or diplomatic support from his own country. Accustomed to such French institutions as the Bureau of Longitudes, which had long received the support of kings and emperors, he went first to Washington, the seat of government. There he introduced himself to Ferdinand Rudolph Hassler, a crusty old Swiss who was just assuming the full direction of the first government-supported scientific agency in the United States, the Coast Survey.[4]

Nicollet worked for several months with Hassler, who remained his lifelong friend, but the Frenchman was not interested in any position that might compromise his freedom to carry out a great plan, which was even then taking shape in his mind. It was, he later wrote, to make "a scientific tour . . . with the view of contributing to the progressive increase of knowledge in the physical geography of North America." Very soon after his arrival in the United States he determined on a study of the Mississippi River system.[5]

In selecting this objective, Nicollet's concerns were primarily philosophical. Although trained in the exact sciences, he thought of geography in its most inclusive sense. To Nicollet physical geography was a study of the climate, the watercourses, the soil, the terrain, the vegetable and animal life, and even the human uses of any region of the globe. In devoting himself to such a study he saw himself as an instrument in the eventual realization of God's purposes for man. He greatly admired the energetic Baron Alexander von Humboldt, to whom he referred as "the Nestor of scientific travellers."[6] Humboldt, after scaling the peaks and volcanoes of the Andes and tramping through the jungles of the Amazon, had settled in Paris in 1808 to assemble his encyclopedic volumes of related facts, including geology, meteorology, oceanography, and ethnology.

[4] For Hassler, see *Dictionary of American Biography*, 8:385 (New York, 1932).
[5] For the quotation, see Joseph N. Nicollet, *Report Intended to Illustrate a Map of the Hydrographical Basin of the Upper Mississippi River*, 3 (26 Congress, 2 session, *Senate Documents*, no. 237 — serial 380). This was also published as 28 Congress, 2 session, *House Documents*, no. 52 — serial 464. It is hereafter cited as *Report*. See also an unpublished memoir of Nicollet written by John J. Abert in 1844, in the archives of the American Philosophical Society, Philadelphia. This is hereafter cited as Abert Memoir.
[6] *Report*, 95.

From the twentieth-century view, Nicollet stood on that great intellectual divide between the general knowledge which was once called natural history and the organized and specialized bodies of fact which have become the science of our day. The gap between his thinking and that of the technological age already dawning seems at times wider than that between him and the Stone-Age men he was to encounter in the North American wilderness. Transportation was a leading topic of conversation among men of affairs in the United States of the 1830s, but although railroads were even then carrying passengers, Nicollet along with many others continued to think of a country interlaced with canals like his native France. In his mind waterways would always control the movements of goods and people. Hence his interest in the Mississippi reflected important practical concerns as well as the romantic view of the great river shared by many Frenchmen since their countrymen had first discovered it.

The lack of geographical information in America was, he realized, as staggering as the distances which stretched between the centers of habitation. There were only a few published works which he might study if he looked for understanding of the country west of the Appalachians. Nearly thirty years had passed since the Lewis and Clark expedition had reached the Pacific. Less remarkable in scope, but a part of the emerging policy of the United States government to support exploration of the West, had been the expeditions of Zebulon M. Pike, whose orders to proceed up the Mississippi to its source were issued while Lewis and Clark were still making their way up the Missouri in 1804. Nicollet was unable to obtain a copy of the publication resulting from Pike's expedition, although maps of the northern country and particularly of the upper Mississippi — with which the journals here reprinted are concerned — still depended in large part upon Pike's observations.[7]

In 1823 the expedition of Lieutenant Stephen H. Long, made under the auspices of the United States Army but including civilian scientists, penetrated what was thought to be the wasteland between the Mississippi and Missouri rivers, following the Red River north-

[7] See Zebulon M. Pike, *An Account of Expeditions to the Sources of the Mississippi* (Philadelphia, 1810). Nicollet refers in his diary to his failure to obtain a copy of this volume. See below, p. 50.

ward to the forty-ninth parallel of latitude and returning eastward along the Canadian boundary to Lake Superior. The published narrative of this journey, largely written by a professor of mineralogy and chemistry, William H. Keating, was a model for future publications, combining geographical reporting with admirable passages on the Indians and on geology.[8]

In 1820 an expedition led by Lewis Cass, then governor of Michigan Territory, had traveled into the region west of Lake Superior where traders — French, English, and American — had long been active. Accompanying Cass had been a young mineralogist, Henry R. Schoolcraft, who on his return published a narrative in which the most readable and informative passages were about the Indians he had observed.[9] Cass had believed the source of the Mississippi to be a body of water which later came to be known as Cass Lake. Schoolcraft, however, was sure that the river flowed into the lake from a source yet farther to the north and west.

In the summer of 1832 while Nicollet was in Washington, Schoolcraft, as Indian agent at Sault Ste. Marie, Michigan, led another expedition to the sources of the great river. Cass, who was by this time secretary of war in the cabinet of President Andrew Jackson, had authorized Schoolcraft's expedition under the Office of Indian Affairs. Later that fall, Nicollet had an opportunity to read the official geographical report of Lieutenant James Allen, a young civil engineer who traveled with Schoolcraft and who had been responsible for the maps. Schoolcraft's own narrative had not yet been published, but Nicollet in 1832 could have learned from Allen's report that the source of the Mississippi was thought by Schoolcraft to be a small lake which that gentleman had named Itasca.[10]

Nicollet began his American travels in December, 1832. Although he had received no direct help or encouragement from the government, he carried with him a letter of introduction to commanders

[8] William H. Keating, *Narrative of an Expedition to the Source of the St. Peter's River* (Philadelphia, 1824).

[9] Henry R. Schoolcraft, *Narrative Journal of Travels through the Northwestern Regions of the United States* (Albany, 1821).

[10] James Allen, *Journal of an "Expedition into the Indian country,"* to the source of the Mississippi, made under the authority of the War Department, in 1832 (23 Congress, 1 session, *House Documents*, no. 323 — serial 257). For Nicollet's comments on Allen's work, see below, p. 41, 103, 121, 130.

of military posts which he might visit along his way. His barometer and chronometer were procured for him by Hassler.[11] His goal was St. Louis, the booming, cosmopolitan Mississippi River city which was then the mecca for all would-be western travelers, but rumors of cholera caused him to delay his arrival there until the summer of 1835.

Traveling from Savannah, Georgia, through the mountains to Nashville, Tennessee, he went down the Cumberland, Ohio, and Mississippi rivers to Natchez and New Orleans. The geographical position of the great river's mouth had not yet been accurately determined and he knew that his subsequent work depended upon this knowledge. In 1834 he went far out of his way to return to Georgia to observe an important eclipse of the sun and also to study the Gulf coast of Florida. His purpose in this as in other detours was always scientific.

He was hospitably received along the way by many French families as well as by the Catholic clergy, with whom he often made his home away from home. Scientists in small but hopeful institutions welcomed him eagerly. From the beginning of his tour he kept the astronomical and meteorological notebooks through which we may trace his itinerary and which were the basis of his geographical work during the rest of his life.[12]

Latitude and longitude — determined by celestial measurements and by chronometer — were not his only observations. He found the measurement of altitude by barometer one of the "most interesting subjects for investigation that present themselves in the vast field where pure mathematics are applied to physical phenomena."[13] His method of establishing barometric stations throughout the country for accurate reference was new to America in the 1830s. It is a method not much changed today, although technology has consider-

[11] Abert Memoir; Nicollet to Hassler, November 17, 1835, Ford Collection, in the New York Public Library. The Minnesota Historical Society owns a barometer carried by Nicollet, but whether it is the one Hassler gave him is not known.

[12] These notebooks, along with correspondence, fragments of what may have been a personal journal, and other miscellaneous papers and sketches, are among the Nicollet Papers in the Library of Congress. Unless otherwise indicated, the notebooks are the source of information on Nicollet's movements. All are in French. Quotations from them have been translated by the editor unless otherwise noted.

[13] Report, 94.

Nicollet (left) with Henry D. Rogers, professor of geology at the University of Pennsylvania. Drawn by Augustin A. C. F. Edouart, a French silhouettist who worked in the United States from 1839 to 1849.

ably increased the accuracy of the instruments and lessened the discomforts suffered by scientists from wind, mosquitoes, and fatigue.

In August, 1835, Nicollet started up the Missouri, leaving St. Louis on an American Fur Company boat. He was favored by the co-operative policy of that company, as had been earlier distinguished travelers such as George Catlin, painter of Indians, in 1832, and the Prince Maximilian of Wied-Neuwied and his entourage in 1834.[14] Nicollet's excursion, however, ended in disaster. Before he had entered Indian country, he was stricken with malaria and forced to return to St. Louis. This recurrent affliction, so common on the frontier of that day, was to incapacitate him during the following winter and to harass him most inconveniently in the northern woods, as his diary discloses.

Weakened by his illness, he remained in St. Louis and Natchez through the fall and winter of 1835. During these months he wrote a "Sketch of the Early History of St. Louis." It remains, according to a modern historian, "the best of the early accounts of St. Louis"

[14] See George Catlin, *Letters and Notes on the Manners, Customs and Condition of the North American Indians*, 1:14 (London, 1841); Reuben Gold Thwaites, ed., *Early Western Travels*, 22:14 (Cleveland, 1905).

and "an authentic attempt to write history."[15] Its purpose was to interpret the early French character of the rapidly changing metropolis. "This respect for France," wrote a traveler in the United States in 1835, "is a gallant sentiment [of Frenchmen] and shows off particularly well when they are far from the country whose honor they assert."[16] Nicollet was certainly no exception to this general observation.

He also read widely in the literature of exploration. Traces of his reading may be found in his notes, and at the time of his death, his library of more than sixty items — maps, pamphlets, and books — included a number of important titles from the early literature of western travel by both English and French authors. References in his *Report* indicate that he was familiar with many more. In 1838 he wrote to a friend asking for more books on the Indian whatever the price.[17] He was particularly moved by the letters of the Jesuit missionaries, and his notebooks reveal that he carried with him a volume or two of the *Jesuit Relations*. He burned with indignation at Americans who maintained that the Jesuits cared nothing for the red man beyond achieving a momentary acceptance of the rituals of the Catholic faith. Paraphrasing a letter by Father Pierre Gabriel Marest, he wrote in his journal: "[We must try] to make first *Men*, then Christians, and to conduct [them] by degrees toward the benefits of civilization."[18]

Nicollet also carried with him to the upper Mississippi country a copy of Schoolcraft's narrative of his trip to the sources of the great river, which had been published in 1834. This volume he used constantly to compare with his own observations. Schoolcraft's contacts

[15] John Francis McDermott, *Early Histories of St. Louis*, 24 (St. Louis, 1952). The "Sketch" was printed as part of Nicollet's *Report* (p. 75–92).
[16] Tyrone Power, *Impressions of America during the years 1833, 1834, and 1835*, 69 (Philadelphia, 1836).
[17] Nicollet to Henry H. Sibley, February 6, 1838 (translation), Sibley Papers, in the Minnesota Historical Society. This and seven other Nicollet letters in the Sibley Papers are preserved only in English copies. The identity of the translator and the disposal of the originals are unknown. See Jane Spector Davis, *Guide to a Microfilm Edition of the Henry Hastings Sibley Papers*, 21 (St. Paul, 1968). A selected list of the books relating to the Indians which Nicollet owned at his death is given in Appendix 3.
[18] Diary fragment dated July 8, 1835, Nicollet Papers, Library of Congress. For a translation of Father Marest's letter, written November 9, 1712, see Reuben Gold Thwaites, ed., *Jesuit Relations and Allied Documents*, 66:219 (Cleveland, Ohio, 1900). Nicollet was to repeat the idea yet again. See below, p. 252.

with the Indians were to engage Nicollet's interest deeply, but as a cartographer he also read with care the explorer's description of the tableland where the Mississippi's sources were found — the *Hauteurs des Terres*, from which waters flowed in three directions to the sea. It was, Nicollet reflected, "an interesting region almost unknown geographically."[19] Shown on the map which accompanied Schoolcraft's volume was the source of the Mississippi — Lake Itasca — a narrow two-pronged body of water hanging like a barb on the end of the great fishhook bend of the river. Cupped beneath the lake was a semicircle of little cone-shaped hills called "Hauteurs des Terres Mountains." Lieutenant Allen's map, accompanying the official report which Nicollet had seen in Washington, had showed these hills as a part of a great north-south ridge dividing the waters of the Mississippi from those of the Red River.

In June, 1836, Nicollet left St. Louis on the steamboat "St. Peter's," traveling upriver to Fort Snelling in what is now Minnesota with a number of St. Louis people bound for a holiday. The tourists were doubtless encouraged in this venture by the enthusiastic report of George Catlin who had returned to their city the previous fall from the fort and who described in glowing superlatives the rugged and picturesque scenery of the upper Mississippi and the pleasant circumstances under which he had been able to observe Indian tribal customs.[20]

On July 2 the "St. Peter's" reached its destination — the massive stone fort at the junction of the Mississippi and Minnesota (called the St. Peter's River in Nicollet's day) which was an outpost of civilization on the edge of the northern wilderness. While it had never been engaged in military action, Fort Snelling had guarded United States interests since its establishment in 1819. It deterred British fur traders who still encroached upon the area and served as a check upon the intertribal Indian wars which had for many years distressed the authorities and disrupted trade. The post's com-

[19] Nicollet to Joseph Rosati, October 15, 1836. The original, written in French, is in the private collection of the Reverend Peter J. Rahill of the Diocese of St. Louis, Missouri. Schoolcraft's account was published as *Narrative of an Expedition through the Upper Mississippi to Itasca Lake* (New York, 1834).

[20] Lawrence Taliaferro Journal, July 2, 1836, in the Minnesota Historical Society. Catlin's visit at Fort Snelling is described in his *Letters and Notes*, 2:129–140. See also Theodore C. Blegen, "The 'Fashionable Tour' on the Upper Mississippi," in *Minnesota History*, 20:378 (December, 1939).

manding location was, wrote Nicollet later, "in my opinion the finest site on the Mississippi River. . . . Fort Snelling is located on the rocky point at this confluence of the two rivers, the sight of which inspires a sentiment of self-protection in the civilized man thus confronted with the wilderness." Looking north to the fort from a point above the Minnesota — possibly Pilot Knob — Nicollet had a splendid view of the broad valley. He later wrote, "Looking to the right of the Fort, we behold a continuation of the valley of the Mississippi, whilst to the left begins that of the St. Peter's. The former has a character of sternness, produced by the denuded and abrupt escarpments of its banks, the wear of which forms rude taluses at their bases. The latter is more graceful, having gently sloping borders, divided into natural terraces, covered by a luxuriant, grassy sward." On the south bank of the Minnesota stood the well-proportioned house of native yellow limestone just built by Henry H. Sibley, chief representative of the American Fur Company in the area since 1834.[21]

Nicollet carried his well-worn official letter of introduction to the commanders of military installations as well as letters addressed to Lawrence Taliaferro, Indian agent at Fort Snelling, from St. Louis friends. The major, as he was called (a courtesy title accorded all United States Indian agents), had been at Fort Snelling since 1819 and was a controversial figure on the Minnesota frontier. Scrupulously honest and devoted to what he regarded as the interests of the Indians under his charge, he was also sensitive, proud, and opinionated. He was not a scholarly man. Nicollet always wrote to Taliaferro in English, although nearly all of his other letters were in French, a language familiar to most cultivated people of the day.[22]

The letter of recommendation which Nicollet carried, wrote Taliaferro in his journal for July 2, 1836, requested the commanding officers to help the Frenchman in his "scientific pursuits under order of the French government." Taliaferro was not the only one among those who met Nicollet on his travels to make this statement about the Frenchman's orders from his country's government. He could scarcely, under the circumstances of his self-imposed exile, have carried any such directive, but it is barely possible that he had a

[21] *Report*, 68; June D. Holmquist and Jean A. Brookins, *Minnesota's Major Historic Sites: A Guide*, 9–11 (St. Paul, 1963).
[22] For a sketch of Taliaferro's life and character, see Helen McCann White, *Guide to a Microfilm Edition of the Lawrence Taliaferro Papers*, 5–7 (St. Paul, 1966).

letter of recommendation or approval from the French minister in Washington. That a Frenchman of Nicollet's obvious learning and talent should be traveling on so unusual a mission without official support of any kind was surprising to most Americans, and it must at times have been difficult for him to explain his position.

Taliaferro installed the "distinguished French gentleman" in his own family quarters near the Indian agency. Nicollet was to use the agency house to store his instruments and "carry on his observations at his leisure."[23] Nearby stood the council house where Taliaferro met with the tribes. Within a few weeks of his arrival, Nicollet had seen in the course of daily routine representatives of the two nations of the region. These were the Sioux, or Dakota, who lived largely in the prairies to the west and south of the fort, and the Chippewa, or Ojibway, people of the lakes and rivers to the north.

Relations between these tribes from the time white traders penetrated the Great Lakes region had been characterized by implacable hostility. Driven from their homes in the eastern woodlands around the St. Lawrence River by the fierce Iroquois, the Chippewa, a people of Algonquin stock armed with guns, had pushed west and south from the head of Lake Superior. They drove the Sioux, who were still a hunting people with a Stone-Age technology, from the favored lands of water and forest onto the open and inhospitable prairies. As the white traders advanced with their incalculable and inevitable effect upon native life, the Sioux also gained possession of firearms and struggled desperately to retain their ancient homelands. They were decisively defeated, according to Chippewa tradition, in a battle at Crow Wing, in east-central Minnesota, which took place sometime during the decade of the 1760s. Since that time the conflict had continued in bloody, if seemingly haphazard, encounters.[24]

In 1825 at the ancient meeting ground of Prairie du Chien, on the plain formed at the mouth of the Wisconsin River as it flows into the Mississippi, a thousand chieftains from all the Indian nations of the upper Mississippi Valley had gathered. There, under the supervision of United States commissioners, they agreed upon boundaries between their hunting lands. The Sioux and the Chippewa were to be separated by a line drawn on the map across what is now the state of Minnesota from the Red River in the west, passing north

[23] Taliaferro Journal, July 2, 1836.
[24] William W. Folwell, *A History of Minnesota*, 1: 82–84 (St. Paul, 1956).

of Fort Snelling, eastward beyond the Chippewa River, and then southeastward to the junction of the Black River with the Mississippi. Among Nicollet's papers in the Library of Congress is a handwritten copy of the "survey of the Indian boundary line between the Sioux and Chippewa nations" made under a contract entered into with General William Clark on April 23, 1835 — ten years after the conference. To the Indians, whose geography was concrete and visual, this imaginary line remained completely unreal. The sporadic warfare continued as it had before.[25]

According to Catlin, the Sioux around Fort Snelling were a sorry lot. Liquor, disease, and diminishing game had undermined their native way of life. To the north, however, Nicollet had before him the prospect of observing a people who "better than any tribe of the upper Great Lakes region, survived the impact of the white man's civilization, diseases and wars." Throughout the active and profitable period of the fur trade — which by 1836 had largely passed into history — the Chippewa had preserved a remarkably unadulterated, persistent, and widespread culture.[26]

Nicollet's preference for the culture of the Chippewa is clearly stated in a number of places in his Indian notes. As he wrote them, during the winter of 1836-37, he based his remarks upon the observations he was able to make of the Sioux who visited the fort. Perhaps, too, he had formed his impressions through what he had heard of them from their enemies. Later, however, in 1838 and again in 1839, he was to travel across the prairies and to live and make friends among the Sioux as he had among the Chippewa. The notes which he made of their life and language have unfortunately not survived, but in his diary he was to recognize the harsh terms of their battle with a hostile environment and to recall with sorrow the lakes of the north, lively with the boats and nets of Chippewa fishermen and with the summertime villages which dotted the shores.

In 1827, much to Taliaferro's disgust, the Chippewa had been removed from his supervision and placed under Schoolcraft, who administered the upper Mississippi bands from a subagency at La Pointe on the south shore of Lake Superior. The tribesmen, however,

[25] Folwell, *Minnesota*, 1: 146.
[26] Taliaferro Journal, June 20, 1836; Catlin, *Letters and Notes*, 2:131. The quotation is from George I. Quimby, *Indian Life in the Upper Great Lakes*, 126 (Chicago, 1960).

finding the trip eastward long and arduous, continued to drift down to their former agency at Fort Snelling. The arrangement was a constant irritation to the major and did not increase his affection for Schoolcraft. Indeed, since the conference at Prairie du Chien, he had suspected his rival of selfish and ambitious machinations against him.[27] Nicollet gave to his host Schoolcraft's new account of his Itasca journey. It is perhaps indicative of the disagreeable relations between Taliaferro and Schoolcraft that the former had not seen the book before. Burning the midnight oil, he sputtered with rage as he read it, scribbling defiant self-vindication in his strong, flowing, illegible handwriting. Particularly irritating to him was the reported speech of Flat Mouth, a powerful chief of the Chippewa at Leech Lake, who had, according to Schoolcraft, accused "persons on the waters of the Upper Mississippi, of giving advice to the Sioux to go to war against the Chippewas."[28]

Nicollet made good use of his time at the fort. On July 5 he began his astronomical observations. Over and over again, he computed the longitude of his position by measuring the distance from the edge of the moon to the sun, to Spica, and to Altair. The average of the results which he obtained at this time differed only slightly — less than four seconds of an arc — from the value which he gave in his *Report* after making additional measurements two years later. Modern maps indicate that Nicollet placed the mouth of the Minnesota only some five miles too far east. From repeated measurements, largely of the altitude of the North Star and the altitude and azimuth of the sun, he obtained data for determining the latitude. These results did not differ significantly from those published in his *Report* nor from the modern value.[29]

One cool July day Nicollet, Major and Mrs. Taliaferro, Colonel William Davenport, the commanding officer of the fort, Mrs. Davenport, and several officers traveled through the lake-studded countryside to lunch at the "celebrated" Falls of St. Anthony. Nicollet was to add his own description of the falls to those of other travelers, writing that "with the noisy boiling of its waters, rebounding in jets from the accumulated debris at its foot, its ascending

[27] White, *Guide to a Microfilm Edition of the Lawrence Taliaferro Papers*, 8.
[28] Taliaferro Journal, July 12, 1835; Schoolcraft, *Narrative of an Expedition*, 86.
[29] *Report*, 116, 124.

vapors, and the long and verdant island that separates the two portions of the falls, with the solitary rocky island that stands in front,
[they] altogether form a grand and imposing spectacle." [30]

While the rest of the party caught a few sunfish and perch in the
lakes and at the falls, Nicollet examined the rocks, collecting, as the
major wrote, "specimens of various kinds of formations." The interest in geology here evinced by Nicollet had grown steadily during
his travels. In the summer of 1836, making his way north into the
watery forests where bedrock is found only in the river channels
and there only at rare intervals, he was to describe carefully and
originally the formations which he examined. These are the first
extensive geological field notes we have from his pen, and in view
of his later reputation in this science, they are an important indication of his method. [31]

As Nicollet lingered at Fort Snelling his ambitions and talents
together with his obvious want of preconceived plans made him the
subject of much discussion. It was Mrs. Taliaferro who finally
brought him to a decision. At Fort Snelling, as had been the case
in many other places where he had depended upon the hospitality
of friends, his sociable nature warmed to the feminine touch. For
Elizabeth Taliaferro he had a "tender affection." One day he was
questioned, as he had been many times before, about what he desired
to accomplish by his visit and where he most wanted to go. Taliaferro
recalled the following exchange:

> Could he go to the settlement of Selkirk? Yes. Could he go to
> the source of the Mississippi? Yes, sir. "Well," said he, with a
> pleasant smile, "you American beat de dev. Suppose I say can
> I go to h--ell, you say yes." Here his friend Mrs. T. remarked,
> "None of us will send you that route if we can prevent it."
> "Well, then, madam, change my route to the upper Missis-
> sippi." [32]

On July 24, Nicollet announced his intention to embark for the

[30] Taliaferro Journal, July 10, 1836; *Report*, 68.

[31] Taliaferro Journal, July 10, 1836. See also Martha Coleman Bray, "Joseph
Nicolas Nicollet, Geologist," in American Philosophical Society, *Proceedings*,
114: 37–59 (February, 1970).

[32] Nicollet to Taliaferro, September 20, 1837, Taliaferro Papers, in the Minnesota Historical Society; Lawrence Taliaferro, "Auto-Biography," in *Minnesota
Historical Collections*, 6: 242 (St. Paul, 1894).

sources of the Mississippi within the next few days. The plan was encouraged by Taliaferro, who hoped that the Frenchman would serve as his emissary to the Chippewa of Leech Lake. It is more than likely, too, that he hoped Nicollet's superior scientific and intellectual training would put Schoolcraft in his place. In any case, he wrote out a list of questions which he wished Nicollet to address to "Flat Mouth or any of the leading men of Leech Lake." Though these questions have not survived, Nicollet was to find out for the agent exactly what Flat Mouth had said to Schoolcraft.[33]

Taliaferro also busied himself with practical details of preparation for the journey. "We procured for him a complete outfit," wrote the Indian agent in his journal. A receipt to "Mr. Nicolas" from the fort sutlers is marked "paid in full" and includes such essential items as three tin pans and two tin cups (at a total price of $2.38), a tin kettle, calico and beads for trading with the Indians, flints, salt, sugar, tobacco, bacon, coffee, brandy, and blankets. Nicollet later expressed his thanks to Sibley, Taliaferro, and the officers of the First Regiment at the fort "for the removal of all difficulties which might be expected to present themselves to a solitary traveler."[34] There is no record as to whether this helpfulness included actual financial assistance from any of these gentlemen, but evidence suggests that members of the Chouteau family of St. Louis, through their close affiliation with the American Fur Company, helped to finance Nicollet's later expeditions. Whether he had received money from them at this time is not clear.

The selection of Nicollet's small entourage was not complicated. He began by bargaining with one Francis Brunia to take him to Leech Lake for $80 to $100. Nicollet had no cause to regret his choice, later describing Brunia as "a giant of great strength but, at the same time, full of the milk of human kindness, and, withal, an excellent geographer."[35] At the last moment, "a Frenchman named

[33] "Memorandum of Lawrence Taliaferro to Flat Mouth, Leech Lake," addressed to "M. Nicollet, July 26, 1836," Nicollet Papers, Library of Congress.
[34] Taliaferro Journal, July 27, 1836; Receipt from Stambaugh and Sibley dated July 27, 1836, in Nicollet Papers, Library of Congress; Report, 53. From May, 1836, to April, 1839, the sutler's store at Fort Snelling was operated under a partnership arrangement between Sibley and Samuel C. Stambaugh. See Francis Paul Prucha, "Army Sutlers and the American Fur Company," in Minnesota History, 40: 22–31 (Spring, 1966). Nicollet's receipt was signed by N[orman W.] Kittson, chief clerk.
[35] Report, 54. This source gives the name as "Brunet." The form used by

Fronchet, belonging to the garrison, and known to his comrades by the name of *Desiré*," presented himself to Nicollet, hoping not only to help the explorer but also to trade with the Indians. Nicollet received "good testimonials of his character" and accepted Fronchet as a member of the party, afterward remarking on his "activity, patience and cheerfulness." A number of officers also expressed a wish to accompany the expedition, but they were required to stay at the fort. Three lieutenants did, however, escort him as far as the Falls of St. Anthony because, wrote Nicollet, they "were desirous of extending to me the final shake-hand before my departure." [36]

Nicollet had barely started when misfortune overtook him. At the falls he was robbed of his provisions and his canoe by some Sioux. Determined not to regard this as a bad omen, and, more important, not to return to the fort, Nicollet wrote to Taliaferro and sent Brunia off with the letter. The agent, much mortified at the inconvenience caused his friend by those whom he called his "starving rice" children, promised that, if possible, the canoe and other property would be found and returned. In the meantime Taliaferro replaced the articles. While he waited for this disaster to be repaired, Nicollet occupied himself with astronomical observations, making his station in "the little house which the United States has built at the foot of the fall to provide shelter for two soldiers of the Fort Snelling garrison who are guarding the mill and a herd of cattle." [37]

The story of the journey to the sources of the Mississippi is told by Nicollet himself in the diary which follows. He found Schoolcraft's identification of the source to be generally correct, although he delineated for the first time a number of small streams flowing into Lake Itasca. Nicollet's geographical investigation was much more intensive than that of the American, and it is significant that he spent three days at Lake Itasca while Schoolcraft had spent only

Nicollet in his diary is followed here. Taliaferro mentions both a Brunia and a Brunet, but François (or Francis) Brunia is the man who accompanied Nicollet. See Taliaferro Journal, July 23, 1836.

[36] *Report*, 53; Taliaferro Journal, July 27, 1836. Nicollet made a brief note that Désiré Fronchet was born near Calais, France, and that his parents lived in Paris. He had been employed in the Commune of Lucienne by the owner of a flower garden from whom he had a good reference. Undated fragment in Nicollet Papers, Library of Congress.

[37] Astronomical Notebook, July 28, 1836; Taliaferro to Nicollet, July 28, 1836, both in Nicollet Papers, Library of Congress.

a few hours. On the tree stump where Schoolcraft had planted the American flag, Nicollet hung his barometer.

The most important single cartographical contribution of the 1836 expedition was Nicollet's correction of Pike's earlier distortion of the position of the mouth of the Crow Wing River, a distortion which had, Nicollet said, "created great disorder in the geography of this region." Pike had placed this point twenty-seven minutes too low in latitude and thus, wrote Nicollet, "from the Falls of St. Anthony upwards, all the river mouths bear too much to the west," and even the sources of the Mississippi had been "three quarters of a degree too far to the west." The triangle of land between the Mississippi and the Missouri which Nicollet was eventually to map had been thus contracted "in a singular manner." Nicollet also carefully delineated on his first map of the watery, forested country through which he traveled in 1836 the *Hauteurs des Terres* which he had studied so keenly on earlier maps. He described this geographical feature in his *Report* as determining the "hydrographical basins of all the innumerable lakes and rivers that so peculiarly characterize this region."[38]

The drainage system of the river was indeed the heart of his work from the beginning. He showed the Red River of the North as flowing from Elbow Lake, in what is now northern Becker County, Minnesota, and separated from Lake Itasca by the *Coteau du Grand Bois*, a part of the *Hauteurs des Terres*. In the *Report* he developed in more detail this relationship when he wrote, "The waters supplied by the north flank of these heights of land — still on the south side of lake Itasca — give origin to the five creeks of which I have spoken above. These are the waters which I consider to be the utmost sources of the Mississippi. Those that flow from the southern side of the same heights, and empty themselves into Elbow lake, are the utmost sources of the Red river of the North; so that the most remote feeders of Hudson bay and the gulf of Mexico are closely approximated to each other."[39] He could have obtained this information about Elbow Lake only from the Indians, yet he presented the stream patterns of the region much more accurately than had been possible before his exploration. In fact, his map is surprisingly similar to modern ones of the region. Here, as throughout the whole

[38] *Report*, 57, 109, 110.
[39] *Report*, 58.

area he explored, he achieved his major aim — the determination of the extent of the various watersheds. Although his interest in these features was principally due to their supposed importance to navigation and perhaps to agriculture, he was emphasizing a concept which has become increasingly important in modern studies of water resources for a population greater than he could have imagined possible.

Nicollet's purpose was not universally received with enthusiasm. The Congregational missionary at Leech Lake, William T. Boutwell, with whom the Frenchman stayed for seven or eight days, granted that his guest understood the use of the sextant, barometer, and chronometer, but said that beyond these skills his education was "superficial." Stating that Nicollet had decided to explore the sources of the Mississippi only after learning at Fort Snelling of the expedition of Schoolcraft and Allen, Boutwell expressed some suspicion that the foreigner's object might be more than "scientific observation." He found Nicollet "a social and well bred man . . . given to flattery and fond of notice."[40] Nicollet, on his part, seemed unaware of any animosity felt by his host. He described his days with Boutwell as full of "quiet and happiness."

Returning from his trip, Nicollet wrote Taliaferro from the Falls of St. Anthony on September 27: "I arrived last evening about dusk, all's well, nothing lost, nothing broken, happy and very successful journey. But I am done, exhausted, and nothing can relieve me but the pleasure to meet you again under your hospitable roof and to see all the friends of the garrison who have been kind to me." He went on to say that he was writing particularly to give the agent "very extraordinary tide[ings]." Flat Mouth and ten of his men were with Nicollet, and their purpose was to visit Taliaferro. Nicollet begged the agent to give the Indians a good welcome until an explanation of what had transpired among the Pillagers could be given. He assured Taliaferro that he had "not trespassed" his instructions, that he had behaved as a "good citizen of the United States," and that Flat Mouth himself would give the major full satisfaction regarding Schoolcraft's statements.[41]

[40] William T. Boutwell Journal, September 9, 1836. The original of this journal has been lost, but a handwritten copy made by J. Fletcher Williams for the years 1832–37 is among the Boutwell Papers in the Minnesota Historical Society. Boutwell had accompanied Schoolcraft in 1832.
[41] Nicollet to Taliaferro, September 27, 1836, Taliaferro Papers.

When Nicollet and the chiefs arrived at Fort Snelling at noon on September 28, a council was held. Six weeks earlier, Nicollet had never met a tribesman living in Indian territory. He was now trusted by one of the most influential Chippewa chiefs to present his case to an American agent — a case upon which hung the familiar issue of peace or war. "We found M. Nicollet in our country and when he left we felt disposed to follow him," said Flat Mouth, according to Taliaferro. The French scientist had, indeed, as the agent reported, "tranquilized the turbulent savage."[42] For his part, Nicollet wrote of the Pillagers: "There were 19 of them. They called me Father! Dieu! What pretty children I had there. They left me several days ago, dear children, and may the great Manitou accompany and guard them — far from me!"[43]

Nicollet had a very personal relationship with an Indian named Chagobay, or Shago-bai, who with his ten-year-old son accompanied the explorer as far as Leech Lake. Chagobay revealed to Nicollet the secrets of the medicine ceremony, a confidence few white people received. In fact, Chagobay's confidence in Nicollet was such that this revelation was made at some risk to himself. On September 29, 1836, Nicollet jotted in the margin of a sketch map that a special ceremony was held at which Flat Mouth relieved Chagobay of guilt for this breach of trust. The following letter, dictated by Chagobay to Boutwell, was received by Nicollet on May 29, 1837.[44] Its perfect simplicity permits no paraphrase:

Friend Nicolette:
The Little Six wishes me to write a line for him. "My friend I think of you so much. I shake hands with you. I

[42] Taliaferro to Henry Dodge, September 29, 1836 (copy), Taliaferro Papers.
[43] Nicollet to Gabriel Paul and Jules de Mun, November 1, 1836, Jules de Mun Papers (Birdsall Collection), in the Missouri Historical Society, St. Louis.
[44] The original of this letter and a handwritten copy of the answer to it are among the Nicollet Papers in the Library of Congress. The first is clearly in Boutwell's hand; the second is less distinctive but may well have been written by Sibley. Shagobay is mentioned by Boutwell, who noted in his journal on June 4, 1836, that "Shagobe and family, this morning visited us, bringing with them a corseau of sugar, to make me a present for medicines &c that I furnished him with last winter." A chief of the same or a very similar name lived in the vicinity of Snake River and was among those who signed the Chippewa treaty of 1837, but there is no evidence that they were the same individual. See Boutwell Journal; Schoolcraft, *Narrative of an Expedition*, 286; Charles J. Kappler, comp. and ed., *Indian Affairs. Laws and Treaties*, 2:493 (Second Edition, Washington, D.C., 1904).

send these bear claws which I take from my heart that you may remember me. When I was young I loved what I send you. When I was young I dreamed, if I kept this little animal's skin I should live long, and now I send it to you that you may remember me. We will be friends while we live and meet in that good place and be friends after we die. I wish you to send me another shell by Brunette such as you gave me last fall. Write me by Brunette that I may hear from you yourself. I am afraid I shall not be able to pay my credit if I don't hunt this spring or else I would come and see you before you leave.

The last time I saw you I was poor. I am still poor now. I have not tobacco to fill my pipe.

I shall still look for what you promised me in a small box.

Shâgobe, his mark   X

Nicollet's answer, which was written in English, probably by the hand of his friend Sibley, reads as follows:

My good friend Shagobe:

I received your kind talk in the letter you sent by Mr. Brunet. From the first time we met in your nation — I placed you near my heart.

I have you still resting in the same spot, and have often thought and spoken of you, and my dreams have been with you and our friends at Leech Lake.

My friend, I thank you from my heart for what you have sent me, for it will, when the great waters divide us, serve to remind me of a good friend (and cheerful traveling companion) [the parenthetical words are inserted in Nicollet's own handwriting] in the great nation of the Chippeways.

My friend, I remember all things. I cannot forget. I have sent you something to fill your pipe, and as soon as the steamboat arrives I will not forget to fulfil all, and keep even friendship forever between us.

My Friends, I wish you to remember me to all my friends at Leech Lake, and I send word that I hope they will listen to the good and true words sent by Brunet as your Father at St. Peter's speaks the Heart of your great Father at Washington. [No signature]

Nothing can speak more eloquently of Nicollet's relations with the Indians than this exchange of letters. Why was he so successful in gaining their confidence? [45] First, and most obviously, he was a Frenchman — a nation of whom the Chippewa had happy memories handed down from earlier associations in the fur trade. His "Frenchness" helped to foster a temperamental affinity between Nicollet and the Indians, and there is evidence that they also recognized his sincerity and his selfless devotion to the goal he had set for himself — the pursuit of knowledge. The Parisian, fond of music and sophisticated conversation, could enjoy a joke with a woodland tribesman in a boggy wilderness somewhere beyond the edge of the world. Fun is shared only by equals, and Nicollet alone among the scholars of his day wrote of the wit and gaiety of the Indian. Of the *Jisakan*, or ceremony of the juggler, which was described by numerous other writers as the deception it was, he wrote: "The natives are greatly amused by it, but nevertheless they believe in all the mystery that takes place. Anyone attempting to turn them away from these beliefs would be running a risk." [46] Play and ritual, pretending and belief — Nicollet understood instinctively their indivisible nature.

The Frenchman was not unique among his contemporaries in his intellectual interest in the fast disappearing life of the native American, nor was he alone in his conviction that the Indian was inherently no more depraved or vicious than other people. He recognized, however, that "The difficulty of studying the Indian . . . is in direct proportion with the importance of doing it." Like the Jesuits before him, he knew that one must share such a life in order to learn about it, and that "Courage, physical strength, and unique perseverance" were necessary. Courage and perseverance Nicollet had, and an almost superhuman patience when observation demanded it. His physical strength was small, but he was willing to spend it without the slightest hesitation. He may well have envied the "blackrobe" the outward habiliment of dedication, for his own devotion was also to the spiritual welfare of *"mes enfants des forêts."* The phrase

[45] In sharp contrast to Nicollet's rapport with the Indians was the experience of George Catlin, who had visited Fort Snelling for the second time while Nicollet was on his way up the Mississippi. With Taliaferro's assistance Catlin made a trip to the pipestone quarries on the prairies to the west. The Sioux had been incensed by this invasion of their sacred meeting ground, and Catlin never personally succeeded in gaining their confidence. See Folwell, *Minnesota*, 1: 119.

[46] See below, p. 218.

sounds patronizing to twentieth-century ears attuned to psychological implications and accustomed to attitudes of social and political equality, but Nicollet used it as did his predecessors of the Roman Catholic church. "Children of nature," he said, and he meant children of God, living in "unconstrained liberty" under a natural law "inspired into men." [47]

As might be expected of a French gentleman of sophisticated interests, Nicollet was touched by the fashionable literary romanticism of Chateaubriand. There are passages in the diary of the geographer describing love affairs between lakes and streams and flowers opening to the caresses of the sun. Such personification of nature is strange, if not offensive, to modern readers. But while Chateaubriand wrote such idylls as *Atala*, of primitive peoples whom he had never met, Nicollet recorded his personal experience: "There is a charm in the life of the Indians. A man much accustomed to exercising his mind relaxes joyfully as he participates in the confusion of a hunting expedition, as he runs in the woods pursuing wild beasts, or as he builds a hut. Kindling a fire and preparing a meal beside a spring — is it not a great source of pleasure? Thousands of Europeans have experienced it and have no desire for any other. A native dies heartbroken if he is brought to the city. Man is therefore essentially more active than contemplative. In his natural environment he has few needs and he finds an inexhaustible source of happiness in the simplicity of his soul." This was, as modern campers will recognize, the therapeutic experience which comes to those who deliberately seek in the wilderness an escape from the complexities of civilization. Alone in the wilderness, Nicollet experienced a genuine sort of animism which enabled him to suspend all intellectual preoccupations and to feel as if he "were living as a part of the great all, sprouting among the trees and flowers." It was, as he said, a "*tristesse* of happiness," and may well have preserved his sanity when he thought of the distance which separated him from all his accustomed pursuits among the world of men.[48]

He soon returned, however, from these dreamy moods to the purpose of his journey. In the geographical names given by the

[47] For quotations, see Appendix 5, p. 251, 253; *Report*, 66.

[48] Nicollet's papers in the Library of Congress include a number of undated reflections which he called "*melanges*" or "various thoughts." They are separate from his diary. The quotations here given are from these *melanges*.

Indian, the French, and the American, Nicollet was quick to recognize an important record of a land and of the people who lived and traveled in it. "It is of great interest to the history of geography to preserve the relationship of these names, [to] retain their etymology and recall their origin," he wrote. And he noted that "the geographic language of the Chippewa is richer than ours."[49] Nicollet was, in fact, the last explorer of the Northwest who saw the landscape through the eyes of the Indian.

He was well aware of his opportunity and of his singular capacity to make use of it. Lest he should "weaken the impressions which the description of places ought to conserve — their characteristic stamp and color," he decided after much searching of heart to spend the winter at Fort Snelling. He was convinced he should publish soon. His map rested "on nearly 2,000 astronomical barometric observations" and presented "more than 300 rivers and new lakes with their relations, the routes of winter and summer, opening all parts of the region to civilization which will soon be knocking at the door." He would, he wrote jubilantly to friends in St. Louis, arrive there with "a volume and map in my hand, near to being wound up for publication." An article about Nicollet appeared in a St. Louis paper, saying that his map had been examined by a "correspondent of ours" and was found to be "most perfect." It would be, reported the paper, "useful . . . to the whole scientific world." Nicollet was encouraged, and he embarked upon the long, cold northern winter in a confident mood. "Study, calculations, editing will make the hours fly," he wrote.[50]

Taliaferro noted that his guest seemed "pleased with his situation in our little family." It was to Nicollet an "enchanted spot." On November 30, he signed as witness to a convention and treaty among three Sioux tribes. Both the Chippewa and the Sioux, being at relative peace that season, visited the agency, and Nicollet was able "to assist" at their medicine dances and their winter and spring ceremonies. The results of his observations are plainly set down for us in his notes. Where and how he learned of their customs of war is less clear.[51]

[49] See below, p. 47, 149.
[50] Nicollet to Gabriel Paul and Jules de Mun, November 1, 1836; *Missouri Literary Review*, October 24, 1836.
[51] Taliaferro to William Clark, November 2, 1836 (copy), Taliaferro Papers;

Taliaferro told Nicollet many Indian tales, among them one which he wrote out "expressly for M. Nicollet." It was the story of a Sioux chief who had accompanied the agent and a deputation of his own people to Washington in 1824. This unfortunate man was visibly affected by the more than usually grievous wailing of an old woman who predicted on his departure that she would never see him again. On the journey his gloom increased as he dreamed three times of his own death. Taliaferro kept close watch over him, but he escaped from the boat and made his way back to St. Louis, where he was placed on a keelboat bound for Prairie du Chien. Again separating himself from his companions, he fell in with a Sauk lodge. He was offered hospitality, but while eating he was killed by a hatchet driven into the back of his skull by his host.[52]

This weird tale must have been called to mind by Nicollet's speculative interest in the effect of dreams upon the Indian's behavior. Another long story, that of Ohitika, touches on the nature of Indian justice and love of liberty. Although incomplete, it is reproduced in Appendix 5 (p. 260). Letters written to Taliaferro by various Indians were copied by Nicollet from the agent's notes and kept for future reference. The geographer's plan for a serious work on Indian culture was growing, as can be seen by the questions listed in Appendix 5.

There were four inches of snow by November 1. Sometimes Nicollet worked at the agency where, as he wrote to friends in St. Louis, "I squat in a little house prepared for me, wrapped in a bearskin, my head covered with a wool cap to receive the visitors who come to me from Fort Snelling or the Sioux." Sometimes he stayed with Sibley across the river, where he worked on his map. "His devotion to his studies," wrote the trader, "was intense and unremitting. I frequently expostulated with him upon his imprudence in thus over-tasking the strength of his delicate frame, but with little effect." Nicollet, however, was aware of no hardship great enough to interfere with the "magnitude of the enterprise in which he was engaged."[53]

Report, 67; "Convention with Wahpaakootah, Susseton, and Upper Medawakanton Tribes of Sioux Indians, November 30, 1836," in Kappler, comp. and ed., Indian Affairs, 2:482.
[52] The manuscript of this tale, dated July 7, 1837, is in the Nicollet Papers, Library of Congress.
[53] Nicollet to Gabriel Paul and Jules de Mun, November 1, 1836; Sibley, in Minnesota Historical Collections, 1:151.

During the long winter evenings at the major's house, Nicollet played the violin, accompanied by Mrs. Taliaferro at the square piano. At bedtime, his hostess would provide a welcome supper of wild rice, mush, and milk. Such a treat was balm to Nicollet's all too frequently distressed digestion, and he wrote to his friends that he had never been so well in his life in spite of temperatures which on one occasion reached 30° below zero.[54]

His diplomatic skills were called into play, too. Between the uncompromising Taliaferro and the competent and honest trader, Sibley, there arose a number of serious disagreements. Nicollet mediated between his friends. In February a delegation of Indians from Lac qui Parle, site of a mission on the upper Minnesota River, came to Taliaferro complaining of Sibley who was at that time visiting the area. Because of the illness of the agent, Nicollet saw the Indians and conveyed the major's judgment in writing to Sibley: "I make it a pleasure to send it to you without delay because . . . there should be no misunderstanding . . . between two men whom I esteem, honor, and love."[55]

As the slow northern spring held back the warmth of summer, however, Nicollet's restlessness and loneliness increased. He longed for good food, wine, and music — but most of all for news. He wrote despairingly to Hassler, "I can't tell you the sufferings I endure in being deprived of news of my friends. . . . But God of Mercy, the end of these torments is almost near." From St. Louis, he said, he planned to return east by way of the Great Lakes and to visit Boston. In anticipation of his departure he sent three boxes of his valuable collections — one containing Indian war implements — to St. Louis in June on the steamer "Palmyra."[56]

He stayed on, however. In July he made an examination of a cave eight miles below the fort on the east bank of the Mississippi which had earlier been described by the English explorer Jonathan Carver. On July 29 he again signed his name as witness to a treaty with the Indians. Twelve hundred Chippewa and several hundred Sioux gathered in an arbor erected near Taliaferro's agency, and the Chippewa

[54] Taliaferro, in *Minnesota Historical Collections*, 6: 242; *Report*, 67.
[55] Nicollet to Sibley, February 23, 1837 (translated copy), Sibley Papers.
[56] Nicollet to Hassler, April 19, 1837, Ford Collection; Nicollet to Taliaferro, September 20, 1837.

ceded to the United States an area comprising most of northwestern Wisconsin, as well as the land between the St. Croix and the Mississippi north of the 1825 boundary between their land and that of the Sioux.[57]

Once more Nicollet's personal desires were to be set aside in favor of the "magnitude of his enterprise." On August 2, he left the fort to accompany a party of traders who had attended the treaty signing and were returning to Lake Superior by way of the St. Croix. Much as he longed to return to civilization, he could not refuse this opportunity to make the first geographical study of the St. Croix — the Mississippi's highest important eastern tributary. "I could not hesitate to profit from it," he wrote a friend.[58] Again, the story of the journey is here told by Nicollet himself, although his record is a meager one; comments on geology and a struggle with the rapids and bogs dominate his entries. The only record of his return trip to the fort, made by way of the St. Louis River and the wearisome Savanna Portage, is a series of readings recorded in his astronomical notebooks.

Nicollet drew a small map of the region drained by the St. Croix — a region included in his published map — but the physical exhaustion he suffered on the tedious trip with its many portages and swampy meanderings was a high price to pay for information about a country so distant from the rich agricultural lands which were to attract settlers. The St. Croix remains today one of the few wild rivers of the United States.

Before Nicollet returned to Fort Snelling in early October, Taliaferro had left the post to go to Washington with a delegation of Sioux to sign before the secretary of war a treaty which would cede to the United States all of the tribe's lands east of the Mississippi. Sibley, too, had left for the East, finding it expedient to represent the interests of the American Fur Company at the treaty table. Nicollet was bitterly disappointed at not seeing his friends again. Sick at heart, he stayed at the fort only long enough to make preparations to embark in a "little birch bark canoe" which carried him

[57] *Report*, 72; Kappler, comp. and ed., *Indian Affairs*, 2: 493.
[58] Nicollet to Rush Nutt, October 18, 1837 (copy), Joseph N. Nicollet Papers, in the Minnesota Historical Society. The original is owned by Mrs. Leslie K. Pollard of Madison, Wisconsin.

and trader William A. Aitken, who had been "kind enough" to wait for him, down the river to Prairie du Chien. Thus he said farewell forever — or so he thought — to the land of such arduous labors and great satisfactions.[59]

At St. Louis he found that the box of Indian implements he had sent earlier was missing. "Where is it?" he wrote Taliaferro in anguish. His letter traveled eastward with a delegation of Winnebago bound for Pittsburgh. He recovered the precious box, but no one knows into whose hands its contents eventually fell. As winter was closing in by the time he found all of his belongings, he abandoned his plan to go by way of the Great Lakes and traveled east by the shortest route — up the Ohio River on the steamboat "Maryland" with his "instruments, pebbles, plants, birds, reptiles, quadrupeds, medicine bags, mocassins [sic], calumets, etc." Pierre Chouteau, Jr., partner of the American Fur Company in St. Louis, traveled with him.[60]

Nicollet's year in the swamps and forests of the North marked the "great divide" in his American career. Before him lay the sunlit plains and a brief but productive period of public service. He placed his map before Secretary of War Joel R. Poinsett, a cultivated South Carolinian with whom the Frenchman conversed happily about many things. Nicollet not only received payment but, to his great delight, he received orders on April 7, 1838, from the Bureau of Topographical Engineers to lead an expedition for the purpose of collecting "additional materials for the map now in hand, of those parts of the United States and their territories which lie west of the Mississippi."[61] This meant the triangle of land between the Mississippi, the Missouri, and the Canadian boundary. Within it lay the unmapped Coteau des Prairies, a rise of land in whose southern reaches the Des Moines River was thought to have its source.

The summer of 1838 saw Nicollet again at Fort Snelling on his way to explore the country at the headwaters of the Minnesota and Des Moines rivers. He returned through the region of lakes and hills drained by the river now known as the Cannon. In 1839 he traveled from Fort Pierre on the Missouri across what is now North Dakota

[59] Quotations from Nicollet to Sibley, November 27, 1837, Sibley Papers; Taliaferro, in *Minnesota Historical Collections*, 6: 217–219.

[60] Nicollet to Taliaferro, September 20, 1837; to Sibley, November 27, 1837.

[61] *Report*, 4.

to Devils Lake and south across the Coteau des Prairies. Accompanying him on both of these trips was a young lieutenant, John C. Frémont, whose later assignments to explore the Rockies were a direct
result of his scientific training under the French cartographer.[62]

When Nicollet returned to Washington early in 1840, he was in
a position to enjoy a well-earned reputation among American scientists. He was given every opportunity by the government to complete his map and report, but he suffered from an obscure stomach
ailment (possibly cancer) and was overwhelmed by the struggle to
organize the vast amount of material he had collected. Unhappy
with the delineation of the topography on the small-scale engraving
of his map to be printed with his report, unable to include his Indian
material, gripped by anxiety and depression about his lost reputation
in France — a state of mind accentuated by illness — he modestly
claimed for himself the distinction of being "the first traveller who
has carried with him astronomical instruments, and put them to profitable account, along the whole course of the Mississippi, from its
mouth to its sources." He died in Washington, D. C., on July 17, 1843,
mourned by the many friends who were well aware of the extraordinary scope of his talents.[63]

Nicollet had been in the United States eleven years. When he
arrived the rivers, plains, and uplands of the Mississippi basin were
generally known, and the responsibility of the United States government to provide and encourage further exploration was widely
(if reluctantly in some quarters) accepted. But there lay ahead a tremendous task. Of the mineral resources, the soils, the watersheds,
and the regional distinctions which would make it possible to develop industry and agriculture and to build an effective transportation system, little had yet been learned. The men who were to provide
this knowledge — engineers, scientists, physicians, and devoted lay-
men of many occupations — struggled with hardships and difficulties
less spectacular perhaps than those met by the earliest explorers but
in reality no less demanding of time and strength. In the 1830s the

[62] *Dictionary of American Biography*, 7: 20 (New York, 1931). For Nicollet's
account of these expeditions, see *Report*, 9–52; Frémont gives an account in his
Memoirs of My Life, 1: 34–54 (New York, 1887). Both have been reprinted with
an introduction and annotation by Doane Robinson in *South Dakota Historical
Collections*, 10: 69–129 (Pierre, 1920).
[63] *Report*, 59. The 1843 map contained much less of Nicollet's careful hach-
uring than did the 1845 map.

nation's first state geological surveys were under way.[64] Men of scientific training — many of them recent refugees from Europe — worked in frontier towns under primitive conditions of travel and often without support from any governing body. The public was naturally concerned with more immediate matters.

To this chapter in the accumulation of geographical and geological information on the United States Nicollet, through enormous labor and intelligent observation, contributed not only a bit of the expertise which drew men of science together into working institutions, but he made also several concrete and valuable additions to the knowledge of the continent. The first, of course, was his splendid map, whose value to our day as well to his own has already been discussed. His contributions to meteorology and geology were equally recognized by his contemporaries, but it is in the latter science especially — the "liveliest" of his day — that his reputation has survived. He made important statements on the limits of the Carboniferous and Cretaceous formations and accurately described the "erratic *deposite*" or what is known today as the glacial drift which covers the upper Midwest as far south as the Missouri River. He did not, however, accept the theory of the glacial origin of this peculiar formation.[65]

Less tangible, perhaps, but of more interest to the social historian is Nicollet's position as a transitional figure in the changing government policy toward the support of science for other than military purposes. He was the first civilian to be appointed leader of an expedition under the Corps of Topographical Engineers, whose responsibilities were more and more of purely civilian concern.[66] Not the least of Nicollet's accomplishments was the training of young Captain Frémont, by whom he was held in great affection and respect, and who carried on Nicollet's work after the geographer's death.

Nicollet's appointment was the direct result of the map which he produced during the long, cold winter of 1836–37 at Fort Snelling.

[64] George P. Merrill, *The First One Hundred Years of American Geology*, 127–208 (New Haven, Conn., 1929); Bray, in American Philosophical Society, *Proceedings*, 114: 37–59.

[65] *Report*, 8.

[66] The Corps of Topographical Engineers was created by act of Congress, July 5, 1838. For an account of its duties and status, see William H. Goetzmann, *Army Exploration in the American West, 1803–1863*, 11 (New Haven, Conn., 1959).

"A map of so unknown a region and from so competent a hand excited no small degree of curiosity," wrote Colonel Abert.[67] That Nicollet's was a competent hand he had himself established as he made his way for four years toward his goal, the Mississippi River, talking and working with American scientists wherever he could find them. Nicollet's story is an inseparable part of the growth of scientific professionalism in America, and nowhere is his own standard of professionalism more strikingly illustrated than in the solitary pursuit of knowledge in the wilderness of Minnesota recounted in the documents here printed.

Professionalism, however, is not always a matter of formal training. Nicollet entered the then new world of geology through his own observations without the benefit of earlier teachers. His attitude toward the Indians foreshadowed the emergence of a science yet unborn. Not until 1879 was the founding of the Bureau of American Ethnology to mark the final "emancipation of ethnology from geography and geology."[68] With the publications of this bureau the culture of the American Indian was documented more fully than that of any other primitive people. Nicollet with his enormous talent for significant observation was the first professional to record the customs of the Chippewa. His notes corroborate much of the work of later ethnologists and add a number of details which would otherwise have remained unknown. It is to be particularly regretted that his "copious grammars" of the Ojibway and Dakota languages which he mentioned to a friend have been lost.[69] Although a translator was hired by Abert to write up Nicollet's notes, nothing more was heard of them.

A map of a segment of country larger than half of Europe, a place in the growing scientific community of what might then have been called an underdeveloped country, observations of permanent value which record a vanishing culture—any one of these might be called an extraordinary accomplishment. Nicollet, accomplishing all three in only eleven years, was indeed an extraordinary man.

[67] Abert Memoir.
[68] Claude Lévi-Strauss, "Anthropology: Its Achievements and Future," in *Knowledge Among Men*, 112 (New York, 1966). That Nicollet himself was aware of the emerging discipline is indicated by an undated memorandum among his papers which notes the existence of an "Ethnographical Society of Paris" devoted to "Ethnological investigation."
[69] Nicollet to Rush Nutt, October 18, 1837.

Expedition to the
Source of the Mississippi
JULY 29 – SEPTEMBER 21, 1836

LEFT THE FALLS OF ST. ANTHONY on Friday, July 29, 1836, at 11 o'clock in the morning. Lovely weather with a fresh wind blowing from the north. From 11 o'clock to 11:28, northwest bound, we coasted along through rocky islands for one mile. The banks gradually decline and level off at the height of the great primitive deposits of rolled gravel.[1] Chagobay and Brunia pointed out to me the *manomini*, or wild rice, which grows in the shallows of the river wherever the reeds or little rushes have not taken over. At 11:28 we headed N and soon bore NNW, till 12:25. Fifteen minutes were lost while on this course, spent making a more even distribution of the gear on board. Another fifteen minutes were lost when we met four canoes manned by Sioux Indians descending the river asking to talk. They informed us that some of their men had just killed several Chippewa. We had hardly left the four canoes when a large flotilla of the same people emerged. I counted thirty-eight canoes in the course of a mile. I refused to stop again. They passed by quietly, all

[1] Nicollet here uses the language of amateur geologists of his day in describing the glacial drift which covers much of the country he traversed. The terms "primitive" and "transitional" (p. 67) were soon to be abandoned by geologists as the new ideas of stratigraphy, now the basis of historical geology, became accepted professionally. In his *Report* (p. 8) Nicollet was one of the first scientific writers in America to employ the term "erratic deposits," the French description of glacial drift.

31

except one canoe on which there was a furious individual who fired
a rifle shot and made horrible contortions as he cried out that he
wanted to speak to us. We hurried away. It appeared that these
parties of Sioux, composed of bands from Lake Calhoun on a hunting expedition, were now afraid of the consequences of the crimes
recently committed against the Chippewa and as a result had decided
it would be wise to break camp and return quickly to their villages.
No doubt we shall soon meet a party of Chippewa heading for
St. Peter to report these acts to the Indian agent. When the canoes
within calling distance noticed we did not intend to stop, we were
suddenly confronted with men and women demanding to know the
identity of the young native accompanying us. They believed him
to be a Sioux child we had kidnapped. This child happens to be a
charming ten-year-old paddling in the front of my canoe with his
father, Chagobay.[2]

At 12:45 the river bore N till 2:45 with a NNW variation
halfway.

Fifteen minutes were lost on this stretch, resting the paddlers
and awaiting William's canoe.[3]

At 2:11 the right bank of the river held to its northern course;
the left bank, on the other hand, withdrew, making way for three
islands. The islands are densely wooded, and the river which up to
now had been barely a quarter of a mile wide is at this point one
mile wide.

At 2:45, as we left the islands behind, a rivulet [Rice Creek]
about thirty feet wide entered the river from the left. Its shores
are adorned with beautiful white lilies. Chagobay told me that it
winds back to the vicinity of the Falls of the St. Croix River, being

[2] Later (p. 44) Nicollet says that these Sioux included a band from the Six
Villages as well as Lake Calhoun. The former (actually a single community)
was located near the present-day town of Shakopee, whose name is derived from
the Dakota word shakpe, meaning six. The village at Lake Calhoun was estab-
lished in 1829 as an agricultural community under the patronage of Taliaferro.
It was abandoned in 1839 because of its exposed position in the continuing war-
fare with the Chippewa. See John P. Williamson, comp., An English-Dakota
Dictionary, 208 (New York, 1902); Samuel W. Pond, Jr., Two Volunteer
Missionaries among the Dakotas, or the Story of the Labors of Samuel W. and
Gideon H. Pond, 37, 146 (Boston and Chicago, 1893). The boy's name was
Nankanâbitauk (see p. 42), which Nicollet also spelled "Nankanâ" (p. 48)
and "Nankatâ" (p. 57).

[3] No further identification of William has been found.

Voyage,

De St Pierre aux Sources du Mississippi.

1836.

N.B. Les noms des lieux où j'ai fait des observations astronomiques, sont donnés dans ce registre tels que je les adopte et tels que j'entends les mettre sur la carte du voyage. Je renvoie à mon journal pour l'origine de ces noms et les motifs qui ont déterminé leur adoption.

Falls of St Antony, Wisconsin territory, Sioux Nation.

Jeudi 28 Juillet 1836.			Jeudi 28 Juillet 1836.		
haut. ☉ à l'ouest.			2me Série.		
3ʰ. 46ᵐ.25ˢ	64°.18'.30"	0.1503677	3ʰ. 51ᵐ.50ˢ	62°.21'.50"	B = 29,020
47.27	63.55.45	0.0239301	52.53	62.00.30	th = 73,5
48.40	63.29.45	9.4390762	53.51	61.40.15	0.1503677
49.58	63.01.30	9.8262378	54.47	61.20.30	0.0239280
50.52	62.43.00	9.4396118	55.58	60.54.45	9.4380822
3.48.49,0	63.29.42,0	9.7178059	3.53.51,8	61.39.34	9.8300582
	31.44.41,0	31°.38'.22"		30.49.47,0	9.4358840
		63.16.44			9.7276920
	+15.46,4	4ʰ.13'.06",98		+15.46,6	32°.17'.20"
+M.30'+	32.00.27,4	+6.7.75	+M.45"+	31.05.33,4	64.34.40
	−1.18,2	4.19.14,88		−1.21,8	4ʰ.18.18",66
	32.◯.39,2	3.48.40,00			+6.7.74
	44.58.20,1	retard = −30 34,88		48.◯.49,6	4.24.26.38
	31.59.03,2	34,88		31.4.11,6 ret.= −30 34,88	3.53.51,80
mem de coll.	−1.30,0	−30.34,62		−1.30,0	
	31.57.39,2	26 St Pierre --- 29".6,62		31.2.41,6	
	44.58.50,0	1 jour en voyage --- 1.6,69		44.58.50,0	
	71.7.14,0	1 jour repos --- 39,57		71.2.16,7	
	148.58.43,2	retard St Pierre = −30.52,88		147.10.48,5	
	74.02.51,6	retard aux chutes = 30.34,62		73.36.24,2	
	58.57.39,2	Diff. longit. = 18,26		31.2.41,6	
	43.5.42,6			43.52.42,6	

N.B. J'ai trouvé le soir, après les observations, une erreur de collimation = −1'.30" ajoutée de la hauteur. Cette erreur n'affecte pas les observations de la page suivante faites sur la même station.

The first page of the astronomical notebook kept by Nicollet on his journey to the source of the Mississippi

separated from the latter by only a short portage. Its course links
several lakes, while irrigating a land abundant with wild rice where
the Sioux gather their yearly provisions. The Sioux call it in their
language Wild Rice River, and the Chippewa *Manominikan Sibi*,
which means river where one reaps wild rice.

From 2:45 to 3:04 we halted at the mouth of Wild Rice River.
For the next one and a half miles upstream the Mississippi is half a
mile wide. It is a beautiful sheet of water with a still surface, its
borders parallel and without vegetation, the left one higher than the
right. There are prairies on either side. It is a cheerful scene. During
this mile and a half, the course of the river is due north by the compass. We traveled this distance from 3:04 to 3:20. From that time
till 3:45 (a mile and a quarter), the river maintains its width, and
its course is NW ¼ W. Right here, Chagobay's son leaned on me
and shot down a dove more than sixty paces away with a rifle I had
exchanged that very morning because I had found it too heavy.

3:47. We passed three islands dividing the river which during
this stretch bears NW. The channel becomes narrower and faster.

4:05. Last point of the above islands. Our bearing is NW. At
4:10 it is NNW.

4:20. Another group of islands appeared. The river is half a mile
wide. We stopped for fifteen minutes.

4:47. The mouth of a river appeared on the left bank (right
bank looking upstream) or on the same side as Wild Rice River.
The river bore N here and more islands appeared. They are numerous and of all sizes. There are some pretty views along the straits
they form. The river is almost three quarters of a mile wide. At
5:10 our bearing, which had turned slightly toward NNW, then
returned due N, veered W, and more islands appeared one after the
other. The left bank veers suddenly, while the right is deflected to
a lesser degree from its original direction. Well-wooded islands fill
the angle thus formed on the left. We stopped here to visit an abandoned Indian camp used during the summer hunting trips. Chagobay, who had stayed ashore for an hour, returned loaded with turtles
and various herbs admirably arranged in braids or packages. He said
they were for making infusions and remedies. Chagobay informed
me the river we had just passed is called by the Chippewa *Kitta-
jouan* or Little-big River [*Coon Creek*]. It does not come very far;
neither does it connect with any lake. It is formed by the many

streams that crisscross the land of high prairies it waters. Its course is almost north and its length thirty to forty miles.

At a distance of a quarter of a mile from the apex of the right angle we have just traced and on the side heading west, the islands disappear and rapids begin. The rapids broken by the last island are approximately two miles long and bear WNW. The powerful current and the shallow waters at the bottom of which lie huge rolled stones make hard and dangerous going for bark canoes. At the beginning of the rapids appears a beautiful sheet of water, perfectly straight, the kind Canadians call an "avenue." The left bank of this "avenue" reveals a cove covered with water plants so thick and so high as to be impenetrable. Myriads of mosquitoes escape from them. We searched for a place to spend the night and stopped three or four miles below Rum River.

The night was still, the sky full of stars, and I regretted the site of our camp did not lend itself to making astronomical observations. As I remained idle, I listened to my Indians, who were talking excitedly, and I asked what they were talking about. Brunia told me that Chagobay was teaching him to recognize the stars. I found room among Chagobay's disciples and he taught me first of all the four cardinal points which are: *Kiou-etten* (north); *Chaouanon* (south); *Qua Banon* (east, the wind of the day); and *Gabé Hen* (west).[4] I inquired if there were not any other winds, and the master replied that they did not know of any others. Then lifting his gaze toward the sky he pointed out to me *Odgi-ganank*, the constellation of the Great Bear. *Odgi-ganank* is the Chippewa name for the little quadruped called pekan (fisher). The Chippewa apply the name to the seven stars. Three of the stars represent the tail of the animal, the others the paws. We then arrived at *Mascouté-gouan*, head of the dragon [*Drago*].They think this constellation resembles the head of a bear, hence their name for it. He further pointed out the constellations of the Eagle and of the Dolphin which follow one another closely, just as an osprey pursues another osprey. Hence their name for both groups: the ospreys or *Nouâ-tehi-mangoued*. Last of all he indicated the North Star, *Kiou-hatten-nanank*, or the star that does not move

[4] A standard source on the Ojibway language gives the cardinal directions as *giwédin* (north), *jâwan* (south), *wâban* (east), and *ningabian* (west). See Frederick Baraga, *Dictionary of the Otchipwe Language*, 1:84, 181, 238, 286 (Montreal, 1878). This will henceforth be cited simply as Baraga.

as the others do. I asked him if this star really does not move. He replied through his monitor, Brunia, that they do not say it does not move, but that they believe it does not. Such a reply is endowed with reason and most remarkable. This first lesson seemed to emphasize that the Chippewa have some sense of observation, or at least certain traditions concerning the stars. I was eager to pursue my observations, but it was 10 o'clock and our teacher was yawning. We had to separate. Brunia and William told me that the natives have their constellations, which they name after animals they know, belonging to their own region.

SATURDAY, JULY 30, 1836. I got up at 3:30 in the morning. I awakened Désiré and my Chippewa. We broke camp and by 4:30 were afloat. The day promised to be fine. The Mississippi was covered with vapor, forming a mist six to eight feet high, not dense enough, however, to prevent us from finding our way. The temperature of the river water was 68.4° and that of the mist 58°. Complete calm. At 6 o'clock we arrived at the mouth of Rum River situated on the left bank: the *Chkodéouâbo Sibi* of the Chippewa, which has its source at Mille Lacs. We stopped here so that I could make a geographical reading at this confluence while breakfast was being prepared. The site is charming. The view is unobstructed on the left bank, which is higher than the densely wooded right bank. There is an endless prairie on one side and an impenetrable forest on the other; obvious sterility on the left, seeming fertility on the right. It looks as if one part awaits the plow and the spade, the other the ax and fire.

Looking southeast, I can see on the right bank at one-third of a mile from the mouth of Rum River a stream [*Elm Creek*] emerging from the low forest. Chagobay tells me it meanders away in a northwesterly direction, linking several lakes, two of which he has visited — the two southernmost and closest to the Mississippi. The two mouths are opposite each other. This stream has not been named yet. It is the fourth worthy of notice since St. Anthony Falls. I did not mention the first [*Bassett Creek*]. This escaped me. It flows from the right bank, just after the rapids above the falls as one goes upstream.

[Nicollet's diary for the evening of July 30 is missing. Accord-

*ing to his astronomical notebook for July 31 the party camped at
the mouth of the Elk River, which Nicollet designated the "St.
Francis or Parallel River."⁵ Next evening the diary continues with
several entries that are disjointed and fragmentary.*]

SUNDAY, JULY 31, 1836. Cloudy, then later a beautiful sky
with a northerly wind. At 8:30 some northern lights appear. A large
arc spans the horizon culminating at 10°. Both extremities, NW and
NE, lean upon the horizon. Three clouds assemble between the arc
and the horizon. At about 9:00, a column of light rises from each
of the clouds. The reddish light is emitted by spells and it is more
intense above and below the arc than it is in the neighboring regions
it crosses. The moon rises, preventing me from following the progress of the phenomenon. Only the arc remains visible.

Sunday, July 31, 1836. *Migady-ouin Sibi Ouissen*: Little Battle
River [*Otter Creek*] on the right bank of the Mississippi in Sioux
country. Between *Migady-ouin* River and *Ka Ouâkummik* [*Clearwater*] River, the two following rivers appear on the same side of the
Mississippi.

1. The *Sibi-ouissen* or Little River [*Silver Creek*] flows in approximately halfway.

2. The *Kibiskabitigoué-yag*, or Meander River, also called Big
Point River by the Canadians [*Fish Creek*], appears three-fourths
of the way upstream.

MONDAY, AUGUST 1, 1836. *Ka Ouâ Kummik Tigoue Yag*,
Clear Water River on the right bank of the Mississippi, Sioux country. I made my observations in a swamp where we were forced to
camp, facing the river.

TUESDAY, AUGUST 2, 1836. It rained all night and it is still
raining today. Of necessity we stay in our camp till Wednesday,
the 3rd, in the morning.

⁵ Today the northeast tributary of the Elk is called the St. Francis. In another
entry in his astronomical notebooks, July 31, 1836, Nicollet refers to this tributary
as "the Leaf River of Pike," and "the *Kâbita Oui Tigoué Yâg*, river beside
another," or Parallel River. On the 1836 map the entire river is the St. Francis
with an East Branch and a Parallel Branch. On the 1843 map the Elk is the
Kabitawi and its northeast tributary is the St. Francis or *Wichaniwa*.

WEDNESDAY, AUGUST 3, 1836. *Osâgis* or *Sâgis Sibi* of the Chippewa [*Sauk River*], also called Sâkis, Sauks, Sawkis by the Americans, and Sâks or Sacs by the French. On the right bank of the Mississippi in Sioux country.

The "g" in Sâgis is pronounced as in the word "guide," but it is not surprising that the Americans and French wrote Sâks, Sâkis, because the Chippewa harden this letter very much, making it sound like a "k." The name Sâgis or Sâkis is given by all the native nations to the Sâkis natives. It recalls the inhabitants that lived at the mouth of this river.[6] The name was given to the river following a solemn and friendly meeting that was held there between the Chippewa and Sâkis Indians.

THURSDAY, AUGUST 4, 1836. Ouâtab or Wâhtab is the name of a Chippewa still living on the east of the Mississippi who would hunt the beaver on this river when there were still beavers about. The Indians respected such territorial hunting rights brought about by time and custom. It was in his memory that they gave this name to the river.

Thursday, August 4, 1836. We left the mouth of Sâkis River this morning at 6 o'clock. Fifty-eight minutes later we reached the mouth of Little Sâkis [*Watab*] River. I estimate the distance to be three good miles. We had breakfast and I made some observations. At 10:30 we started out again. Along the three miles that follow Little Sâkis River there are some rapids that are not bad enough to call for portages. They are still difficult to overcome because of strong currents and of the difficulty in finding quieter channels where rocks are less of a menace. It is at the upper end of these rapids, where the river is narrow and where a cove begins, that the brother of [Joseph] Renneville, the trader of Lac qui Parle, a Sioux half-breed, was killed by a Chippewa ambushed in the brush overlooking the river.[7] A quarter of a mile above the rapids, on the

---

[6] See Warren Upham, *Minnesota Geographic Names*, 51 (Reprint Edition, St. Paul, 1969). According to Upham, "The origin of the names of Sauk river and of Osakis lake . . . was from refugee Sauk or Sac Indians, who came to Osakis lake from the home of this tribe . . . in Wisconsin."

[7] Nicollet refers to this incident again on p. 52. There is no record that any relative of Joseph Renville died at this time, although his brother Victor is said to have been slain near Little Falls a decade earlier. See Thomas Hughes, *Indian Chiefs of Southern Minnesota*, 81 (Mankato, Minn., 1927).

Detail of the Mississippi between Sauk Rapids and Little Rock Creek. Nicollet's notes on the sketch include descriptions of the river and the surrounding country as well as geological observations.

left bank, a small creek [*Halfway Brook*] flows forth. It is difficult to spot it because its mouth is entirely concealed by tall reeds and other water plants. One and a quarter miles beyond the creek, on the same side of the river, a hill of primitive rocks rises (syenite and porphyry). It is a mile long, one quarter of a mile wide, and one side forms the bank of the river. The fact that it is the first rock rising high from the ground since St. Anthony Falls makes it all the more pleasing to behold. Some day, when the arts will contrast its height with the surrounding flat country, it will be a picturesque sight of admirable beauty. This hill is called the Rock or the *Kouâbikâ* of the Chippewa.[8] The same name is given to the natural irregularities surrounding it. The large and beautiful island preceding it is called Rock Island (*Kouâbikâ*). The creek that flows from its base toward its extremity upstream is called Rock Creek [*unnamed*], and the river emptying from the same bank half a mile up is Rock River (*Kouâbikâ Sibi*) [*Little Rock Creek*]. It comes from quite far away. The height of its tallest peak that one cannot see from the edge of the river is ninety-three feet above the water level. At 1:00, the barometer on this summit reads 29, 190–64, 6–64, 6. There is an abundance of Cryptogamia to be found. Pine trees also appear.

The famous Prairie au Jeu de la Crosse forms a lovely cove at the mouth of the river.[9] We spend the night there making observations. There is a creek [*unnamed*] one or two miles beyond this point on the right bank.

FRIDAY, AUGUST 5, 1836. We left the mouth of Broken [*Platte*] River at 9:26. I have just been informed by Mr. William that near the spot where we met the Chippewa last Wednesday, only a little farther up, is a river very much traveled by the natives

[8] This feature was also known as the Peace Rock from its proximity to the boundary negotiated between the Sioux and Chippewa in 1825. The entire area was often referred to as "Little Rock," because of numerous outcroppings of granite and syenite that form small knobs and hills. See Upham, *Minnesota Geographic Names*, 52.

[9] This prairie was noted by Pike, who found "immense herds of elk and buffalo" in the vicinity and by Beltrami, who called the Little Rock River "*Bikabikao-sibi*, or Shuffle-board." The latter is the only other reference found to this prairie as a site for games. See Elliott Coues, ed., *The Expeditions of Zebulon Montgomery Pike*, 1:316 (New York, 1895); J. C. Beltrami, *A Pilgrimage in Europe and America*, 2:468 (London, 1828).

that I had overlooked. It does not have a name yet and comes out on the left bank.[10]

At 10:08 we paddled by the mouth of *Sagatagan Sibi* or Spunk River, named after an Indian, Sagatagan, who regularly hunted on it. *Tondre* in French, or *sagatanan* in Chippewa, is also the word for a certain kind of tinder used in making fire. The river is on the right bank and must be long, since it is used for hunting. It winds back to and goes through Spunk Lake, or *Sagatanan Sagahagan*. There are two miles, or very nearly that, between the mouth of this last tributary and the preceding one. We rested seventeen minutes, time enough for a pipe.

At 11:46 we reached the mouth of the *Kânichô (jô)-tigoué-ahâ*, a river thirty feet wide on the right bank. It twists back far to the west or northwest and is linked to several lakes. Within five minutes, farther upstream and on the same side, appeared another river coming from a less remote place. Because they are so close and because of their distinct features, the Indians have given these rivers a mutual name: *Kanijô-tigoué-hâ*, or Two Rivers from *kanijô* meaning two, and *tigouéhâ*, river. Indians frequently use the Two Rivers, racing or hunting with their canoes. It is six miles from the *Sagatagan Sibi* to the first of the Two Rivers, and one third of a mile separates the first from the second.

The *Sagatagan Sibi* and the Two Rivers are probably the waterways tentatively represented on maps as Wolf Creek and Rocky Creek.[11] Their positioning on these maps is not exact, and furthermore the latter, or Rocky Creek, is shown only as a single river when in reality there are two, both forming the Two Rivers, a familiar name with all the natives, traders, and white people in the country. It is true that the mouth of the second of the Two Rivers is difficult to see because it is obscured by islands around which canoes cannot navigate, and had I not been warned by Brunia, William, and Chagobay I would have missed it myself. Lieutenant Allen's map gives an indication of the rivers that is poorer yet, and

[10] "Last Wednesday" would have been August 3, when Nicollet traveled between the mouth of the Clearwater and the mouth of the Sauk River. Since no streams of any importance enter the Mississippi from the east in this area, the statement must have resulted from some misunderstanding.

[11] Wolf Creek appears on the map of this area in Henry S. Tanner, *New American Atlas* (Washington, D.C., 1825). Tanner took his information from Pike's map.

he does not name them. The numerous instances of negligence I have noted on this map from St. Peter to here prove that good science cannot be accomplished by traveling a hundred miles a day. Why go to the trouble of mustering a national expedition and end up throwing confusion over the work done by the brave Major Pike thirty years earlier? I hope the country I have yet to cover in the course of this expedition will give me the opportunity of restoring the high regard I had acquired for Lieutenant Allen while reading his report to Major [General Alexander] Macomb.

I left the second of the Two Rivers at 12:08. Soon we began to feel the force of the current caused by the rapids we would have to negotiate that day. After a mile's navigation we met a succession of small rapids that merely make furrows through the river for half a mile, and after another half a mile we reached the foot of the big rapids called by the Canadians: *Rapide Coûteau*, or Cutting Rapids, (rapids cutting up the canoes as it were).[12] We made no portage, but we all disembarked so as to lighten the weight in the canoes.

Désiré, the young Missâbays[13] and Nankanâbitauk began to tow while Brunia, his brother, and Chagobay labored in water up to their waists, pushing the canoe over the crests of the impetuous waves swelled here by the sudden drop of the water level. We carried out this passage near the left bank of the river where rock-formed channels, the easiest to clear, are to be found.

During the halt we made at the foot of the rapids to prepare for the ascent, I noticed on the bank trickles of water oozing from under the rocks, suspending a kind of blue sand, brilliant, very fine, and sustaining afloat a matter very soft and oily to the touch when one stirred the liquid. It is a talcous sand resulting from the dissolution of a steatitic schist, rich in infinitely small talcum flakes, all filtering the oozing water referred to above. This steatite is crossed by veins of quartz and it seems to rest on the shales forming the bed of the river in these parts.[14]

This simple circumstance brings with it the opportunity of

[12] This is shown as Knife Rapids on Nicollet's 1843 map.

[13] Here and below (p. 48) Nicollet's use of this term is unexplained. He apparently referred to several young Chippewa who were members of the party and may have meant to use the word *missinabés* (see p. 114). Elsewhere he defines *missabay* as giant (Appendix 5, p. 255), and *missabé* as the manito of hunters (p. 212). Baraga (2:252) gives *missâbe* as giant.

[14] Nicollet used the French word *schist* which means both schist and shale, but here and elsewhere in the diary he meant shale.

reflecting upon the relative value attached by the human species to objects supplied by nature for its needs. The discovery of this sand caused me to reflect on the progress of the sciences and arts which are useful to society. William, the trader, the merchant, saw in it a veritable gold mine, and among the natives it awakened ideas of pleasure and vanity, inciting them to knead the sand, thus creating colors with which they daubed their faces, arms, and hair and smeared their foreheads, their clothing, and their canoes. Chagobay, in particular, drew on his cheeks a series of strokes equal to the number of illustrious deeds he had accomplished and decorated his chest with symbols of the medals of honor that had successively been granted to his ancestors and himself by the kings of France and England and the presidents of the United States. Brunia alone, an interesting man, a being halfway between the savage and the civilized man, remained calm and neutral in the middle of the three different orders of enthusiasm caused by this event.

It was in this new fashion, now entirely barbarian, that our canoes passed *Rapide-coûteau*, Knife Rapids or Cutting Rapids. Immediately after these rapids, two lovely brooks made their appearance, one after the other.[15] Their entrance into the river is concealed by tall grass, but their murmur is audible. I visited the first, which formed a cascade seven to eight feet high in a very wild site ten to fifteen feet away from the left bank of the river. For a mile after Cutting Rapids we met, in turn, places of uniform and gentle currents, then places where the currents are quickened by sudden changes in the river level. Whenever there is a little bay or curve one must use extra strength to maneuver the canoes.

Finally, during a fourth mile, we undertook and passed the rapids of the River of the Swans [*Pike Rapids*], the last ones on this part of the river. Here again the left bank is the side permitting an easier passage. It was nearly 5 o'clock when we reached the mouth of Swan River. Therefore we spent five hours coming from Two Rivers to Swan River. One and a half hours were devoted to resting and making the necessary preparations for each ascent. This left three and a half hours used traveling a distance I estimate to be four good miles, climbing up rapids and strong, free currents.[16]

[15] These brooks are shown but not named on the 1836 map. They do not appear on the 1843 map, and they are unidentifiable today.

[16] According to modern measurements this distance is 7 miles. See United

Because the rapids end here, and also because islands and accumulations of floating trees obstruct it, the entrance into Swan River is unapproachable. We set up camp a mile upstream, on the right shore of the river, near the house where the American Fur Company now has a trading post run by a Chippewa of mixed blood, Monsieur Cravasson.[17] The sky, which had been beautiful for the first half of the day, clouded over for the rest, and the wind was blowing from the south. It rained considerably during the night.

SATURDAY, AUGUST 6, 1836. Because the sky remained overcast and also because it rained heavily all night long, I was not able to make any observations. This morning the sky was still threatening. I decided we should stay at this camp. In these wild surroundings where I have ventured, I am ignorant of the destiny Providence has in store for me. I do not wish to leave anything undone that might delay me as I return, if indeed I do return. So I shall await the sun of the day or the stars of the night. My men needed the rest anyway. We all have some laundering and drying to do, and I have many notes to file and update.

It comes to mind that the day I left St. Anthony Falls I met thirty-eight canoes manned by Sioux from the Six [Villages] and Lake Calhoun on a hunting expedition. They had learned that Sioux Indians from the St. Peter River had committed crimes against the Chippewa (the Pillagers of Leech Lake with whom they are still at war), and they told me they had interrupted their hunting expedition to return hastily to their village, fearing war would inevitably break out between the Sioux at large and the Chippewa of Leech Lake.[18] It may be remembered that a few days after this encounter,

States Army, Corps of Engineers, *The Middle and Upper Mississippi River*, 286 (Washington, D.C., 1940).

[17] In the astronomical notebook under date of August 5, 1836, Nicollet calls the river the West Swan and records an observation from the mouth. He also wrote: "I made my camp between two trading houses which were established here this year to set up trade with the Indians." "Cravasson" was probably Peter Crebassa, who was listed as clerk in charge of the American Fur Company post at Fond du Lac during 1836–37 but had apparently been shifted to the new location. A list of trading licenses issued in 1838 includes Swan River and indicates that John Aitken was then in charge. See Grace Lee Nute, ed., "The Diary of Martin McLeod," in *Minnesota History*, 4: 380n. (August–November, 1922); licenses issued by Miles Vineyard, May 25, 1838, in Sibley Papers.

[18] Various origins have been given for the name "Pillagers." Schoolcraft

I met fifteen to eighteen more canoes, manned this time by Chippewa Indians from Sandy Lake, members of the party of Strong Head, their chief, who informed me that the news of the crimes was false and that none had been committed.[19] We now find out here that the crimes were real. However, the number and the circumstances remain unknown. The only positive fact is that a Chippewa on a hunting trip with his wife and children fled the Sioux whom he saw approaching, and the latter, unable to catch him, vengefully killed his wife and children and looted and burned down his hut. The poor man returned to Leech Lake, naked and exhausted. Ashamed of not having defended those so dear to him, he did not dare tell of his misfortune for several days. Finally, the party of the chief, Flat Mouth, rose up in arms. When I reach Leech Lake I shall probably find that this chief has departed with a group of his warriors to avenge the deed perpetrated on a family of his tribe.[20]

Three o'clock in the afternoon. The Chippewa from Sandy Lake and the Sioux from the lakes around St. Anthony Falls often live on good terms and part only in case of general belligerency between the two nations to which they belong. So it was with the two parties I met successively on my way here. In the course of their hunting expedition, now interrupted, they had fraternized every evening in those abandoned camps I inspected on this trip as mentioned in my notes of the previous days.[21] I found out that they danced every evening, but I arrived too late to see these dances. They separated following the news of the crimes committed at large in the land, and, not knowing what consequences these events might bring, the

(*Narrative of an Expedition*, 90) lays it to the "robbery of a principal trader." William W. Warren in his *History of the Ojibways*, 256 (*Minnesota Historical Collections*, vol. 5, 1885) ascribes it to a general reputation for bravery. Nicollet accepted Schoolcraft's explanation. See *Report*, 62.

[19] If Nicollet noted this incident, the entry has been lost. In writing "La Tête Forte" here and later (p. 47, 78) he probably meant Strong Ground, the chief of the Sandy Lake band. Taliaferro noted in his journal on August 6, 1836, that he had received a letter from Nicollet carried by Strong Ground. Schoolcraft calls this chief Soangikumig (*Narrative of an Expedition*, 115), and Warren in his *History of the Ojibways*, 470, refers to him as Songemomik.

[20] Flat Mouth was one of the most famous and respected chiefs of the Chippewa. See Schoolcraft, *Narrative of an Expedition*, 80–83; Warren, *History of the Ojibways*, 17, 45, 477, 478–481; William T. Boutwell Journal, May 24, 1835. He was absent when Nicollet arrived at Leech Lake, but not making war upon the Sioux. (See below, p. 84, 198.)

[21] See above, p. 34.

wives of the Sioux had urged their husbands to go back home, while the Chippewa women had let their husbands go down to St. Peter while they themselves returned [north] with their children. In the last two days, we have been joined by ten canoes filled with women and children. They travel in our company, setting up their camp next to ours. They are most reserved, very modest, and full of mirth. They display an extreme tenderness for their children. Their becoming way of dressing and talking is very much in contrast with that of a nation from the south.[22] They have nothing to eat and yet they are very merry, very talkative, and verify Chagobay's words: "You shall see poor people, but they shall be happy, gay, proud, and hospitable. That which you shall give shall be well received; nothing shall ever be asked of you and you shall receive for that which you offer." Right now, these women, who have camped on the other shore since this morning to be with other families settled there, have just crossed the river to bid us farewell. They brought their children and took particular care of those still in their cradles. There they are, sitting in a circle around the fire, the youngsters huddled around their mothers every which way. The strangeness of this spectacle is heightened by the way the newborn have been arranged in their cradles and by the way their mothers turn them over and over without ever jarring the poor little creatures. I distribute several measures of ribbon, and the little flotilla composed of seven bark canoes recrosses the river. I watch with anxiety the orange line formed by these light gondolas checkered with hieroglyphics painted native style. I fear it might be cut off by the south wind that is blowing quite strongly. No, God protects these innocent navigators! The orange line becomes shorter and shorter. Each dot detaching itself vanishes into the reeds. There goes the last one. I sigh with relief.

The Chippewa name for Swan River is *Ouâbisi-oui-sibi* from *ouâbisi* meaning swan, and *sibi*, river.[23] In general, I note everywhere that the names given to places in these regions by the French or the Americans (the latter translating from the French) are of

[22] Nicollet had encountered tribes in Missouri, Arkansas, and Iowa. He might also have meant the Sioux he had seen near Fort Snelling.

[23] On a scrap of paper filed among his notes, Nicollet recorded that this name was given to him by "Cravasson." The same source is credited with the name *Omokoso Sibi* for the Little Elk River. (See p. 52 for a variation.)

Indian origin and no more than a mere translation of these native names into both modern languages. Therefore, it is of great interest to the history of geography to preserve the relationship of these names, [to] retain their etymology and recall their origin.

There is on this campsite a portage leading from the Mississippi to Swan River. It is a mile long and is used by the Indians and traders to circumvent the difficulties and obstacles encountered at the mouth of the river. The river is a popular hunting ground. It is long and connects with a lake [*Big Swan Lake*] of the same name. Both continue to be abundant with swans as they have been since time immemorial. I saw many bundles containing the plumage of these creatures brought to the American [Fur] Company trading post near my tent. My campsite is [in] a pretty little wood composed mostly of sugar maples, ironwoods, and white woods (basswoods). It is hardly convenient for my observations, neither is it agreeable in damp weather. I could have selected a better one, either closer to the house of the factor or on the opposite shore among the natives, but we came here accompanied by William, who was about to leave our group to settle in this very wood to trade with the natives as a representative of the Baker Company at St. Peter, a competitor of the American Company.[24]

Because it was necessary to exchange a canoe, an operation that only William can facilitate, I felt it wise to postpone our separation till now. The canoe I have used thus far would prove to be too large for the rivers I am going to navigate during the coming week. His is a more convenient size. He accommodatingly gave it to me with the same eagerness he has always shown when giving me information about the country we have crossed together.

Before sunset, I left to visit the native women and the village on the opposite shore where they had settled while they waited for the return of their husbands. I saw the old mother and the sister of the chief called Strong Head [*sic*], and the grave of one of his aunts, who had died a few days before. The face of this chief had indeed

[24] Benjamin F. Baker, a native of Virginia, arrived at Fort Snelling as a schoolteacher in 1822. He soon became a trader and in 1825 built a post near the mouth of the Crow Wing River, where Schoolcraft and Allen found him in 1832. In 1834 he moved to the vicinity of Fort Snelling, where he operated a store until 1838. See Donald Dean Parker, ed., *The Recollections of Philander Prescott, Frontiersman of the Old Northwest 1819–1862*, 47, 80, 153, 168 (Lincoln, Neb., 1966); Allen, in 23 Congress, 1 session, *House Documents*, no. 323, p. 53.

been daubed with black paint when I met him going to St. Peter with his warriors. He had decorated this aunt's grave with glorious trophies: a long pole with fourteen rings notched into the bark, denoting that he had been at war fourteen times; six white rings proved he had returned pure from war (without success, I suppose) by as many times; but eight red ones indicated he had drawn blood (or *fait le coup*—made a killing as the Canadians say) eight times.[25] He did not forget to place some tobacco on the grave so that his aunt could smoke during her long journey.

Returning to my canoe to cross the river, I found two basins full of blueberries that the native women had placed there. I enjoyed them. They are very sweet berries, of a pulpy and juicy consistency, the size of our beautiful red currants in France. They are a great source of help to the traveler when they are ripe. The natives provide themselves with great quantities of them and spread them to dry on rush matting for consumption during the winter. They are considered to be nourishing and wholesome. Natives and white people eat baskets full of them without experiencing the slightest inconvenience.

At dusk the sky seemed about to clear. I took the necessary steps to make some observations, but hardly had I made a series of elevations when the sky clouded over and began to threaten rain. I went to bed.

SUNDAY, AUGUST 7, 1836. This morning at dawn, the young Missâbays and Nankanâ were already up and about. This was extraordinary. Today we were not supposed to break camp. Whenever we do leave early it is impossible to extract them from the mousetrap where they snuggle up every night, in the end of an upside down canoe serving as a tent. A moment later Brunia and Chagobay both appeared, one of them drying his clothes, the other inspecting the sky with nothing on to dry. There ensued a conversation between the two fathers and the two sons, the tone of which sounded terribly gloomy. I sat up on my behind, right in the middle of a puddle of water, and said to Brunia, "What is all this about? Aren't you lighting a fire? The children aren't playing, and Chagobay is not singing. *Omâ-mônay*. What's happening?"

"We are soaked."

[25] For a discussion of the custom of "counting coup," see p. 170–172.

"So am I."

"We could not get any sleep."

"I couldn't either."

"During the night we were lifted up into the air."

"So was I."

"So was I."

And "So was I," repeated William, his mother, and Désiré.

The fact was, the night that had just gone by had been a night of terror and fright. Torrents of rain had poured down for hours accompanied by thunder, lightning, and hail. The hailstones hurled forth during eight to ten minutes had dismembered several trees around us, and at about 3 o'clock lightning had struck a forest of pine trees bordering our little wood. It appears that this bolt was the cause of the commotion that had jolted us all, the effects of which still showed on the sad faces of my companions in sleeplessness.

As I straightened the disarray into which the night had thrown my luggage and provisions, I noticed that the latter, since my departure, had diminished at the rate of a geometric progression, while the distance to be covered had diminished at the rate of an arithmetic progression only. It was clear Désiré had been overly generous and that he had made many friends among the native men and women at my expense. Only travelers in the desert can comprehend the sensation felt when the negative results of such an inventory are suddenly realized. I think it is somewhat similar to the sensation the beautiful ladies of Paris wish to express when they say, *"Ah! ma chère, j'en ai en la barre!"* [*Oh! my dear, it came like a stroke!*] It seems to me Désiré is a crafty Frontin.[26] He justified himself, saying I was the one who started being generous and reassured me by saying he would go hunting.

At about 8 o'clock it stopped raining. I walked down to the edge of the river to find a path among the reeds that would lead to the nearby forest. I wanted to examine the trees struck by lightning. I arrived in the nick of time to help two acquaintances descend from the bark canoes they had used to cross the river. One was a little seven-year-old native girl, the other her five-year-old brother, both children of one of the women who had visited us the evening before.

---

[26] Frontin was a familiar French comedy character, usually portrayed as a bold and witty valet.

They offered me a basket full of blueberries. I took it, saddened by
the thought that there was certainly nothing in their hut for breakfast and that there had probably been nothing there for supper the
day before—the weather had been so bad and the men away. I was
sorry I had given away ribbons when there must have been hopes
for something more substantial. My heart was bleeding. And I had
just scolded Désiré, so what could I do? I did find a way without
his knowing about it. Then I climbed aboard the little canoe and
my two little guardian angels, who seemed to be so happy because
they had made me happy, led me toward the lightning-struck trees
so that I could examine them. They dropped me off carefully on the
shore, holding back the canoe by hanging on to reeds with their
little hands, and returned safely across the river, although the south
wind continued to blow strongly.

During my travels in America, I have often admired the preco-
cious skill with which the children of the natives living along the
shores of lakes and rivers maneuver their canoes; but I have to admit
I did not expect as much on a river such as the Mississippi. Only
yesterday, it was evident how afraid I was, although it was the
women who manned the canoes. But this is what one observes every
day and at any time of the day on the Mississippi wherever Sioux
and Chippewa Indians are to be found.

At 11 o'clock the clouds seemed about to disperse. I took the
necessary steps to measure the meridian sun and requested that our
departure be organized. All went well. I had hardly finished making
my observations when the sky clouded over again, and it stayed
cloudy for the rest of the day. At 12:30 we bade farewell to Mr.
Cravasson and Mr. William. The latter's mother was on her way
to Red Lake so we took her with us. And so we left Swan River.
It is marked on Tanner's map as the place where Major Pike spent
the winter of 1805 to 1806.[27] I am anxious to read the diary of Pike's
expedition. For the past three years I have been traveling in the
South and West, but I have never been able to lay my hands on it.

Two miles after Swan River on the right bank there emerges a
stream called Little Falls [*Pike*] Creek. It is named thus because of
the presence of a waterfall three miles above. At this point, five

[27] See Tanner, *New American Atlas*. Folwell gives Pike's wintering ground
of 1805–06 as "four miles south of Little Falls on the west bank of the Mississippi,
80 rods below the mouth of the Swan River." (*History of Minnesota*, 1:95.)

miles from Swan River, that is, there are indeed some rapids extending across the full width of the river [*Little Falls*]. They are less difficult than the previous ones, and they are the last of the series of obstacles of this nature in the way of steam or sailboat navigation on the upper Mississippi. The western extremity of these rapids is unmanageable because of a waterfall four or five feet high made up of an accumulation of pebbles, but the passage can be easily negotiated along the left bank where a canal is formed by an island and the bank, avoiding all danger and sparing the strength of the crew.

A quarter of a mile below the rapids, a rock eight to ten feet high is to be seen on the left bank. Its vertical façade bears Indian inscriptions drawn with red chalk.[28] Brunia volunteered first to give an interpretation of the hieroglyphic escutcheon: there were two bars more or less vertically parallel, followed by a circle under which was drawn a closed hand seizing something. Brunia believed this meant a party of Chippewa were descending the river to negotiate some important matter either with the Indian agent who represents the American government at St. Peter or with the Sioux they were hoping to meet. In which case, the circle represented the sun, the bars indicated two suns, hence two days, and the hand completed the statement which was that in two days the party descending the river would shake hands with the people they were going to see. This discourse from Brunia brought an ironical smile to Chagobay's lips. He could not conceive of Brunia's inattentiveness and assailed him severely. There followed between the two a discussion which made for me an interesting parody of the lofty literary criticisms exchanged between the young Champollion and Claprott on the subject of Egyptian hieroglyphics.[29] The two bars, insisted

[28] The existence of this rock had been noted by others. According to Pike the place was known as the Rapids of the Painted Rock, and Beltrami designated it "the Great Rock." In 1820 Schoolcraft reported a "Painted Rock upon which the Indians have drawn a number of hieroglyphics and rude designs." He located it, however, between Elk River and the Little Falls on the west or right bank of the Mississippi. The feature was described in detail by Warren Upham in the state geological survey. He confirms Nicollet's location, placing it "on the east shore of the Mississippi, about a half mile south of the middle of Little Falls village, and about a fifth of a mile south from the end of Mill Island." See Coues, ed., *Expeditions of Pike*, 1:316; Beltrami, *A Pilgrimage in Europe and America*, 2:466; Schoolcraft, *Narrative Journal of Travels*, 267; Newton H. Winchell and Warren Upham, *The Geology of Minnesota*, 2:596 (St. Paul, 1888).

[29] Jean François Champollion (1790–1832) was an illustrious French Egyptologist. The editor has been unable to further identify his colleague, Claprott.

Chagobay, represent two nights; the Chippewa count time by the number of nights and not by the number of days.

"Furthermore your sun is no other than the bare head of a man; don't you see," he told Brunia, "that the circle shows nothing suggesting light as it does when we use this sign begging it to be favorable to us, to give us good weather on our voyages. I am telling you," he said, "this circle symbolizes a shaven head, a 'scalped' head. As far as the hand is concerned it is closed, suggesting that it holds something. It is not extended as a hand when we present it to the white people. Therefore the true construction of the meaning of these signs is as follows: after two nights, or on the third day, a head of hair was taken from a Sioux. I say a Sioux, because we wage war only on the Sioux.

"Last of all," says he, "the event these markings refer to is that of the death of Rainville, the brother, that occurred at the Little Rock, and of whom we spoke a few days ago.—Don't you recall," he added for Brunia's benefit, "that so and so (a Chippewa whose name I have forgotten) on his way back from St. Peter found abandoned on the shore of the river the body of a Sioux he recognized as Rainville's; that he took its hair and drew these signs on the rock to tell the Sioux he only took it on the third day, and also to tell them what cowards they must be for not having rescued the body of their chief for so long a time. Finally, don't you remember they held dances for several days at Leech Lake when the head of hair was brought there?"

Chagobay's knowledge floored my poor Brunia and what seemed to increase the confusion considerably was the necessity for Brunia to translate into French everything Chagobay said. He did it most graciously, and we all finished by laughing at the academic quarrel. The subject kindled much animation and interest in our canoe for the following five miles as we traveled from Little Falls to La Biche River (Elk River), the *Omoschkôs Sibi* of the Chippewa [*Little Elk River*]. It is still a living tradition of the natives to name this river after La Biche, a Frenchman the Sioux killed near there many years ago. Hence, to be authentic, one should write in English, La Biche River. In the course of these five miles we joined a canoe manned by two handsome natives, brothers from the osprey family.[80] They

[80] Warren lists no such family or totem. See *History of the Ojibways*, 41–53.

took part in the discussion and were of the opinion of Chagobay. They left us two miles before we reached La Biche River, where I set up camp hoping to take our geographical position during the evening. Barely two hours after leaving us, the two natives returned with a bear and a doe they had killed in that short time. They pitched camp with us, and bear meat was our menu for supper.

[*At the point there is another gap in the diary, and the entries are not resumed until August 11. On August 10 Nicollet recorded an "accident" in his astronomical notebook. This no doubt accounts for the interval, which is nevertheless bridged by fragmentary and hasty entries made on the pages of a smaller notebook. These have been inserted in his diary at this point but are now so faint as to be barely legible. The portions of them that could be deciphered follow here.*]

SUNDAY, AUGUST 7, 1836. We left Swan River at 12:36. Two miles upstream on the right bank I found a little river which is called Little Falls Creek [*Pike Creek*], or Little Rapid Creek because of its proximity to the rapids we are going to encounter. At 2:12 we pass the Little Falls formed by gravel or small rocks which obstruct the Mississippi. This is not a waterfall but a sudden declivity all the way across the width of the river. At 2:38 we are one-fourth mile above the rapids. A quarter of a mile below the rapids is a rock eight to ten feet high on whose face the Indians have drawn the following hieroglyphics with red chalk: [*Sketch too faint for reproduction.*]

WEDNESDAY, AUGUST 10, 1836. We left at 4:14 the east bank of the Mississippi across from Crow [*Crow Wing*] Island and took the south branch of the Crow [*Crow Wing*] River as it enters the Mississippi.[31] We enter this branch at 4:17. Arrive at the junction of the north branch at 4:30 [*Here there is an illegible map.*] We halt to meet with some Indians. [*Two lines illegible.*]

[31] In his *Report* (p. 54) Nicollet explains that he chose this way because "I could not but reflect that the Mississippi before me had been thoroughly explored during the expeditions of Major Pike, General Cass, and Mr. Schoolcraft. . . . I thought, therefore, that it might be advisable to attempt another route across the country." He makes no mention of the trading post of the American Fur Company on Crow Wing Island, a spot which had been a wintering place for traders and voyageurs since 1771.

5:00. Detour by N to NE passing by an island; river one-fourth mile wide, three to four feet deep. Flat all the way to its source.

[*Here follows an illegible page.*]

5:20. Group of islands. Course W. Beautiful country. Left bank high and the river's path is wooded with a curtain of pines suitable for lumber.
5:35. Turn from W to SW
5:50. Detour W–NNW
5:57. NW and NNW
6:12. Gull River or Riviere La Mouve [*old French for* mouette]

[*The last line on the page above is illegible. The entry in the astronomical notebook for August 10 is given below.*]

The entrance of Chippewa Crow [*Crow Wing*] River into the Mississippi is divided into two navigable arms by a very beautiful island, known by the name of Crow [*Wing*] Island. The astronomical station is on the east bank of the river, opposite the arm of the river which empties into the Mississippi north of the island. I was not able to make better observations at this important station.[32] An accident which made me very ill and which might have cost my life, combined with the foul weather which has pursued me ever since I left Swan River.

THURSDAY, AUGUST 11, 1836. We started up the mouth of Gull River at 5:42. There was fog on the river; it was cool. Our general course was north. Rapids. Pebbly bed. River sixty to eighty feet wide, three feet deep. The men take to the water and drag the canoe. Fallen trees increase the difficulties. Zigzags. At 6:05 no more obstacles. The river penetrates upstream into an open flat country of a most cheerful appearance. The section we have just traveled since we left Crow River, among rapids, high dunes, and densely covered areas was created, as it were, to prepare our eyes for the agreeable surprise we experienced when we reached this plain. Here

[32] Despite this statement, Nicollet's astronomical notebook indicates on August 10 that he determined the latitude at this place by two methods and altogether made three astronomical observations from different points at this station. This is significant, because in his *Report* (p. 109) he takes credit for correcting the latitude as given by Pike, which he said was 27' short.

the river is no more than thirty to forty feet wide, but it is deeper, more serene, easier, and safer to navigate. It meanders every five or ten minutes across open prairies hemmed by woods. The water is extremely transparent. Its characteristics of freshness and excellence of taste are a valuable compensation for the hardness and warmth of the Mississippi water which has grown tiresome after several days of use.

Until 6:35, or three miles after we left the mouth of the river, our course was directed between N and NNE, between N and NE, then ENE and toward the end, close to E. At 7:42 the course suddenly bore NNW and soon returned to fix itself between N and E. Then it evolved to SE and back to E and then again SE and back to E. Then N, NNW, NW, and W and back to N for a mile till 7:45. We stopped for breakfast. I estimate the distance traveled during those two hours to be a good eight miles. We have been advancing steadily and at a good pace. We left after breakfast at 9:57, heading N right away, then bearing full S and returning due N, both times by W. Chagobay armed the tip of his pole with two darts for spearing the fish that are so abundant in this river: small carp like those in France, sunfish, perch, pike, and other species. And the children from time to time dived into the water, bringing out various kinds of shellfish that emit iridescent colors from the bottom of the water. At 11:30 we rested. We had traveled five miles just since breakfast. Our fishing and hunting parties had been fruitful and entertaining. The average bearing was NE.

At 11:45: en route. At 12 o'clock the small valley widened; the little hills branched away, introducing a vast horizon of reeds. Here the river's meanderings follow every imaginable direction of the winds, but they inevitably return toward the general course, which is north. Some way back, trees fallen across the river had forced us to plow our way through the reeds. A boat gliding across a prairie must have been quite a sight. But soon the river divided into small canals and we lost the main stream. Chagobay, still standing at the bow spearing fish, stretched himself on the tips of his toes to find the river, but, overtopped by the reeds, he could not see anything. He grasped his son and in no time stood him up on his shoulders, and right away the child indicated with his finger the direction we must take, as well as the innumerable zigzags of the river.

Chagobay then declared that we would need the whole day to

get out of this if we did not take the shortest way which would be to navigate in a straight line across the fields of reeds. Nankatâ pointed toward the first field, and we tackled it, the natives filling the air with wild shrieks of joy. Once started, the roars of laughter continued and when water began to shine through the denseness of the aquatic forest, cries of joy and triumph resounded anew. We traveled approximately three miles in this manner. At one particular moment the reeds and rushes were so tightly interwoven that they formed a matting so thick and spongy that our canoe was actually lifted out of the water. It was necessary to use a hatchet on both sides to launch it again. In the course of this peculiar way of navigating, Chagobay, Brunia, and his brother continued to use their poles and the rest of the time widened our path by separating and pushing back the rushes.

When we reached a place where difficulties of this nature began to diminish, and where the little hills on both sides of the valley converged only to diverge again, I was surprised to see near the right shore a hillock that definitely had the appearance of having been made by the hands of man, very much like those Indian mounds that are so common in the United States. Our canoe could not reach the mound. So Brunia took me on his back and let me down at its foot. I examined it and was soon convinced it was man-made, on a deep swamp, out of the sand filled with small pebbles so typical of this region. The raw material must have been quarried from the little hill nearby behind the mound. The latter is set there like an island. Vibrations resound when you stamp its surface with your foot, suggesting that there are cavities within.[33]

But the great prize of this short visit paid to the mysterious and ancient relic was the view I was able to enjoy from its summit, which is no higher than fifteen feet above the river. The countryside we had crossed since noon and all the country that lay ahead was composed now not only of small valleys, but of one long and large valley, spacious and airy—a vast blanket of verdure sliced by silver waves and framed by two long black lines of pines fading away on the horizon northward and southward. The valley from north to south is nearly six miles long.

[33] There are numerous burial mounds in the Gull Lake area. Although no specific mound can be identified as that described by Nicollet, he was probably correct in thinking it to be man-made.

It was 2:30 when we left this sea of greenness and resumed the course of the river that had become more uniform and regular. Chagobay has been overloading our canoe with gorgeous fish. It is odd that he should not miss a single one when spearing from the canoe in motion and that he should have had no success today whenever we stopped paddling so as to enable him to aim.

At 3 o'clock we made many strange turns. The average bearing which had been to the N with deviations to the E, now veered N, swiveled to the W, S, and E, reaching as far as ENE, then swung rapidly back to its original setting. We then arrived at the foot of rapids a quarter of a mile long, almost breaking my canoe into little bits. In these rapids the river is wider and barely one-and-a-half feet deep. Huge rolled stones that often show themselves above the water garnish the river bed. After the rapids, the river bears N, then NNW, and reverts to its former state—flat. The new profile on which it runs is horizontal and higher. Two miles above the rapids, the horizon, which had been limited all day long by the little hills crowned with pine trees, began to spread out before us. Suddenly the river was deeper, and to such a degree that we were forced to abandon the poles in order to maneuver the canoe. We took to the paddles and the crew of seven cleared the last two miles in a short time. We reached Gull Lake at 4:15. The average bearing these last four miles was NW. We pitched camp on a point of land separating a bay from the lake, leaving a channel between it and the opposite hills several hundred *toises* wide.[34] I estimate the distance traveled today, by the route shown by Chagobay across the reeds and rushes of the swamp, to be twenty-five miles. The distance from Crow River to Gull Lake following the river cannot be less than twenty-eight or thirty miles. This is the distance that Mr. Baker of St. Peter had indicated. Allowing for the detours of the river, I expect the distance by water is about double the distance of a straight line drawn from our point of departure to that of our arrival.[35]

This has been a great day, different, and a merry one for everybody. The impression it has left still clings to us as I write this at 7 o'clock.

[34] A *toise* equals 1.949 meters or 6.395 English feet.
[35] According to modern maps the straight-line distance between Gull Lake and the Crow Wing River is approximately seven miles. The length of the Gull River is shown as about twelve miles, but the maps do not indicate all the windings followed by Nicollet.

Sketch map of the Gull Lake area

FRIDAY, AUGUST 12, 1836. Yesterday evening I barely made enough observations to establish the geographical position of Gull Lake when the sky clouded over completely. Lightning, thunder, and rain soon followed and lasted until midnight. It is obvious that the atmosphere is not treating us like spoiled children, and it is also true that if we are handed some joyful moments, we are not deprived of misery either. That single lovely day yesterday made me forget what I had suffered in the course of my work, which is nearly always accomplished in swamps or in dew as damp as rain, accentuated by incredibly rapid temperature changes and in the presence of irritating mosquitoes whose itching bites cause our blood to boil. Hence it is not surprising that we should all be more or less indisposed. This morning I hardly felt any better. The trembling I experienced all night continued. I know what the remedies are, but first of all I must leave this wild country we are crossing – such a lost and unknown land. I gave myself a minimum of treatment so that I could save time and continue our voyage.[36]

Around 11 o'clock I got the impression that it might not rain for a few hours, and we made the most of that by crossing the lake [*Gull*] to carry out a portage toward another lake [*Mayo Lake*] by means of a small river. It flows into Gull River a little distance above the entrance of the latter into the lake. At 12:04 we left the camp on the point where we had spent the night. We crossed the lake lengthwise, following a line drawn through our camp to the mouth of Gull River. At the same time I made approximate topographic readings of the hills enclosing the lake. The average elevation of their summits placed around the perimeter of this beautiful sheet of water is forty-five feet. The trees adorning these hills are for the most part red and white pine, a few red cedar on the points, birch, oak (blackjack), and [*one word illegible*], white ash trees, etc. At 12:43 we passed the first point on the left [*Rocky Point*], where Mr. Baker's trading house is to be found, abandoned.[37] Our general course is NNE.

Twelve minutes later we glided by the second point. At 1:34 we

---

[36] Nicollet suffered from malaria, which he had contracted in St. Louis the summer before. See above, p. 7.

[37] Baker apparently had an unlicensed post at Gull Lake as early as 1828. Nicollet makes no mention of an American Fur Company post which reportedly was operating in the vicinity in 1836. See Grace Lee Nute, "Posts in the Minnesota Fur-Trading Area, 1660–1855," in *Minnesota History*, 11:372 (December, 1930).

penetrated the little bay at the end of which Gull River makes its entrance into the lake. The bay runs north and widens eastward toward its extremity, the entrance of the river forming a narrow channel which we entered at 1:48. We lost twenty minutes. I estimate the distance from here to the camp to be five miles, plus two miles from the camp to the bottom of the southwest bay — seven miles altogether. We rested at the entrance of Gull River. At 2:07 we left the entrance of Gull River and traveled upstream. A third of a mile farther the river forms a deep cove, admitting a little river [*Home Brook*] on the right bank. After another third of a mile and on the same side appeared a creek [*Stony Brook*]. The course up to now, for a mile altogether, has been N with detours toward E rather than W.

Immediately after this creek, a mile and a quarter from the entrance, we came to a lake [*Upper Gull*], an expansion of the river half a mile wide with a point penetrating from the north. The lake is one and a quarter miles long. The direction of its axis is SSW–NNE. We emerged from the lake heading upstream on Gull River and a quarter of a mile later, leaving Gull River, we took a small river, or branch, flowing into it from the left (right bank of Gull River).[38] A quarter of a mile later we left it to carry out a portage, one mile long in a N, NNE, and NW direction. It took us over a hill of pines with Gull River at the foot of the other slope emerging from Long Lake, *Kâghino Gamac* [*Mayo Lake and Sibley Lake*]. We accomplished this portage to avoid rapids and obstructions that make navigation unmanageable on these parts of Gull River.

We started our portage at 3:10. It is three miles from the mouth of Gull River to this point. We had to disembark on a soft and spongy meadow with matted reeds concealing the water. Three trips were necessary to complete the portage, and this brought us to 6:30 in the evening. It was too late to attempt crossing Long Lake, however much we desired to do so. And the men were too tired. We convinced ourselves we should spend the night at the entrance of the lake. Five miles on Gull Lake and three on Gull River, plus a one-mile portage, nine miles in all.

SATURDAY, AUGUST 13, 1836. Yesterday evening after sun-

---

[38] This stream is not named on modern maps, nor is the stream which Nicollet calls the Gull River, connecting Mayo Lake with Upper Gull Lake.

set the clouds lifted for a while. I was sorry this did not coincide with a better state of health on my part and a geographical site of more importance. At approximately 7:30 northern lights began to gather. Huge masses of luminous clouds of indeterminate shapes touched the horizon from northwest to northeast. A little later these masses united and formed an arc which rested on the northeastern horizon while its branches rose from the northwest and the northeast. Soon it broke into several fragments, some shaped like clouds, others like columns inclined at various angles. Three of them, vertical but short, sustained very small compact clouds of a luminosity far more intense than the rest of the phenomenon. Soon the whole mass of clouds stretched upward and rose northeast as high as the constellation of Cassiopeia. This took place at 8:30. The phenomenon seemed to be progressing steadily toward some stage of stability that I was anxious to see. But I was in a forest, and I had to run from one place to another to obtain a clear view of all its parts. This wore me out and caused such convulsions that I rolled to the ground. When this crisis had passed, I returned to the aurora borealis. The spectacle was still about the same. However, a particular circumstance made it more interesting. There was a black cloud suspended on the horizon. Shaped like a horizontal wheel, it gradually dispersed to the north. There, the particles of the cloud scattered, to be slowly drawn away by a gentle westerly breeze that left their shape and color unaltered but guided them across the aurora all the way to its northeastern edge. There the clouds faded away and vanished completely. The western cloud had been exhausted and lightning and shimmering sheets of light replaced it. They would gleam from time to time while the northern lights maintained their confused form from end to end. The climax of this chain of events produced so great a luminosity that the shadows of the trees were sharply projected, and I could clearly see in the water the reflection of those on the opposite side of the lake. It was 9:15. Nothing had changed. But I was chilled and I had to retire to my tent. I must not forget to point out that the little atmospheric clouds which passed, as I said, across the aurora borealis actually did have this motion, thereby proving beyond the shadow of a doubt that they were closer to earth than the luminous matter against which they were silhouetted.

Although this morning my pulse was beating at a feverish pace, I did feel much better. Yesterday evening's crisis and a long sleep have produced this beneficial effect, a good omen. At 6 o'clock we left the southern end of Long Lake and at 7:35 we had reached the northern end. The lake is a good five miles long while its width varies from a quarter to a half mile. Its course is N and S. Near the middle of its length, the lake is strangled by encroaching hills and becomes as narrow as a river. A mile before reaching the north end we passed by Gull River [*Mayo Creek*] on our left. It winds away westward and northwestward. Where to? I don't know.[39]

At 8 o'clock we began our portage which is a good two miles long. Crossing pine hills, it leads to a charming round lake, its diameter three quarters of a mile long.[40] This portage distance of two miles between Long Lake and the round lake has an ENE average bearing. The sky which was so clear when we left our camp this morning is covered again with clouds driven in by a strong wind from the northwest. I wonder if I will be able to make some observations of the sun at noon while my men complete the portage of the luggage. The hills on this portage are the highest I have seen since St. Peter and in order to determine their height I made some barometric readings on the topmost peak as well as on the shores of the lakes they separate.

Yesterday, as we crossed Gull Lake we noticed on some little rocks which form two small islands ospreys, bitterns, gulls, pelicans, cormorants, and all those species which live on fish and reptiles and which abound in this lake. Today we find along the swamps that border Long Lake some beautiful cranes which, regretfully, we had no time to hunt down.

As I bid farewell to Gull River, I should really pause to describe with some detail the things I have observed since we left the mouth of Crow River. However, I note that the land that lies ahead has the same physical characteristics as the land we are leaving, and I plan to incorporate all those details in a general survey of the region which I shall draft at a later date. It will cover the topography of the land, its physical irregularities, the products of the water, the ground,

---

[39] Mayo Creek rises in Moose Lake, some twelve miles to the west of Sibley Lake.

[40] On Nicollet's 1843 map this is called Lake Gratiot, for Brigadier General Charles Gratiot (1788–1855), chief of the Army Engineers. On the 1836 manuscript map it is named Circular Lake, and Lake Gratiot is indicated as being a body of water west of Leech Lake. This is now Upper Hay Lake.

and the air, the formation of the lakes, the weather system—storms, blizzards, etc.

We set out at twelve minutes past 3:00 on the circular lake called *Kawâ-we-é Gamag*, the round lake of the Chippewa [*Upper Hay Lake*]. It is a cheerful and charming lake, where one may be at peace and rest, or meditate and study, or dream and love. In the surroundings of Paris or London, the hills embracing it would sell for about 100,000 francs per fifty square feet. Crossing it we were tossed about by a violent wind from the northwest. The waves were just high enough to bring shrieks from one of our affected ladies from *La Chausée d'Antin!* [41]

This pleasing little lake is fed by a river flowing in from the northwest called by the natives *Manito Sibi Ouissen* (Manito River) [*Hay Creek*].[42] One can reach Pine River from the lake by taking either one of two routes. The shortest starts with a portage of two and a half miles heading north and leading to Hay Lake, *Kâmuskusi Wâ Gamag* [*Deer Lake*]. The lake is crossed in a matter of minutes to be followed by another portage, three quarters of a mile long, at the end of which is Pine River. The other way is longer but there are no such tedious portages.[43] It suits us perfectly since we are not equipped for portages, and also because we shall be crossing some regions which are particularly interesting for my work.

So we take it, making our exit from Round Lake by Manito River, which is not only the lake's sole tributary, but also its only outlet. The Manito River exit is to the northeast of the lake, thick with obstructions composed of rushes and reeds. We had traveled only some hundred yards when a path of flowers and a garden of greenery opened before us. The surface of the water was completely concealed by the large round leaves of white water lilies crowned with their striking flowers, the size and brilliance of which vie with

[41] Chausée d'Antin was a quarter of Paris known for its population of wealthy bankers, where "newly rich luxury . . . contrasted with the simplicity of the aristocratic salons." See Guillaume de Bertier de Sauvigny, *The Bourbon Restoration*, 262 (Philadelphia, 1966).

[42] Throughout his manuscript Nicollet used the letter "d" in place of the "t" in manito. The editor has substituted the more accepted spelling.

[43] Apparently the Indians considered the northern route shorter and better under ordinary conditions. It would probably have gone by way of modern Nelson and Deer lakes. Because of high water at the time, Nicollet's party was able to canoe down Hay Creek from what is now Upper Hay Lake to Lower Hay Lake and on into Whitefish Lake without making portages.

those of the *grandiflore magnolia*. A curtain of green trees bordering the left bank projected its jagged shadows across the wide ribbon of green and white. Everyone seemed affected by this pretty landscape. Chagobay himself, in the front of the canoe, was afraid of damaging the flowers. He would hold his paddle up, and the other paddlers would do the same and our galley, at the mercy of the current, would glide lightly over the bed of greenness leaving unharmed the yellow-hearted white corollas, unwinding gently their flexible stems.

After this enchanting scene, which lasted for more than a mile, Brunia began to sing a native barcarole. Chagobay accompanied him in a low voice, or rather, with a sort of humming frequently interrupted. I had noticed several times that natives sing very little or not at all when on water. Chagobay strongly confirms this opinion, for he who is such a good amateur singer, whose voice is so full, and who delightfully entertains me every evening with his songs of war, death, and scalping, sung in bed, especially when it rains, only murmurs when afloat. The reason for this is that a native paddling or exposed to the winds has his sense of hearing and sight too keenly on the *qui vive*, is too preoccupied by outward objects to be able to concentrate on a regular song. I have also invariably noted how he automatically surrenders to the impulse he receives from the songs of others. Game flying in the air, the wild animal in the forest, the fish in the water hold more sway over him than the melodies uttered by Brunia and Désiré. There is a constant unobserved play of his hands that switch from the paddle to the rifle or the pole armed with a dart.

In the evening it is a different matter. Even though nobody is listening, he lies on his back, sings, and marks time with his fists on his chest. Today he seems to have enjoyed gliding through the flowers because the horizon was brought up close to us by the curtain of pines following the meanderings of the river and also because the water was invisible.

I was so hypnotized myself by the scene that I forgot I had a compass before me and that I was supposed to chart the direction of the river. I was quite startled when, an hour after having left Round Lake, I heard more cries next to me announcing our entry into Manito [*Lower Hay*] Lake. It is twice as big as the other, its high banks following upon each other less regularly but nevertheless forming a circle. We made our entry bearing NE and followed the chord of a little arc of the lake leading us to the exit of Manito River on the same bearing.

We expected to encounter great difficulties descending this river, which after one-third of a mile vanishes into Whitefish Lake.[44] We thought we might have to make a portage, but the waters were high, our canoe with its load could float down, and we only needed to maneuver properly through the obstructions of driftwood encumbering the river. To do this, Chagobay, Brunia, and his brother stepped into the water. The latter waded first, calling attention to the obstacles, brushing aside those that could be moved.

After a few minutes we perceived the flash of the waters of Whitefish Lake through the foliage on the strip of land separating us from it. This bar soon narrowed enough to allow the waves whipped up by a violent northwest wind to break their foamy waters upon us. We ran into trouble making our entry into the lake. The impetuous wind would drive us back into the forest, and the waves wanted no part of us. Finally my crew mastered the raging waters, and we set up camp near the mouth of Pine River which we have to ascend. The wind subsided, and a startling sunset presided over an hour of contemplation which we devoted to an examination of the lake. Three hours such as those we had just spent in cheerful adventures, in innocent and astonishing delight, would be enough to draw a man from his grave. Also the fever that had seized me again on Round Lake went unnoticed. I thought about it at suppertime and found it had left me. Thus, although it was cold, there was no risk in making observations that led me far into the end of the day. And I slept well all night.

All the country we have seen since we left Crow Island and especially since Gull Lake is completely unknown. Indeed, there are only a few natives who are familiar with it. Its sterility and the absence of big game keep them away, and they only use these parts

[44] Lower Hay Lake is now in effect a bay of Whitefish Lake. Here and elsewhere throughout the area Nicollet traversed, the topography has been greatly changed by the erection of dams. Many small private ones were built during the lumbering era, but the major alterations are the result of a comprehensive system of reservoirs constructed at the headwaters of the Mississippi by the Army Corps of Engineers in the years after 1880. The purpose was to regulate the level of the river and improve navigation. The Pine River dam, which raised the level of Whitefish and many connecting lakes, was completed in 1886. See Lucile M. Kane, *The Waterfall That Built a City*, 128–132 (St. Paul, 1966); 50 Congress, 1 session, *House Executive Documents*, no. 1, part 2, p. 1681.

as a steppingstone leading to other places. Brunia and even Chagobay knew nothing about the land beyond Gull Lake, and it was only
thanks to information obtained with difficulty that our adventurous
expedition turned out to be a complete success. However, this will
not prevent this region from becoming very important some day as
an opening for shorter and easier communications with the northwest.

SUNDAY, AUGUST 14, 1836, When I decided to come and
visit these parts, the prospect of seeing some northern lights was one
of the considerations that weighed heavily in convincing me that
the trip was necessary. It appears I shall be served to my heart's
content. Some extraordinary ones developed last night. But they
deserve special attention, and the rapid notes I take down in this
diary of my voyage are no place for that description.

We arose this morning amid torrents of rain. Our present situation compared to that of last night is pitiful. We decided to camp
for the day. I assembled my general staff in my tent. Brunia and
Chagobay took a seat and smoked. I opened my portfolio to take
paper and pencils, and my two cartographers plotted the land
through which we must find a way tomorrow. Désiré, the young
natives, Brunia's brother, and William's kind, elderly mother took
refuge under the canoe as they waited for the waterfall from the
skies to subside so that they could light a fire and prepare breakfast.

After long deliberation my council concluded that we already
recognized six routes by which we could go to Leech Lake starting
from Crow [Wing] Island and that these routes would multiply as
we advanced. However, there are many doubtful points, and we
were in dire need of natives to clarify them. Unfortunately we had
not met any for three days. What would they be doing on these
sterile grounds — a land that one cannot but admire, yet where there
is nothing to eat unless it be laboriously earned?

I did not want to find merely any kind of a route to Leech Lake.
I wanted the shortest, the easiest, and the one that would contribute
the most to the development of trade and the arrival of the civilization that will soon be knocking on the door of these solitudes. And
that is why our council was so laborious and long, filled with as many
anxieties as are the councils of kings on the eve of war.

From here there are two routes. One consists in ascending Pine

River, at the mouth of which we are now situated, by passing beyond the portages of Hay Lake already mentioned, and by taking to the right four portages from river to lake, from lake to river, from lake to lake, most of them through swamp. Judging by the present state of the river waters and the abundant rains, this route must be quite impracticable. In addition to these usual difficulties, an interminable succession of rapids would be encountered by ascending Pine River. Having taken all these facts into consideration, the council decided we should take the route that will be described tomorrow as we travel it.

MONDAY, AUGUST 15, 1836. We left the astronomical station at the entrance of Pine River into Whitefish Lake at 6:06. Cloudy weather but calm. The surface of the lake was as calm today as it was rough when we arrived the evening of the day before yesterday. There lingered a hazy and drizzly fog. The cold hit us as soon as we were in open water and lingered on until we were out of it.

The shape of the lake as a whole is very unusual. It is composed of two sections connected by a channel four to five hundred yards wide, partly obstructed by reeds and other plants of high growth. Each section of the lake taken separately is very beautiful, and the contrast of each one bordered in the same style by hills, forests, and varied hues makes the comparison all the more beautiful. In size it compares well with the lakes of the first order in this region west of the Mississippi. Its name indicates the predominant species of fish haunting its depths. It also contains trout. The bottom of the lake is of sand, that same sand which characterizes all these parts and results from the disaggregation of primitive rocks and transitional phyllites. The shells in abundance are three or four species of small helixes.[45] Pebbles are to be found only on the shore battered by north and northwesterly winds, between the mouths of the Pine and Manito rivers.

The distance by water from the entrance to the exit of Pine River is eight miles and this is merely four-fifths of a dotted line that would measure the longest span of water passing through the narrows. I

---

[45] "Phyllites" is the technical English translation of *phyllades*, the word Nicollet used. It refers to hard rocks like slate, which one can easily divide into leafy segments. His use of the word *désagrégation* shows his exact knowledge of the composition of the granites which he then called primitive rocks. In 1836 a helix might have been any spiral shell with a moderately high spire.

made a survey of the lake and drew a good sketch, and I can thus dispense with giving a description of the course followed.[46] As we leave the lake we sail along Pine River for eight miles in a very strong current. The river in some places is a hundred feet wide and two feet deep. Then we enter into a small lake [*Rush Lake*] from which we make a prompt exit among thick rushes and reeds, leaving aside on our left a pretty little bay with a smooth surface and a high, picturesque shoreline.

We are back on Pine River again for a mile. Here the transparency of the water is grayish due to a pebbly bed coated with some kind of substance. The entrance into Lake Travers [*Cross Lake*] is cut off by a point composed of an accumulation of enormous rolled stones. We stopped on it for lunch. Lake Travers is oval shaped with a four-mile-long perimeter. Its longest axis runs N and S. The characteristics of the landscape are those already noted on the other lakes in these parts. However, the shores on this one furnish the geologist with samples of every variety of rock that has contributed to the formation of the sands and rolled pebbles composing the great deposit recalled so many times.

During my travels in the United States, I have always displayed great reserve and abstained from imposing names on places even when in the interest of my work dedicated to the progress of general geography it was necessary to do so. Now I find I am obliged to overcome this reluctance, and I begin today. I hope the people of the United States will confirm the names of my preference, all the more so since they will have been chosen from their midst as tokens of my respect or esteem, of my friendship or gratitude.

Here is another Lake Travers. The natives give this name to any lake that cuts off their natural path over land or water. I come across some every day, as well as Otter Lakes, and Turtle Lakes. There is no end to them. This confusion must be dissipated, but as I do so I shall pay all due respect to the places with names that, because of impressive characteristics or situation, or as a rendezvous for traders, have already found their place on geographical maps and in history. Therefore this lake shall be Lake Davenport, named after that brave colonel, lover of sciences, now in command of Fort Snelling.

[46] Even allowing for alterations in topography, it appears that Nicollet overestimated the length of the lake by nearly half, as he also did the distance traveled on the Pine River. His sketch has been lost.

We entered Lake Davenport following an eastern bearing. We made an exit under the same bearing passing into a stream [*Daggett Brook*] that should be considered one of the main tributaries of Pine River. Pine River itself is an important river for its length, its volume of water, and its transversal direction that links the Mississippi with all the central part of this region lying between the Mississippi, its sources, the *Hauteurs des Terres* and Crow River.[47] In the course of the first four miles we travel on this branch of the middle section oriented ENE two other lakes make their appearance one after the other, both charming to the eyes. Their waters are as transparent and pure as crystal. Stripped, no doubt, of their sheltering soils washed off as alluvium, the abandoned quartz, talc, and steatite that now coat the bottom of the river bed dazzle us with their pearly, unctuous, and delightful radiance.[48] Chagobay now stands on the tip of the canoe, and his first strike today brings in a five or six pound pike, also a golden carp weighing one and a half pounds.

Three miles beyond the lakes mentioned above we find the river closed off by two recently fallen pine trees. It would take longer to cut them than to make a portage, so we do not hesitate and twenty minutes later we are back on our way. These three miles start out with an ENE bearing but veer to NNE for the last mile.

Four miles up, following a northerly bearing, we make an entry into a third lake [*Mitchell Lake*] on the river. It is practically round, bordered with hills, one of which on the northwest side reaches a hundred feet after a slow and smooth climb.[49] The view of this little mountain is rendered all the more ravishing at this time by the combinations of colors displayed by short and long twin-leaved pines [*red or jack pine*], birch, cedar, and other species of trees that have suffered from scattered forest fires. This lake is a veritable miniature;

[47] Here and in a few other places Nicollet spelled the phrase *Hauteurs de Terre*. For the sake of consistency, however, the spelling used in his published *Report* will be followed throughout this work.

[48] From Nicollet's statement that they appeared "one after the other," it would seem that these must have been Daggett Lake and Little Pine Lake. They are now virtually one because of the heightened water level from the Pine River dam.

[49] The lake here described must have been Mitchell Lake, although its shape is no longer round, and it is the fourth, not third, lake as one ascends Daggett Brook. Nicollet failed to mention Eagle Lake. The fact that the latter is dammed at its outlet suggests possible changes in topography since 1836.

it deserves a name, but this shall be the prerogative of the happy people that some day shall dwell on its borders.

We find here the entrance of two rivers, one coming from northeast [*Spring Brook*], the other from northwest [*Daggett Brook*]— both tributaries of the lake from which branches the river we have just ascended. The river on the northwest crosses three lakes, the last of which, as one ascends them, is somewhat substantial. The Indians call it Otter Lake.[50] We do not take this route but the other one to the northeast.

Before entering the river I must not forget to mention the eleven miles covered since leaving Lake Davenport. This section is what fresh-water navigators might call a good river for canoes and boats of more substantial capacity. We never found less than three feet of water over a width never less than thirty to forty feet. The current is moderately fast. There are no sudden changes in the level of the bed and we found no other obstacles than toppled trees that could be removed from the river in two days' time. Finally, this river is wedged between banks twelve to fifteen feet high, which hold back the water in two or three places where it might have a tendency to wander. The details I have recorded will not be judged useless if all that I see as I advance bears out the important conclusions I am beginning to discern.

I would have found it convenient to set up an astronomical station on the edge of this pretty little lake, not only because it is the meeting place of the two small rivers, but also to confirm the course of our route during the day. But it was only 3 o'clock, and the sky had been improving more and more since noon. We have been delayed so many times since St. Peter that we felt it more reasonable to travel a few more miles.

So we paddled northeast into the little river. We had covered less than two or three hundred yards when we struck some rapids half a mile long. We cleared them without too much trouble, after which my crew began filling their pipes with the intention of smoking as we glided over the quiet surface of a triangular lake that suddenly opened

---

[50] It is impossible to know what three lakes were meant here. Daggett Brook now rises in Cass County (T140N, R27W) and flows through Lakes George and Washburn, both of which might be called "somewhat substantial." Lake Washburn, because of its very irregular shape, might easily have been considered two or even three separate bodies of water.

before us. The shores of this lake, slightly larger than the one before, are well wooded and almost at water level which is in contrast with the lakes we have seen before.[51]

Four and a half miles upstream, following a deviation that suddenly veers and holds north, we crossed another lake with low-lying shores and beautiful water [*Pug Hole Lake*], and half a mile farther, yet another with troubled waters choked by reeds. Half a mile later we found the river so full of obstructions that we were forced to make a portage three to four hundreds yards long. This took us late into the night and led to the southwestern end of a sizable lake whose beauty, illuminated by the glow of the rising moon, prepares our hearts for tomorrow. So many lakes one after the other are nevertheless no cause for monotony or boredom. The wild and untrodden nature that lies between them disposes one's spirit to receive them with charm and pleasure.

TUESDAY, AUGUST 16, 1836. This morning I rose before daybreak, kindled the campfire, and awakened my officers, my young pages, and our kindly old native woman, the lady of honor of our company. The night had glittered with stars. I had been able to make the observations I needed here, and the station to which they referred was more important than the one I had regretfully abandoned. I was happy; a rest of a few hours proved to be enough.

Crooked Lake, or Baltimore Canal [*Lake Roosevelt*], is composed of three parts following one another:

First part. Bearing SW-NE. Its length is very deceptive. Although it seems short, it is at least eight miles long and half a mile wide. The shores lie low and are well wooded.

Second part. SSW-NNE is two and a half miles long and half a mile wide. The western shore is twelve to fifteen feet high and most attractive.

Third part. The bearing is N and it veers NNE. It is one and a half miles long. The total length of the canal is twelve miles.[52] There

---

[51] This lake apparently no longer exists. The description suggests that it was shallow. Nearby Minnie Lake and a number of small ponds in the vicinity may be remnants of it. The same is true of the lake "choked with reeds" mentioned in the paragraph below.

[52] The main features of Lake Roosevelt today are recognizable in Nicollet's description, although the southern section is somewhat wider than he saw it, possibly because of a dam at the outlet. The northernmost end veers NNW,

is not a single stone to lay nor a tree to fell. There is even lumber available for shipbuilding!

By 8:30 A.M. we had reached the northern extremity of the "Canal-lake." We had broken camp at 6:00 and were making very good progress. We paddled along a little section of river, then found a small lake [*unnamed*] which we crossed. We put ashore at the foot of a hill to make a portage that passed over the top, leaving the river to the right as the latter furrows its way into a narrow gorge formed by the hill we are on and the one on the other shore. At this point the river is not navigable. The length of this portage measured with Brunia's stride is 3,500 paces, an average derived from three trips with a margin of error not exceeding four or five paces between trips. One of Brunia's paces equals 2.775 feet. Therefore the portage equals 9,712 feet long or 3,237 yards.

After the portage we crossed a little lake [*Abe Lake*] at the foot of the hills we had just left and started out on another portage, 7,354 feet — or 2,451 yards — long, ending in a second lake [*unnamed*]. The hills on this second portage are a few feet higher than before. They form a water divide between the river we had just ascended and Little Boy River heading south.[53] The spongy prairies bordering the lakes on these portages make for very difficult embarking and disembarking. The men were constantly wading in the water. They sank through grassy surface crusts and got in each other's way. It occurred to me they should form a chain as men do when putting out fires, extending from the canoe to the dry landing place. The idea was new to them, and they used it. It was night by the time we had made the two portages, and the men were exasperated, every one of them having made the round trip four times. Muggy weather, threatening rain, and mosquitoes rendered the last part of the journey quite intolerable. We are enduring literally clouds of mosquitoes that rise higher than the tallest trees I could make out towering above the swamps.

We camped on the edge of the second lake after finishing the second portage. Supper brought the men's speech back and we had a

not NNE, as written in the manuscript diary. He uses the word "*canal*" to describe a long lake or chain of lakes providing a broad, comparatively smooth passage.

[53] These hills are a part of what was later designated the Leaf Hills Moraine. See Newton H. Winchell, *Geology of Minnesota*, 4: plate opposite p. 54 (St. Paul, 1899). They form a watershed as described by Nicollet, except that the stream he here calls the Little Boy River flows north and west, not south.

sentimental evening. Chagobay asked through Brunia if he might have a private conversation with me. He proceeded in accordance with the customs of the natives: he sat down, gave me his hand and said what he had to say. He gave advice on the things we are likely to encounter at Leech Lake and regretted that he must leave me there. He requested that I take him to the sources of the Mississippi and told me why. I told him that was impossible and why. We all slept in my tent, crowded pell-mell, away from the rain that poured all night.

WEDNESDAY, AUGUST 17, 1836. As we left our camp this morning to cross the second little lake, we could see the water of the swampy prairie flowing south to form the lake [*unnamed*] from which Little Boy River makes its exit.[54] Cloudy sky —but the rain has stopped.

After crossing the little lake we made another portage a third of a mile long, thus avoiding the low prairie that conceals the waters forming Little Boy River. This low prairie is difficult to follow. It is surrounded by hills seventy to eighty feet tall and is obstructed by fallen trees of a great variety of species. The portage was easy, going along a fairly well-trodden path over the dry, undulating ground of the hills. This short portage linked us with a third small lake [*Bass Lake?*] that flows almost at once into Philadelphia Canal or Turtle Lake [*Coffin Lake?*] through straits that are the first distinctive feature of Little Boy River. Properly speaking, the third little lake would be part of Turtle Lake if it were not for the current separating them. This being a canal, all these waterways are like one.[55]

[54] At this point Nicollet was not on what present-day geographers designate as the Boy River (or Little Boy River). The latter stream rises in Ten Mile Lake (T140N, R31W) and flows east and north through a series of lakes, including Woman Lake and Girl Lake, into Inguadona Lake, where it is joined by Laura Creek, flowing from the east. The spot Nicollet here describes is one of the unnamed headwaters of Laura Creek. It is now impossible to identify positively the little lakes he speaks of. They may have been an unnamed and unmapped series of ponds in section 34 of Thunder Lake Township, Cass County.

[55] There are now in this area three separate lakes, named on modern maps Bass, Coffin, and Kidney. Older maps show Bass and Coffin linked in one lake, which both Winchell and Upham designate as Turtle Lake. (See Winchell, *Geology of Minnesota*, 4: plate opposite p. 54; Upham, *Minnesota Geographic Names*, 99.) It is possible that this is the same Turtle Lake mentioned by Nicollet and that under the conditions of high water prevailing during his trip, it was connected more or less directly with the southern end of Thunder Lake.

We left the extremity of the portage leading to Turtle Lake at
12:09:

12:09 — 12:21 NNE — first section, canal.

12:21 — 12:24 NE — canal narrows down, rushes and reeds.

12:24 — entrance into an open lake [*Thunder Lake*]. We follow
the NNW chord leaving a half circle on our right. Chord and diameter: [*Here Nicollet left a blank space in the manuscript.*]

12:33 — end of diameter stretch across the half circle of the cove.
We enter another canal — bearing NW.

12:48 — two rounded capes are facing each other. The hills on the
right and left are a pretty sight to behold. They are separated by a
mile, half of which is filled with the capes and coves, the other half
by the canal. We do not hit bottom with our fifteen-foot poles. A
twenty-nine-minute rest. A meeting with some natives. A very short
portage to the right leads to Duck Lake [*Big Rice Lake*], wider and
nearly as long as this one.[56] Here the lake opens up toward NNE and
W. We head straight out, in other words we maintain our NW bearing from 1:17 until 1:39.

The end of the lake on the northwestern side is crowned with
hills that seem higher than all the others. A small river comes from a
lake [*both unidentified*] and then, too, there is a portage leading to
Otter Lake [*Lake George*].[57]

We took Little Boy River flowing from the lake. Much to my
delight the sky cleared, and I stopped to make some astronomical
readings. Here I found some yellow lilies, the first in these parts. Here
also begin what the natives call "their gardens," where they gather
abundant crops of wild rice.

We left this astronomical station at 4:05. We penetrated right into
a wild rice paddy that we crossed as freely as if there were no rice
there. Our bearing is WNW. The horizon cleared, widened, and we
arrived in the middle of a huge expanse of water and rice [*Laura Lake*]

[56] This portage went by way of Little Thunder Lake. In the 1890s Winchell
noted that a lumber company had dammed the outlet of Thunder Lake and had
made a ditch across the narrow neck of land, draining the waters of Thunder
Lake into Little Thunder and Big Rice lakes. This had cut off the flow of water
into Laura Lake, and the latter was drying up. (See *Geology of Minnesota*,
4:58.) Present-day maps show that the natural drainage pattern has been restored.

[57] As his maps reveal, Nicollet was misinformed about the relative distances
in this area. If the trail led to the Otter Lake referred to on p. 70, it could only
have been by way of Little Bass Lake, Island Lake, and several more portages.

bordered by the series of hills we just left. These have expanded and widened to encompass a circular surface of practically five square miles, beautiful to behold. Take away the vegetation covering the water, and this surface becomes a first rate lake for these parts, bordered at the foot of the hills with tamarack. The natives call it Tamarack Lake (Authorn [*Hawthorn*] Lake). Between this lake and the canal we had just left, the river is barely one mile long. When we arrive half of the lake is indeed without rice. At 5:05 we left the lake. I estimate the chord we followed to be four miles long and the diameter five. We entered a river [*Laura Creek*] that continues to wind through wild rice following a northwestern course. Little by little the numerous bends decreased in number as they increased in length. The river is clear, twenty to thirty feet wide and five to six feet deep. The hills that had withdrawn are now closing in. They are crowned with young pines of the best kind with a lovely curtain of young tamaracks spread out before them. Now the river flows in a flat and open valley. We are traveling it at a speed of seven to eight miles per hour but make little headway because of all the meandering. The name tamarack (*épinette*) is the one used here, but the tree thus called is the larch.

At 6:15 we penetrated Little Whitefish [*Lower Trelipe*] Lake. It is a beautiful expanse of water three miles long, three-fourths of a mile wide, and free of vegetation. We have covered eight miles since 5:05 but an actual distance of only three miles on a NW bearing. The longest part of the lake is oriented E to W. We camp here.

THURSDAY, AUGUST 18, 1836. We left our bivouac at 9:15. We spent the night on the edge of Little Whitefish Lake in a beautiful forest set in excellent soil and composed of several kinds of oak, maple, and other trees of mixed variety. Pine, cedar, and larch trees seldom appear on the edge of this pretty lake. The river winds on within the valley of wild rice, always flat and sinuous. This river does not yet have a name. Some half-breeds call it *Petit Enfant Rivière* and such is the name I use later on.[58] A name suiting it better would be Indian

[58] On some maps the stream between Laura Lake and Inguadona Lake is called Trelipe Creek, but the more common name is Laura Creek. The name Laura Creek is also given to the stream flowing south from Oxbow Lake into Laura Lake, and is occasionally applied to the short stream connecting Thunder Lake with Laura Lake.

Gardens River. It becomes wider and wider and remains deep. The valley is now smiling and beautiful.

I do not know what is happening. Since leaving Crow Island we had not met a single native until yesterday evening, when we had a short conversation with a young man and his wife, both fishing. But this morning already, seven or eight canoes filled with young natives have appeared, their hair adorned with feathers, their faces smeared with red. They passed by at an extraordinary speed, cutting off the bends by plowing through the rice paddies, not saying a word, with the obvious intention of getting far ahead of us. We shall see what happens. We are supposed to reach Leech Lake today if the north wind that is blowing so strongly permits.

At exactly 10:15 we entered a lake [*Inguadona Lake*] far bigger than the preceding one. Its longest span, oriented NNE and SSW, is at least eleven to twelve miles with a width varying from one half to two miles. It is a large canal. We would have entered from the southern part of the canal had we taken the alternate route that goes up Pine River from where we were camped at its entrance into Whitefish Lake. This lake, or canal, is also without a name; we come out of it following Indian Gardens [*Boy*] River. We had entered it from a NW direction. The distance from the exit of the preceding lake to the entrance of this one is eight miles by the river, five miles going through the rice — New York Canal.

At noon we arrive at some rapids fifteen to twenty yards long which one could easily eliminate by simply removing the one to three cubic feet of rolled pebbles forming them. Immediately below, the river resumes its normal pace. It is fifty to sixty feet wide and often as much as fifteen feet deep, never less than four or five feet deep in its widest spots. The rapids are approximately twelve miles below the preceding lake.

At 12:30, three miles below the rapids, we negotiated more of them, a quarter of a mile long. Here we have a veritable change in the level of the river bed. Since we had three or four feet of water, we cleared them with no difficulty other than that of steering the canoe away from some rocks that jut through the surface of the water. Here again, it would suffice to move away the rocks to free the current.

At 1:15 we entered another lake [*Boy Lake*]. After a few minutes it becomes a canal similar in its ornamental style and rich surroundings to the preceding one. Its length at first glance is twelve to fifteen miles oriented NNE to SSW. On the south end I found a channel linking it with another section of the canal also very long. By means of a portage this latter section — still one-half to two miles wide — leads to Leech Lake. Since it is parallel to the former canal we made our entry under the same bearing, our exit also, and we then resumed our course in Indian Gardens River. Thus, we have discovered four canals since the day before yesterday which, taken in the order of their discovery and latitude, are: Canals Baltimore, Philadelphia, New York, and Boston.

We entered Leech Lake at 5 o'clock. Very cold northwesterly wind, fine, penetrating drizzle. We barely found time to take refuge for the night on the first peninsula we saw. The next morning, August 19 at 10 o'clock, we came to Otter Tail Point, Brunia's home. It is now the principal village.[59] There is a detailed account to give here of the four days spent on this lake before heading for the sources of the Mississippi.

LEECH LAKE, SATURDAY, AUGUST 20, 1836. The warriors of Leech Lake were having a meeting with their chief. Lattrape (Matchigabo) sent for me requesting that I join them also. I went there without delay accompanied by Joseph Montreuil and François Brunia, who was to serve as my interpreter.[60] Once there, they asked me if I would undertake to transmit to the Indian agent at St. Peter, and to the Great Father, president of the United States, words of a very urgent nature. My answer, "Yes!"

[59] According to statistical tables prepared by the War Department in 1832, the village of Leech Lake then numbered 139 men, 194 women, and 373 children, plus 24 persons of mixed blood. (See Schoolcraft, *Narrative of an Expedition*, 221.) In 1836 Nicollet estimated the population at about 1,000, furnishing 180 warriors. He pointed out that because of the Indians' nomadic habits, this did not necessarily mean an over-all increase of population. (*Report*, 63.)

[60] "Ma-ghe-ga-bo, or La Trappe" from Leech Lake was one of the signers of the Chippewa treaty of 1837. There are several references to him in Boutwell's journal, where he appears threatening and antagonistic to the missionary. Schoolcraft describes him as "a very tall, gaunt, and savage looking warrior, who appeared to be made up, body and mind, of sensualities." Later (p. 199) Nicollet spells the name "Majigabo." Joseph Montreuil (or Montrelle) was an employee of the American Fur Company. He was listed as an interpreter in 1835. See Kappler, comp. and ed., *Indian Affairs*, 2: 482; Schoolcraft, *Narrative of an Expedition*, 102; Boutwell Journal, May 29, 1835; October 19, 1836; "List of Persons in the District of Fond du Lac, September 12, 1835," Sibley Papers.

"However," continued Matchigabo, "there are some stern words. Will you tell them?"

"Yes, if they are fair."

"Will you write down what we shall say to you?"

"Yes."

"All those you see here gathered are our old ones, the most respected in the nation; those who are not here are in agreement with us and we answer for them."

We having agreed upon all this, Matchigabo elaborated on the following points:

"Even if I were to wear you out listening all day to me, there would be no end to the enumeration of the falsehoods told us by the agent of St. Peter since his arrival among us. I have been here twelve years. The agent was already at St. Peter when I came.[61] He said to me he was in no danger, that he had nothing to fear from his enemies. Yes, thus did he talk, but in the spring one of our people was beaten to death by the Sioux. At first I listened with trust, and at Prairie du Chien, at the Great Council, I buried the hatchet. The president of the Council told us that the first village to start a war would be reduced to ashes. This president added, 'My children, behold, these arms of mine are long enough to defend you.'

"Then did we bury the hatchet. Last summer (1835) the commander of the fort [*Major John Bliss*] said to me, 'I have been sent here by your Great Father to strike first at the one who is stupid enough to start a war. My Children, I have the power to seize those who kill one of yours. I shall deliver him unto you to do with what you will.'[62]

"The agent told us, 'The murderers shall be captured. I shall dispatch a native of Sandy Lake carrying a message to Big Ox of Wild Rice, to Strong Head, also to Leech Lake.[63] You shall come down

[61] Lawrence Taliaferro had become agent at Fort Snelling (St. Peter) in 1819, and had served for seventeen years by 1836.

[62] For the council at Prairie du Chien, see above, p. 11. The "president" referred to could have been either Lewis Cass of Michigan or William Clark of Missouri, both of whom were commissioners for the United States government. The events of which Matchigabo talks here and in the following paragraphs are described in Taliaferro's journal, July 11, 1835. Three Sioux had treacherously slain a Chippewa, and the agent promised that he would deliver the murderers to the Chippewa for punishment.

[63] Big Ox of Wild Rice was also called Pe-zhe-ke, or the Buffalo, since the Ojibway word for these animals is the same. He was from the upper St. Croix,

here. We shall deliver the prisoners to you that you may handle them according to your decision.' He added, 'My children, I cannot capture the murderers easily, but I shall take them by surprise, I shall seduce them with cries of joy. And when we are not able to take them, you shall find nought but ashes in the village where they dwell. Indeed, we shall wage war upon them, my children. They can kill me, they can kill another agent, even five of them in all, but the sixth time,' adds the agent, seizing a handful of ashes, 'there shall be so many of us that we shall overpower them. My children, we shall be the first and you shall follow and when all will be done we shall seize the scalps.'

" 'No, my Father,' said the chief, 'we shall help you.' [64]

" 'My Father,' I said to him, 'I listen to you. I give you three years to capture the murderers and if after those three years you still have not caught them, I shall be forced to do as I wish.' "

At this point, Matchigabo comes close to me, sits facing me and holding my hands adds:

"The weight of these falsehoods can no more be lifted than a heavy rock. My Father, my heart mourns the loss of our warriors slaughtered by the Sioux. Were I to lose ten pigs I would be afflicted with grief. If a native lost ten pigs you would put in prison him who stole them. How can you expect us to stand still when those promises you made to us have yet to be fulfilled?

"Behold (speaking to me) the size of this lake. To fill it with presents would be no compensation for the loss of our men killed by the Sioux. My Father, you have contempt for your own heart when you speak falsehoods. I believed the things you said. My Father, it occurs to me that perhaps your interpreter changes the words you pronounce. You raised your finger toward the sky as you spoke, indicating thereby that God was witness to what you said. It was understood the commander was speaking the truth."

[Here Nicollet inserted the following list of names in his diary.]

Flat Face [Mouth], Chief of the Lake — Eche Kibokosè

an area known to fur traders as the Folle Avoine or Wild Rice country. His son Little Ox of Leech Lake, called Pe-zhe-kins or Young Buffalo, may have been the one Nicollet refers to as "Chikins" (p. 82). For the chief Nicollet calls Strong Head, see p. 45n. Baraga, 2:354 (Montreal, 1880); Kappler, comp. and ed., Indian Affairs, 2:482; Allen, in 23 Congress, 1 session, House Documents, no. 323, p. 61.

[64] The identity of this "chief" is not made clear in the manuscript.

Pictorial signatures of three Indians. Left: Flat Mouth.
Center: Chagobay, or Little Six. Right: Hole-in-the-Sky.

The Elder Brother, Tchou Seyâ — at Big Point
Cloudy Sky, Tchiana Koué — at Big Point (son)
Yellow Robe, Ouézookoné — at Big Point
The Chief of the Land, Obiygouâdens — at Otter Tail Point
Lattrape, Matchigabo, Great Speaker — at Otter Tail Point
The Little Ox, Pizzikins (son of Big Ox of Wild Rice) also at Otter
     Tail Point
Bougon — Bear Island
Jeune Homme, Young Man — Bear Island
The Little Shoulder — Bear Island
Chagobay, Gotohassy (number 6)[65]

[65] The Elder Brother is mentioned frequently by Boutwell and also by both
Schoolcraft and Taliaferro. The latter notes that "Oldest Son" had in reality
more authority than Flat Mouth. The Chief of the Land is also mentioned often
by Taliaferro (who calls him "Obiquette") as well as by Pike and Warren.
Both of these chiefs signed the 1837 treaty. Yellow Robe is characterized by
Boutwell as one "who makes pretensions to some importance as a sort of chief."
For Flat Mouth, see above, p. 13, 15, 18, 45n.; for Matchigabo, p. 77n.; for Little
Ox, p. 79n.; for Chagobay, p. 19. The editor has not been able to further identify
the others listed here nor the individual referred to as "Terra Firma" who was
the next speaker. Kappler, comp. and ed., *Indian Affairs*, 2:492; Pike, *Expedition
to the Sources of the Mississippi*, 135; Warren, *History of the Ojibways*, 487;

Question addressed by me, "Why do you hate Americans?"

Solid Ground, Terra Firma, answered saying, "Yes, we hate them. Because wherever they establish military posts to protect the natives they keep them like dogs. Because for the slightest folly we commit they drive us under the ground (put us in prison), whip us with rope, tie cords around our neck and hang us. Our fathers always said they would love to see the French from France again, they who discovered this land and who were the first to be good to us.[66] We long for the French of the other shore, that they may prevent our young ones from exterminating the Americans. We have heard the Americans have bought a land."[67]

They ask me if Mr. Boutwell is sent by the government.[68] Also, they ask why there is opposition to their drinking whisky, and they say some of their young men have heard about it and would like to taste it.

"My Great Father, I take your hand, do all you can to send me some. There is a frontier not far away, and beyond it this beverage flows like water. We do not know if the agent is telling falsehoods of his own or if Washington orders him to tell them. We beg you to write to our Great Father telling him of our intentions, asking him to tell us what his are. We shall seal the letter with one side of the war

Taliaferro Journal, July 10, 1835; Boutwell Journal, October 12, 1834 (quotation); October 15, 1834; March 12, 20, 21, 26, 1835.

[66] The first white contact with the Indians of the upper Mississippi was made by Frenchmen in the mid-seventeenth century, and French dominance in the area lasted until 1763, when possession of Canada passed to the English. During this period the Chippewa, furnished for the first time with firearms by French traders, moved west from the Great Lakes and pushed the Sioux out of northern Minnesota. It was for the Chippewa, therefore, a golden era of expansion and newly acquired European trade goods, and their memories of the French were correspondingly fond. In his *Report* (p. 55) Nicollet notes that the Pillagers referred to him as "a Frenchman of the olden time," or "a Frenchman from beyond the waters," as distinguished from the French-Canadians.

[67] This may have been a reference to the Louisiana Purchase of 1803.

[68] William T. Boutwell operated a mission among the Pillager Chippewa from 1834 to 1837. He had accompanied Schoolcraft's expedition in 1832 and after a year as a missionary at La Pointe, he returned to Leech Lake under sponsorship of the American Board of Commissioners for Foreign Missions. This board represented a joint effort of the Presbyterian and Congregational churches, and therefore Nicollet's later statement (p. 112) that the missionary was Presbyterian was only a partial error. Boutwell was actually a graduate of Andover Theological Seminary, a stronghold of New England Congregationalism. See Folwell, *Minnesota*, 1: 175.

hatchet. You shall carry it to our Great Father, and he will send us his answer on the reverse side. But he that carries the answer must not go through St. Peter. He must come by way of Sandy Lake."

At this point, Chikins spoke and talked directly to the agent [as if he were present].

"I do not have good things to say to you. When I saw you last summer you did not tell me the truth. Summer is long and yet I have forgotten nothing. I placed within my ears those things you said; I was as close to you as from here to there, and I locked these words in my heart. Now I believe you no more. [At that time] the agent said [to me], 'My children, maybe you do not believe in your hearts the words I say, and yet all I speak is the truth.'

"Yes, Father, I trust you no longer. I watched your mouth and eyes carefully as you spoke. You were far away and I still did not believe you. I am ashamed for you, you deceive us so often. My Father, so many children have listened to you, to those words you pronounced which were so many untruths. You said you would stretch your arm across the river to prevent those who trade with the Sioux from ascending the river, and yet they did ascend. Even if you were close to me, and said, 'I shall go,' I am so ashamed for you because of the deceptive words you spoke last summer that I would not believe you. 'Behold,' you said, as you extended and flexed your arm to show your strength, thereby demonstrating that you had the power to do it. Now, I ask you, why did you let the prisoners escape? After so many fine words spoken to us by the agent since he has been at St. Peter, see this bundle of pieces of wood. Take it, and count them. They represent the number of Chippewa killed by the Sioux. I count them and I find forty-eight.

"I dug up my war hatchet seven years ago, when I saw so many of our brothers killed without having been avenged. All the natives of Leech Lake decided to go to war. Seven were killed as they waged war, but it was our fault and they are not included in this bundle. I speak exactly, I do not fear to speak."

"Here is one," says he [*Chikins to Nicollet*], pointing toward Brunia, "who was brought up by us and who knows everything as I do."

[*Chikins continues.*] "Four years later I again seized my hatchet and we fought. We met with the others [*Sioux*], clashed, and another one of ours was killed, but I do not include him either in the bundle.

Those are the only follies we have committed since the Americans interfered to keep us in peace. I would like to know why the agent has repeated to us that we should stand still. Have we not waited long enough to find out if he has sent us something, written a message with an explanation?"

(It appears Brunia bears no news either.)

[*Chikins again speaks.*] "We would then know what to do. I was convinced my Father was a man; he had indeed many people in his fort, and also when I was in St. Peter he unbuttoned his breeches for his needs, and I did see that he was like us, like I am, that he had that which makes a man. Now, I dig up my hatchet again. I want my Great Father to be aware of it. We do not know on whom we can rely."[69]

TUESDAY, AUGUST 23, 1836. At about 10 o'clock in the morning, Matchigabo, Chief of the Land, and Little Ox gathered in a smoking session with seven or eight elders. They sent for me, for they wished to speak to me more. I joined them. There ensued a long conversation about their missing the French, on the excitement caused by my presence among them, on the inner fire kindled by the French, who provided great well-being, a fire that dies down as the Americans advance.

They apologized for the improper words said the evening before by some of their men in front of Mr. Boutwell. They disavowed these words, blaming the indiscreet individuals for them, and said an apology would be made to Mr. Boutwell. They also added that these unwise persons had no rank and were not entitled to give their opinion on such important matters as those discussed that evening with Mr. Boutwell and myself.

Another subject of discussion was how I liked their country, if I found it agreeable, and if I liked being with them. I took advantage

[69] An entry in Nicollet's astronomical notebook for August 19 reads: "This evening and the next day, Saturday, no observation was possible, because of the dances, the harangues, and the assemblies of the natives which I was forced to endure." In his *Report* (p. 54) he wrote: "But, during the first three days of this week, the Chippeways of the lake greatly annoyed me; and, from mutual misunderstandings, even put my life in jeopardy, as my guide scarcely dared to side with me, for fear of exposing himself." Nicollet blames this difficulty on the fact that he brought insufficient presents and goes on to tell of how Boutwell, though kept by bad weather from crossing the lake for several days, at last came to his aid and calmed the Indians.

of the situation to inspire them with notions of work, culture, and religion. I told them how God was generous to them. I drew a comparison between their standard of living and that of many other nations westward and southward whose people live in disheartening conditions because of diseases, the climate, and the absence of natural resources. In order to pluck their sensitive chord, I pointed out that some of these people, being deprived of tobacco, are reduced to smoking buffalo dung, whereas here they only smoke their old pipes and tobacco pouches when they are temporarily out of tobacco.[70]

They present me with a calumet of peace and friendship for the king of France, urging me to talk with him for a long time on their behalf — to call upon him to intercede with the president of the United States for the betterment of their plight. "This pipe is a simple one," they add, "without ornaments. It is the symbol of our poverty. We wrap it in the bark of the trees from our forests to show we have nothing else we can use to warm, shelter, or dress ourselves."

At about 2 o'clock in the afternoon the wind from the south that had whipped up the lake for the last two days, thus preventing me from leaving, showed signs of subsiding. We prepared for our departure and were about to leave for the embarkation place when a canoe appeared in the distance heading in from Little Boy River. The high chief of the lake, Flat Mouth, was returning from his trip to Lake Superior.[71] I had to wait for his arrival, for the Indians convinced me he would be mortified if I were to leave so close to his arrival. I stayed. Flat Mouth disembarked. We shook hands, and he demonstrated his joy at finding me still there. He had heard I was in his country, but feared I had already left. After we had spent some moments together, I noticed that other chiefs were coming in and that before long, following the messages that had been sent to all the closest communities around the lake, he would be surrounded by a great number of people. I begged him to forgive my having to continue my voyage, assuring him also that I would return in eight to ten days and that at that time I would be in a better position to respond to his welcome. This lapse

[70] See Appendix 5, p. 254.

[71] In his *Report* (p. 61) Nicollet states that Flat Mouth had been absent for three months visiting "British trading posts to obtain ammunition to enable him to make war against the Sioux," but that he had been disappointed in his quest. Boutwell notes in his journal (October 18, 1836) the circulation of a report that Flat Mouth "had been at La Pointe this summer, and returned with 5 kegs of powder and two or three bags of shot and ball."

of time, moreover, would not be too long for him, considering he was going to be busy parleying night and day in the course of numerous smoking sessions in which all would participate, not to mention the feasts of the medicine ceremonies that would follow one after the other. I noted that as the natives entered the lodge where I was with their chief whom they had not seen for two months, there was no salutation of any sort, no contact of the hands, no sign of any kind emphasizing the pleasure of seeing one another again. The natives would enter, lie down on the matting, stay quiet, and introduce themselves into the conversation gradually.

At 3: 30 I finally left the point on which I had pitched camp. The lake was still very restless and on two or three occasions its waves threatened to swallow up our canoe with its contents. More than once I was about to turn back but, then, there was as much danger in doing that as in going ahead. So off we went, and we reached the Reverend Boutwell's house at 5: 00. I wanted to see him. He lives at the bottom end of the bay [*Uram Bay*] formed by Great Point [*Stony Point*] and Pine Point a little distance from the house of Mr. Etienne, the trader.[72] From there we passed Pine Point, and since the night caught up with us, and it was impossible to leave the lake on this day, we camped six miles farther up. It was a splendid night. A strong wind from the south rid us of all mosquitoes and blessed us with a mild temperature. It was regrettable that the location of our camp was not suited for astronomical observations.

WEDNESDAY, AUGUST 24, 1836. We broke camp at 6: 00 in the morning. Yesterday I could see in the way the goods had been stowed on board the evidence of our precipitate escape from the inevitable Saturnalia. Today, after putting everything in its proper place, I feel more comfortable, and I can write. Our voyage is peaceful and quiet. There are no children along to enliven us. Our canoe is no more than fourteen feet long and there are only four of us on board: Brunia, Désiré, an old native, and myself. I left Chagobay, my friend and teacher, in the midst of his family and medicines. He told me once more as I left that he would appeal to *Wâbanark* for my

[72] The American Fur Company trader at Leech Lake was William Davenport. He was, however, absent during the summer of 1836, according to Boutwell, and an unidentified "half-breed" was left in charge — probably the "Mr. Etienne" to whom Nicollet refers. Boutwell Journal, June 2, October 27, 31, 1836.

prompt return.[73] The old native taking Chagobay's place with us is called Kégouédgikâ.[74] His beautiful face, his handsome dark hair, almost curly and for which he seems to care, the silver ring pinching the partition of his nose, and his noble bearing all reveal at first glance a respectable personality. This impression is confirmed not only by his own people but also by the whites. Kégouédgikâ is the only Leech Lake Pillager quite familiar with the region I am about to explore. He is the only one who has scoured it while hunting, hence their name for it: the Grounds of Kégouédgikâ. Finally, he is one of the old ones of his nation, a wise man, a mediator, a keen observer — all qualities which lead me to place my confidence in the man.

In three quarters of an hour we went from yesterday evening's camping site to the mouth of *Kâbékanâ Sibi* — the Kâbékanâ [*Kabe-kona*] River that we are supposed to ascend. Its entrance into Leech Lake is two or three miles north of the starting point of the portage which leads to the lakes that give birth to Crow River. Our average bearing from Otter Tail Point to the mouth of Kâbékanâ River has been SW. We had barely covered one mile in a westerly direction on this river when we made our entrance into a lake [*Kabekona Bay*] two or three miles long and three-fourths of a mile wide. The shore on our left is composed of well-exposed hills of a pleasant aspect. Three small rivers, contributing their waters to the lake, flow from this shore in an east-westerly direction. The last of them comes from a lake [*Benedict Lake*] very close by that washes the base of the hills just mentioned at the level where they withdraw from the lake we are crossing. As we leave this lake [*Kabekona Bay*], re-entering Kâbékanâ River, we run into a flat valley irrigated by this river and offering an abundant yield of wild rice. This valley is absolutely identical to the valley of the Indian Gardens washed by Little Boy River. Pine and larch trees adorn its shore line which from time to time is interrupted by hills typical of the country.

After traveling four miles W and two miles NW we crossed a pretty little lake [*Oak Lake*] three-fourths of a mile wide, continued three more miles westward, and entered into beautiful Lake Kâbé-kanâ [*Kabekona*] which lends its name to the river we are now

[73] Baraga (2:390) gives *wabanang* as "morning star."

[74] This name is spelled *Kegwedzissag* in Nicollet's *Report* (p. 55), but since this was translated by others, it is probable that the version in the journal is closer to the phonetic spelling, which Nicollet usually recorded with care.

leaving. The size of this lake is approximately six by two miles. On the west shore are beautiful hills, well wooded, seventy to eighty feet high, and easily distinguished from all others around. The shore to the east is sandy, five to six feet high, on which birch, lime, ash, ironwood trees, etc. thrive vigorously. All the lakes and rivers we have seen today abound with fish. One can catch ten- to twelve-pound pike. Bear, deer, wolves, otter, fox, civet cats, badgers, woodchucks, the moose with a wattle under its throat, many crows, a few raccoons, very few beaver — such are the species characterizing these parts.[75] Game birds abound. Kégouédgikâ killed three ducks, all point-blank.

On the western shore of Lake Kâbékanâ flows first of all a small river [*Sucker Brook*] where the Indians start out on a fifteen-mile portage when they use this route to go to Big Otter Tail [*Ottertail*] Lake situated to the west of the *Hauteurs des Terres*.[76] (Kâbékanâ from *kâbé*, to leave, and *kanâ*, path. Hence, Kâbékana, the place where the lake and canoes are left and where the portage or path begins.)[77] Farther up and on the same side is to be found the mouth of a small river [*Gulch Creek*], which links several of the first lakes [*Little Gulch Lakes*] we will have to cross to go to La Biche Lake [*Lake Itasca*]. These lakes are linked by portages that are used as much to shorten the way as to avoid the difficulties and bends of this river.

At this point I called for a meeting to evaluate our present situation. When we disembark at the entrance of this river we must first of all make a six-mile portage through muskegs and often across swampy shallows. Taking into consideration our total freight and the weight of the canoe, I have to admit it is impossible to transport the lot in a single trip. One or two of us will have to come back and

[75] The civet cat is probably the striped skunk. In the manuscript Nicollet refers to crows as *mâitres*, an allusion to La Fontaine, *The Crow and the Fox*, which starts with the words "Master Corbeau perched on a tree . . ."

[76] On his maps Nicollet shows a string of lakes through which this portage leads to Ottertail Lake, northeast of present-day Fergus Falls in Otter Tail County. He did not travel over this portage and must have obtained his information from his guide. Many lakes in the vicinity of the portage are named on his 1843 map after friends of his, but the lakes on the portage itself bear Indian names. On both his 1836 and 1843 maps Ottertail Lake is shown as the source of the Red River of the North.

[77] Nicollet's *Report* (p. 55) gives this as *Kabekonaug*, from *kabe*, to disembark, and *mikan*, a path or trail.

fetch the things not carried across the first time. Hence for a six-mile portage, some would have to cover eighteen miles, while the others would wait for the duration of a twelve-mile hike. All this meant a lot of fatigue and a lot of time wasted. I asked Kégouéd-gikâ what he thought, and he told me that there are fifteen portages to be carried out before reaching Lake La Biche, two or three of which are four to six miles long and the others much shorter. It is an incredible task, representing six days of stevedoring to bring it to a conclusion, because most of the lakes are mere ponds.

I had almost decided to turn back and take the route through Leech Lake, Cass Lake, and Lake Travers [*Bemidji*], but then I would be traveling a route already known and thus would lose the advantage of opening an interior route quite unknown to geography, trade, and civilization. Fortunately my familiarity with the minds of these natives reminded me that they always travel following a straight line, disregarding obstacles as long as the way is the shortest. So I asked Kégouédgikâ if there is not an easier route.

"Yes," he replied, "but it is longer."

"How much longer?"

"By one day."

"Which way?"

"By way of Kâbékanâ River which we just left and which we can continue to ascend. It will lead us to Lake La Biche by means of three portages. However," he added, "I have not seen this route for a very long time; we shall find it full of obstacles, but none are insurmountable."

Obviously, Kégouédgikâ had based all his reckoning on travel-ing light as natives are wont to do—with a gun, a canoe, and a pad-dle. The native and his canoe play "saddle-my-nag," one carrying the other and vice versa. Little did it occur to him that a poor astronomer is unlikely to be proficient at this kind of sport. After he had thus revived my spirits, though, I could not very well bear a grudge against him for not having mentioned this route when I was about to turn and go back.

"So let's go, let's go," I cried with joy, and we started out at once up Kâbékanâ River which flows into the lake a mere hundred steps to the north of the little river leading toward the lakes sepa-rated by fifteen portages. At 6:00 in the evening we have already traveled ten to twelve miles on the Kâbékanâ from its entrance into the lake of the same name. The first two miles are through a few fallen trees, willows, and thick groves of alders that lean over the water because of the lack of foundation for their roots. These species are sometimes mixed with several others having red berries [*high bush cranberries*] that the natives eat with avidity.

During these first two miles we had to open up a passage, sometimes using the hatchet but most of the time using our hands to break off or push aside the branches blocking our way. At other times we passed below a vault formed by toppled trees, and now and then, as a last resort, the men took to the water and the canoe was lifted over the trunks of these very trees. After two miles such obstacles as these become fewer, and the river runs freely in its bed, bordered by savannas or swamps with thickly matted bottoms filled with water. Its width varies from twenty to forty or fifty feet; its depth is nearly always three to six feet. The water is beautifully transparent; the bed is of sand mixed with very small pebbles. There is no physical obstacle to the river itself, not a stone to remove thus far, and its course can be rid of obstructions by simply using the hatchet to clear its shores.

Several aquatic plants grow in the river without obstructing it. Among them is a plant [*white water buttercup*] the stem of which is proportionate in size with the depth of the water. Its pretty white flower with five petals rises to bloom on the surface where after having radiated its beauty for several days it is fertilized and withdraws into the water with the precious fruit of its passions. At night it closes, but during the day it expands and glows under the light and warmth of the sun. Its stem carries leaves composed of short and filiform folioles forming a brush that opens into a crest. They support the stem in its transversal undulations while the flower floats on the surface. The river right now is bedecked with large tufts of this pretty little flower which reigns in all the places where the current is not obstructed or shaded. None of these aquatic plants disturb the transparency of the water, for there is nothing oozy or slimy about them.

Now is a good time to point out that the temperature of the water of this river is low compared to that of the lakes and other rivers in these parts. During the ten to twelve miles we have just traveled, I always found it to be between 54° and 56°, while that of the lakes and rivers which lie across its path and which I have been measuring for the last few days varies between 64° and 68° and sometimes reaches 70°. The vegetation is therefore proper to the river.

I looked carefully for shells and found no trace of any. There are no fish either; the species abundant in Lake Kâbékanâ into which this river flows never ascend it. Finally, Kégouédgikâ tells me that Kâbékanâ River is always the last to freeze in the country and also the last to thaw. Usually the lakes start freezing between November 15 and December 15. This river does not freeze even in January, but only in February or March. The water of the Kâbékanâ is most delicious to drink. It was such a delight that we kept drinking it, and it served as nourishment for practically the whole day. It is the product of a number of springs oozing from the flanks of the hills that form the valley it irrigates.

The valley is one to three miles wide and the flat base on which the river continually winds from one hill to the other is filled with brushwood—thickets forming what they call here muskegs, in the midst of which the voyageur can see nothing around him.[78] This base seems to lie on a thick bed of peat, the depth of which is bound to increase. All the tree shrubs of many a variety growing on it are smothered and often drowned to such a degree that they cannot develop. There is no doubt that if herds of animals were to trample this base, the water would gather into one single canal two or three times larger than the river is now, and the bottom of the valley would become rich and fit for the first civilized colony to introduce itself into these parts. This valley, because of its water and natural beauty, ranks first among all that I have seen since the junction of the Mississippi and Crow [*Crow Wing*] rivers.

THURSDAY, AUGUST 25, 1836. Yesterday we found it difficult to camp for the night. We could not find our way out of a long muskeg in which we had become entangled at the approach of night. At last, pushing our canoe across the reeds, we found a little channel leading to the edge of a beautiful pine forest, the fore-

---

[78] For muskeg, Nicollet wrote *mosqué*, a French word meaning hidden. The phonetic similarity may have led him to think the term was derived from French. It actually comes from the Ojibway *mashkig*, meaning swamp.

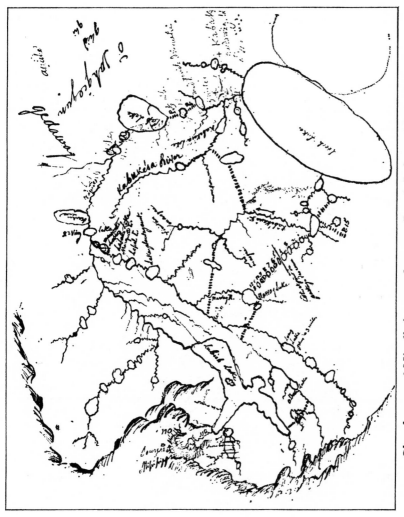

Sketch map of Nicollet's route between Leech Lake and Lake Itasca

ground of a chain of hills that converged with the Kâbékanâ valley formation. It had been a lovely day and the night was equally beautiful. Our position, however, presented nothing that I could take advantage of in the interest of geography. So we made the most of a long and refreshing period of repose which we needed rather badly.

This morning for the first time in my life I attended a terrifying concert performed at dawn by wolves whose bands are wont to haunt these totally deserted and virgin forests. It was like a choir of chilling howls that could be heard in the distance on both sides of the river, spreading far and wide across the echoing solitudes. Such was our source of entertainment for almost an hour during which we did not speak. I know not to what degree such a morning hymn can be pleasing to the gods of nature. As for me, poor Christian that I am, I readily admit it troubled my morning prayers. Had I not recalled that these ferocious animals, well provided for by the abundant game they devour, are more inclined to flee than to attack a solitary traveler, I would have shuddered with fear. Be it as it may, I did notice that this reveille of a new kind had my people up before sunrise and that our canoe was afloat in less than a quarter of an hour.

Soon we were back on the bed of white flowers that had seduced us the evening before. The chilly flowers were closed and shriveled up. Their dismal appearance, coupled with the monotonous sound of the paddle and the terrifying howls resounding yet in the neighboring woods, drove me momentarily into one of those vague reveries with which only the voyageur is familiar. But in a little while the rays of the rising sun began to gild the jagged fringes crowning the forest of green trees to the east. The flowers unclosed their white corollas and opened their hearts to the quickening and love-inspiring warmth. Our muskeg began to clear, the horizon opened, and joyful hills appeared to be closing in. Some birds sang and Kégouédgikâ at last broke the dismal silence that had hovered over our frail craft.

"Over there," he said, "a little river [*unnamed*] flows into the Kâbékanâ from the right."

We were now two miles away from our camp. He would constantly point out fresh trails of deer and wolves, small slides of earth on the edge of the river caused by a heavy bear, the age and size of which he would determine by the track of its paw, or the toppled reeds where otters had reveled, and many others. Kégouédgikâ was inexhaustible. At the height of his excitement at the sight of so many trails of animals inhabiting his domain, there would perchance appear some unfortunate ducks. Busy grooming their plumage, they might let us approach within rifle shot. Down would go the paddle, off would go the gun, and Kégouédgikâ, who the night before had served *canard de France,* unctuous and meaty, for supper, could introduce for breakfast a wood duck, an autumn duck, and a kind of delicate bird called the diver.

At about noon the valley bottom became clear of the muskeg that had obscured our view for so long. The river is only twenty to twenty-five feet wide and is two to three feet deep. The flanks of the hills are totally exposed and a silky greenness seems to flow forth from tamarack and cedar and from the fir trees which prevail where the pine can no longer be distinguished. We stopped and climbed to what appeared to be the highest point on the right bank. I made a barometric reading above the river and measured eighty-five feet. Some summits on the right shore seemed to be twenty or twenty-five feet higher. The hill we were examining is composed entirely of sand, rolled quartzose stones, and transitional shale. The young fir trees covering it form a wood so dense that they suffocate and can by no means thrive. From the summit, I could enjoy across some clearings the view of the Kâbékanâ valley. It is really beautiful and wholly confirmed the opinion of it I had already formed yesterday.

We prolonged our ascent of the river till 6:00 in the evening, bringing today's total traveling distance to about twenty miles. In the course of the last miles we encountered small, short rapids barely a foot deep. For the first time in these parts we came across rolled stones large enough to obstruct navigation. We did not have to make a portage, however. Disembarking from the canoe and pulling it for about a hundred yards proved to be sufficient. Today's travels ended at a place where the Kâbékanâ branches from another small river [*unnamed*] which comes from the northwest and then passes west through some narrows leading to a lake [*Hubbard Lake*] from which it issues to the Kâbékanâ. This lake is situated on the far side of hills that border the right shores of the stream to that point. We abandoned the Kâbékanâ to camp on top of the hill on the right bank facing the river junction.

Here began the portage that will lead us to the waters of the Mississippi. It was a lovely day, a little warmer than the one before. The thermometer climbed to 78° in the shade. The Kâbékanâ waters gave us readings of 54° to 56° till the very end. The night was not favorable for the observations I wanted to make in order to establish the geographical position of the tributary and the starting point of the portage at the same time. Mists veiled the sky just when I needed its clarity the most in order to pinpoint the site.

FRIDAY, AUGUST 26, 1836. We arose early to prepare our burdens for the portage and made do with a little coffee and water for breakfast so as to lunch with more appetite and pleasure after this painful chore. It took four hours to do it, from 7:00 to 11:00. The entire portage from east to west breaks down as follows:

Three quarters of a mile across a forest of fir trees and some swamps.

One quarter of a mile over a pond or around it on foot.

One good mile across a forest and some brush.

One mile over an unnamed lake, the one from which emerges the branch that makes a fork with the Kâbékanâ as mentioned yesterday.

One and a quarter miles across a wood of fir trees with some clearings caused by fire. At the end of this we met a small river [Alcohol Creek] emerging from the south. We waded across some shallows on its edge, etc.

After three quarters of a mile of good portage terrain we encounter another river, larger than the former, also from the south. Both are heading north to join and form Laplace [Schoolcraft] River.

We have done five miles altogether.

These five miles of portage mixed with short, comforting trips over water were carried out cheerfully and without difficulty because the profile we were tackling was most of the time horizontal and clear of handicaps. As we ate I measured some meridian elevations of the sun and then, as I chattered with Brunia and Kégouédgikâ, I discovered with glee we had already reached the eastern branch of the sources of the Mississippi as they are described by Schoolcraft and Lieutenant Allen. Therefore it remains for us to ascend the river [Birch Creek] up to Lake Ossawa [Alice Lake].[79] But before lunching and leaving I

[79] In the diary and in his astronomical notebook Nicollet clearly spells this word Ossawa. It is illegible on his 1836 map, but on the 1843 map and in the

must point out that the portage we just traveled is a railroad route all mapped out for the future, leading from Kâbékanâ River to the Mississippi springs.

We left again at 1:30, making good headway, and by 2 o'clock (two miles later) we reached the rapids and obstructions in the river which have to be detoured by making a portage. The latter is carried out in fifty-five minutes. I estimate that it represents one and a quarter or two miles of the sinuous course of the river. At 3 o'clock we left the rapids. The river is joined by three other ones, quite long, below the lake.[80] For two miles below these junctions it is no more than ten to fifteen feet wide. However, as we ascended towards Ossawa Lake, it became wider and wider. Allen disagrees and yet it could not have changed since he was there. In this section it is six to seven feet deep, never less than two, with a width of thirty, forty, or fifty feet.

The entrance into Lake Ossawa is one of the most majestic I ever saw. There is always an element of surprise on entering the lakes of these parts, but this one we approached through a large and beautiful avenue a mile long, both sides diverging with their extremities dissolving into the lake, embracing, as it were, a beautiful span of water of indefinite width. As we advanced, our gaze fell upon two lovely curtains of green trees bordering the shores for two miles and concealing the tall hills in the distance on either side. The river along this avenue flows through the middle of a flat green carpet, carving itself a deeper bed and broadening its width to more than one hundred feet. At 6 o'clock we made our entry near the place where another small river enters from a westerly direction.[81] We crossed the lake lengthwise and left on the same river which a mile later brought us to the portage that on the morrow was to lead us to Lake La Biche. At the place where we left Ossawa River, the latter was still fifteen to twenty feet wide and four feet deep, with a very noticeable current. We find some buffalo heads that had disappeared seventeen years before.[82]

Report the spelling is Assawa. Allen's journal gives it as Usaw-way. (23 Congress, 1 session, *House Documents*, no. 323, p. 43.) Nicollet here assumes Alice Lake to be the main source of the Schoolcraft River. Modern maps show the river rising in Schoolcraft Lake, farther to the south.

[80] The reference to three streams is not clear. Two streams now flow into the section of Birch Creek traversed by Nicollet — one being the Schoolcraft River, which he considered a tributary, and the other an unnamed stream flowing from Lake Hattie.

[81] This unnamed stream flows from Lost Lake.

[82] The final cryptic sentence is totally unexplained.

Near the river we discovered a fine, well-preserved circular camp cut into the forest. We quartered there for the night, which promised to be as lovely as the day had been — hot, however, with the south wind which had blown all day. I intended to make the most of it in case the weather should be bad tomorrow. But the mosquitoes were so fierce and turned out in such great numbers that by 10 o'clock I had to abandon the battlefield to them, having accomplished but a part of what I had intended to do and that much at the expense of serious inflammation of my eyes and face caused by their bites. (Compare my notes with those of Schoolcraft.) [83]

SATURDAY, AUGUST 27, 1836. Although we arose at 4: 30 to prepare for the six-mile portage lying before us, we were not ready until 6: 30. With some people, the thought of having but one last effort to make gives extra strength and doubles their energy. Today we witnessed the contrary. There we were, lingering, chatting, wasting time. The night had been a hot one, the mosquitoes had been terrible, and we had not rested well. In the morning the barometer dipped rapidly; the sun and south wind heralded much heat and swarms of mosquitoes. As we expatiated upon the misfortunes of the voyageur, we neglected the assembling of the packages each one of us was to carry. Fortunately, Désiré, who is as greedy as a cat and whose hands burn him as long as there remains a single ounce of provisions in a bag, remarked that the coffee drunk on the eve had been of great benefit to us and that there remained enough of it to make a cup for each of us.

"Well," I said, "let's have the rest of the coffee!" In as much time as it took to say it, the coffee was ready and the packages made. We gulped down the former and loaded the latter, and off we went at last.

The first mile of the portage was a short swamp followed by a small elevation covered with white cedars. We then plunged into shallows filled with toppled trees in full decomposition, accumulated there by centuries of time, covered with a thick coat of damp moss mixed with other wild vegetation. One might well call it a buried forest over which there grew yet another. We left this horrible mire and began to tread some sandy, barren ground scattered with pine

[83] The parenthetical statement was apparently only a reminder to himself. In his astronomical notebook for August 26 he says: "I have never suffered so much from mosquitoes in all my life as when making the observations for this time. Also, I fear that they are not sorry."

trees of the most pitiful kind and rising into a hill on top of which we halted for a while.

My men cleared this first mile with joy and courage. They trotted off and twenty-five minutes later arrived, still trotting. Trotting is indeed the cruising speed of the portage bearer. Experience has proved that time and fatigue can thus be minimized. The momentum acquired paves the bearer's way through shrubs, tree branches, over the irregularities of the terrain, while he remains oblivious to these obstacles and preserves the energy he would have to deploy brushing them aside if he were walking.

Brunia, the giant, with the canoe tipped over his head looking like an enormous seal swimming over shrubbery, opened our path. Désiré and Kégouédgikâ could barely follow him and invariably ended up questioning their own efficiency. Brunia's load weighed from 110 to 115 pounds, that of each of the other two, from eighty-five to ninety pounds. Today, as in the course of all our portages, I was given the opportunity of admiring the ease with which Désiré could fulfill such tasks all entirely new to him. Never did he grumble once, and his cheerful disposition sustained him as much as his physical strength did.

As for the astronomer, he was always behind. He would catch up whenever he could, but he was forever behind the others, and this first mile in particular he was far behind the others. It should be noted that on these portages I had selected as my own load all those things that are most precious to me: my instruments and papers. In case of an accident, it was the only way to shield the others from painful regrets and to avoid manifestations of impatience on my part. I carried on my back, the way soldiers carry their bags, a ten-inch sextant in its box, all wrapped up in deer hide. I carried also a barometer slung over my shoulder like a hunting rifle. Over my left arm I folded a big coat, pressing my charts against my left side, an umbrella in my hand. In my right hand I held a basket containing a chronometer, some thermometers, a small pocket compass, a mercury container, the box and cover of an artificial horizon, and some other small objects such as pencils, paper, and a coiled surveying chain. The weight of my load added up to thirty-five pounds.[84]

Although I was the one carrying the least, I nevertheless suffered

[84] This often-quoted description of Nicollet's "accoutrement," rewritten with somewhat more style, appears also in his *Report* (p. 56).

the most. I had been fortunate enough to come thus far without breaking anything or even losing a needle's worth of my things. It was so important that I reach my objective, now so close, with equal success, that I could ill afford not to double my energy and triple the precautions I was taking. One can imagine then the difficulties I had to overcome as I waded through the obstructions of this forest surrounded by swamps, burdened as I was with fragile instruments which, to make matters worse for the little physical strength with which I am endowed anyway, were unevenly distributed over my person.

My men were already resting on top of the hill mentioned above while I was barely starting to scramble through the swamp. There I was, sweeping aside one by one the branches in my way, sometimes sinking through the mossy crust on which I was treading, plunging knee deep into water, at other times falling amidst the slimy decay of big trees on which I thought I had sure footing but which completely crumbled under my weight.

It is indeed conceivable that under the circumstances I was paying more attention to my instruments than to the path I was following, and no one will be surprised to learn that I went totally astray. I wandered erroneously for half an hour without seeing a single overturned leaf, a single bent or cracked branch, or any other clue on the ground that might have guided me back to the trail followed by my men. However, I was aware of the fact that a west southwesterly direction led to the end of our run and was about to head that way when I heard a shot which I concluded must be a signal for me. As it turned out, the gunshot was not fired for me at all. A magnificent bald eagle had been Kégouédgikâ's target as he wandered around waiting for me in the pine forest I was seeking. This put me on another wrong trail. Finally, Kégouédgikâ let out the native cry. I responded and reached the hill, on which I made some barometric readings before 8:30.

We then climbed down the west bank of the hill and climbed up yet another one slightly higher, on which I made more readings. We continued to climb up and down in this way without ever reaching anything higher than the latter hill, and then we came across a little lake [unidentified] filled with the water from the hills surrounding it. From it flowed a little creek [unidentified] leading to Ossawa River. As we canoed across we were given the enjoyment of a ten- or twelve-minute rest, and we then resumed the portage at once. By this time we had covered three miles.

The next three miles are a succession of up and down slopes. In the dips we found small swamps which the bearers crossed in a straight line, wading through half a foot of water, but which I avoided by following the edge of the surrounding forest. Finally we arrived on the top of the last ridge that seemed higher than all those we had passed in the morning. I measured its height against that of Lake La Biche to which we were to descend in only a quarter of an hour, following a very steep slope for the first five minutes. We arrived on the lake just in time for me to set up my barometer for a noon reading and a comparison with the other readings made that morning. Therefore we spent five hours making a six-mile portage from Ossawa River. But I am the one responsible for this long span of time, for my men spent no more than three hours. They did not take their rests as is customary during long portages in these northern regions. They stopped only three times and rested only until I arrived.

The last three miles of this portage cross a territory covered with more vegetation than encountered on the preceding stretches in spite of the fact that this whole hill formation is identical in all respects — sand mixed with talcose and syenitic rock being its foundation.[85] There are more varieties of green trees of a healthier growth and generally less. . . . [*Here one page of the manuscript is missing.*]

MONDAY, AUGUST 29, 1836. Visit to the shores and surroundings of Lake La Biche [*Itasca*]. Discovery of the sources.

After thirty hours of uninterrupted labor during which I only slept two and a half hours, we started out by canoe to visit the shores and surroundings of the lake. We left first of all from the island [*Schoolcraft Island*] at the end of the southwest bay. The axis of this western avenue is two miles long due NNE-SSW. On the right flows a river fifteen feet wide at its mouth.[86] It comes from the *hautes*

[85] Nicollet is here referring to what we know as the glacial drift, which in this area is very likely to contain talcose and syenitic rock. Talcose as used in the past referred to other rocks beside talc, including biotite schist and chloritic greenstones, which are common rock types in the region north of Lake Itasca. Syenitic rocks, similar to granite but lacking quartz, are also common in the area. Professor Glenn B. Morey, Minnesota Geological Survey, to the editor, December 20, 1968.

[86] This seems to have been the unnamed stream which drains Bohall Lake in seasons of high water.

terres that are very near us. We steered to the opposite shore of the bay and noticed another river [*Chambers Creek*] eight feet wide at its entrance. Our canoe could not ascend it because of the many obstructions of wood and debris. We hoisted the canoe and penetrated on foot three hundred steps into the forest which lies beyond the swamps bordering the canal. We discovered it to flow out of a pretty circular lake [*Elk Lake*] with a diameter a good mile long. The lake is bordered with three brooks flowing down from hills forty to fifty feet high forming the foreground of the *hautes terres* beyond, from which the three brooks originate. They fill the lake marked on my map. The brook situated farthest to the east forms a pond at the foot of the *hautes terres* from which it issues to pour forth into the lake.[87]

After this visit we returned to the bay and followed the same shore. Almost at once we came across a river [*Nicollet Creek*] fifteen to twenty feet wide by two feet deep at its entrance. Three hundred feet later it is three feet deep and ten feet wide. Its current is lively, the temperature of the water 54°. That of the water of the lake into which it empties is 66°. We then found tree debris and, fearing it would be too difficult to pass it, we left the canoe, bent on following the river on foot.

Pembina and Red River. Sources of the Mississippi and Red River.

Pembina is the Canadian translation of the Chippewa word *anibimin* (plural: *anibiminum*) from *anibiminagâwozh* (*anib*, white elm, and *min, minum*, berries). It is a kind of white elm growing six to eight feet high over a diameter of one to three or four inches, bearing fruit or berries in clusters of a beautiful red when they are ripe, somewhat sour to the taste but agreeable as a healthy and refreshing nourishment. The leaves of this tree, which is perhaps the *assiminier* of Missouri and Illinois, turn red in the fall and, mingling with the shades of the other species, contribute to the whole admirable harmony of hues the vegetation presents at this time of year.[88]

[87] Warren Upham lists four streams flowing into Elk Lake: Siegfried Creek, flowing from Hall Lake on the west; Elk Creek from the southwest; Clarke Creek from the south; and Gay-gued-o-say Creek (named for Nicollet's Indian guide) from the southeast. The latter stream drains Clarke Lake and Deer Park Lake in seasons of high water. One of these was probably the pond mentioned by Nicollet. *Minnesota Geographic Names*, 130.

[88] The bush Nicollet describes is the high bush cranberry. Keating gives the

It is out of the wood of this tree that the Indians make those special pipestems we find so fascinating. The Indians also greatly prize its berries. It appears that the abundance with which they grow in the valley of the Red River of the North gave origin to their calling one of its tributaries *Anibi-minanisibi* — river of the elms with the berries which the Canadians call pembinas. Hence Pembina River and Pembina, the name of the place at the mouth of this river where only a few years ago the trading post of the North West Company used to be.[89] There, also, passes the forty-ninth northern parallel that separates the British possessions from those of the United States in these parts.

Between the forty-seventh and forty-eighth parallel the main chain of hills called *Hauteurs des Terres* runs more or less in a north northwesterly direction. Toward its southern tip the chain loses altitude and veers east; it then rises again, veering northeast and sprouting into all directions of the eastern horizon those various ramifications that become so many water divides. The waters drain these spurs and gather in the numerous basins and lakes formed by them and their protruding extremities. I have had occasion to describe these extremities before. It is around this bend of the southern tip of the *Hauteurs des Terres*, and in the space of only two or three minutes of latitude and longitude, that the sources of both the Mississippi and Red rivers are to be found.

The very first trickles that will form the Mississippi descend from the north flank of this bend, springing forth at its base at a constant temperature no doubt oscillating between 43.5° and 44.2°. There already they gather into a small lake [*Whipple Lake*] from which flows the brook, Mississippi [*Nicollet Creek*], one and a half feet deep. It then forms a second lake [*unidentified*] several hundred yards farther downstream, at the foot of the chain of hills, from which ooze

same origin for the name Pembina, spelling the Ojibway word for the plant as *anepeminan*. See *Expedition to the Source of the St. Peter's River*, vol. 2, appendix, p. 38. The *assiminier* is identified by Nicollet in a later random note as the *asimin* or pawpaw. See also William A. Read, *Louisiana French*, 79 (Baton Rouge, La., 1931), who gives *acminier* as pawpaw tree.

[89] A number of fur trading posts were maintained at various times and on various sites near the mouth of the Pembina River. The North West Company was active there from about 1790 until 1814. The Hudson's Bay Company had posts in the vicinity between 1803 and 1823, and the American William A. Aitken was trading there as early as 1824. Nute, in *Minnesota History*, 11:366; H. V.

forth other springs of the same temperature heading for the second lake. The temperature of this lake is 48°. It increases the volume of the Mississippi which then flows out of it, boasting a width of three to four feet and a depth of one foot.

From then on this infant stream already shows signs of the capricious and encroaching propensities that characterize its power and course along its various stages of growth all the way down to the Gulf of Mexico. It is testing its strength over a stretch of a quarter mile which it doubles in length by making a series of meanders before coming to rest in a third lake [*Nicollet Lake*] that must cover a quarter of a mile square at certain times of the year. This lake is a composite of the Mississippi and other wild streams emptying into it from the surrounding swamps that fill the bottom of the valley opening into the southwestern bay of Lake La Biche. As the Mississippi issues from this lake, it resumes its meandering across more marshes and two or three miles later enters Lake La Biche, heads north, veers south and descends toward the Gulf of Mexico.

TUESDAY, AUGUST 30, 1836. We bade farewell to our pretty and romantic little island which in itself contains a complete array of all those species of trees that in this region one sometimes only encounters isolated: the spruce, beautiful cedar, white wood (lime or bass), two kinds of oak on the western shore, the long-needled pine (pitch [*jack*] pine), some hazelnut, larch, birch, and those shrubs with red berries. This lake does not have on its shores those large rolled stones that are characteristic of the lakes of a certain size in these parts. The bottom of the lake is of sand mixed with pebbles that are no bigger than a nut. On the eastern side of the lake they are the size of an Easter egg. There are no rocks or stones to be seen on the island except those exposed in the hollows made by toppling trees.

It was eleven minutes after 6 o'clock when we left the island. The day promised to be lovely, but there were signs of change: the barometer that was very low Saturday evening and climbed half an inch yesterday morning, Monday, began to drop again last night, and the wind which was from the west has veered to the south from which direction it is blowing strongly this morning. In eighteen minutes we

Arnold, *The History of Old Pembina*, 52, 85 (Larimore, N. Dak., 1917); E. E. Rich, *The History of the Hudson's Bay Company, 1670–1870*, 2:430 (London, 1959).

passed from the island to the outlet of the Mississippi, and we found the river, already a child, brisk and lively, fifteen to twenty feet wide over a depth of one foot. At 6: 30 I found its temperature to be 62°, that of the atmosphere 56°. An hour after our departure we found the Mississippi to be already thirty to forty feet wide and two to four feet deep.

The water is crystal clear. The river bed which at first was sand and gravel strewn with shells of the single species anodonta now becomes filled with aquatic plants while its flat shores are well wooded with larch, cedar, spruce, ash, birch, and aspen.[90] The valley is quite flat. The reeds on its edges widen its domain, and the river either winds freely through them or flows along its main channel, twenty to thirty feet wide. Here teal and duck of various kinds romp around in great numbers, providing ample food for our breakfast which otherwise might have been a meager one.

At 9 o'clock sharp we stopped to eat at the foot of two very short rapids [*Kakabikans Rapids*] following one another closely. We passed them with no difficulty other than steering our frail canoe with skill among large rolled stones that caused the water to boil while the lowering of the level of the bed increased our velocity. I estimated that we had covered fifteen to sixteen miles since Lake La Biche.[91] The time spent was two hours and fifty minutes. However, I must discount thirty minutes spent hunting and smoking. The current up to this point was moderate and we advanced only at six miles per hour. Let us add for good measure an extra two miles for the sake of those who are inclined to overrate themselves. That makes eighteen miles. Allen says the distance is twenty-five miles. If we are using the same points of reference, one can conclude it was while going over these rapids that this officer lost his compass and that it was on the spot where we lunched that his party camped that night.[92] I forgot to mention that eight to ten miles after leaving Lake La Biche, we encountered on the left bank a river [*Sucker Creek*] coming from the northwest.

At 11: 12 we resumed our navigating. Up to the rapids there are no visible hills near the river, but the countryside is flat and well

[90] Anodonta, at the time Nicollet wrote, might have meant any pond or lake clam.

[91] The distance is actually 7.6 miles. Corps of Engineers, *Middle and Upper Mississippi*, 288.

[92] Allen, in 23 Congress, 1 session, *House Documents*, no. 323, p. 45.

wooded. Beside the rapids the shores are still only mere banks twelve to fifteen feet high. The river narrows, its current is very fast, and because of its velocity there is but little water. From time to time some hills do close in more, and we floated through ten or twelve miles of large rolled stones, little water, and much driftwood. By noon we were about to pull through these obstructions when we had to stop to repair our canoe, damaged by friction that had taken off the tar on the seams of the keel. At 12:30 we were back on the water. The river had improved but still presented obstructions till 1:30.

Meanwhile, the sky that had been so lovely in the morning clouded over. A storm gathered in the southwest and was traveling toward us. We made for the forest, pitched the tent, lit a fire, and by the time the storm passed over us all our luggage and passengers were safely sheltered. At 3:15 we slipped off again.

Soon the river escapes from the narrow valley in which it has been confined since the first rapids. It enters a large valley, opening to our view in the distance the wooded hills that had just shifted away from us on either side of the river. The valley bottom is a flat, marshy prairie broken up by clusters of shrubbery. The current is slower, and there is much water, spreading over twenty to thirty feet in breadth. The river is in a wandering mood. It meanders and sometimes it even doubles back. Since lunch we had encountered a second stream [*Chill Creek*] entering from the right side of the river, and then two more flowing into the marshy prairie — the first from the left [*Bear Creek*], the second from the right [*La Salle River*]. Just before reaching the latter, we noticed a mound bare of trees opening a portage across the *Hauteurs des Terres*, a part of the route that the Indians follow to go from this region to the Red River country. The name of this portage is *Aya-waiway-satagan*. It leads to a large lake [*Upper Rice Lake*] they call Lake Hauteur de Terre, *Ayawaiway Satagan Sagahegain* (lake that intersects the *hautes terres*).[93] From this lake there flows a river [*Wild Rice River*] joining the Red River. It takes seven to eight days to reach the Red River.

[93] The Hauteur de Terre Lake shown on both of Nicollet's maps is not this body of water, but modern Flat Lake in Becker County. Upper Rice Lake is named Rice Lake on his maps. The portage is shown on the 1836 map, which also indicates a smaller lake now nonexistent. This "Portage of the Heights of Land" is also described by William Morrison, a North West Company trader who visited Lake Itasca in 1804. See "Who Discovered Itasca Lake?" in *Minnesota Historical Collections*, 1:343 (St. Paul, 1902).

At 4:30, the forests that have just moved in toward the river present the most beautiful spectacle of evergreens I have ever seen in my life. They are regular, standing upright, some forty to fifty feet high. They form quite a contrast to the frayed larch and pine with branches that often droop. A fresh breeze disperses the mosquitoes that have harassed us so badly today. Truly, in this moment, the valley is beautiful. It spreads away before us but narrows down a little on the sides. The river is more tame; it is gathering strength and begins to impose its will upon the land it waters. A fifth river [*unnamed*], subdued, joins us from the east. I noticed it at 4:50 as it made its entrance, its waters dancing. We are cruising at eight miles per hour. Two ducks, one teal, a bustard, a crane are welcome gifts proffered by the gods of the river to the inexorable Kégouédgikâ.

The valley stayed just as beautiful till 6:30 at which time we decided to take advantage of a suitable site for the night. According to my calculations this place was fifty-three miles from Lake La Biche. Here the hills converge and compress the valley. The river is confined again, showing some rapids in those places where rolled stones reappear. Then the current settles down to a smooth, flat level and the valley expands again.

WEDNESDAY, AUGUST 31, 1836. The place where we spent the night on the right bank of the river presents rounded hills rising higher as they retreat one upon the other. At first, by the river, they are fifteen to twenty feet high. They rise to a hundred and thirty feet within the pine forest that covers them. The same seems to take place on the other shore. Needless to say, their geological nature is still sand and accumulated stone and all the hills in these parts deserve to be called *Hauteurs des Terres* by the natives who mean by this phrase, mountains without rocks in place. It stormed and rained during part of the night.

We broke camp at 5:38, navigated the narrows of the valley, and found ourselves in a landscape identical to that of the evening before. The evergreens have not ceased to be astonishingly beautiful. At 9 o'clock we halted for breakfast after cruising some twenty-five to twenty-six miles. We noticed four rivers and halted for half an hour with natives traveling in eight canoes from Lake Winnipac [*Winni-bigoshish*] on their way to reap wild rice. We ate on the left bank opposite the fourth river observed today. As the sketch on my map points out, its source is near Lake La Biche.[94]

At 10:30 we left our breakfast site and at 11:28 we passed the junction of a river on the left bank. Its course crosses two lakes. There is a lake [Monimin] at this confluence also.[95] The Mississippi is slower, forty feet wide and eight to twelve feet deep. The river it received seems to add much to its volume, resulting in the flooding of eight to nine square miles of this part of the valley. Only the center of this expanse is free from all vegetation, and this is the part I call a lake. That much did we observe today, but I am not aware of what takes place the rest of the year.

At 12:02, or four miles later, we floated by another river [unidentified] on the right bank. In this flat area we have crossed since we left the lake just mentioned, the Mississippi makes numerous detours and keeps doubling back. We managed to avoid most of the long ones by cutting through the marshy prairie. The latter is submerged to such a degree that the reeds pierce the surface of the water by no more than one or two feet. This short-cut traveling method practiced by the Indians has caused the prairie to be crisscrossed in all directions by a multitude of small canals which one has to know how to follow in order to emerge with some advantage out of the maze they form.

At 12:56 or seven miles farther, another river appeared on the left bank. It is a lovely river, twenty feet wide and five to six feet deep.[96] Now the Mississippi is already comparable to some of its tributaries of the second order. It is close to the size of the St. Peter River, equal to that of the Illinois River at its mouth, and larger than the Yazoo River.

We cruised at seven or eight miles per hour. We would have been going at ten if it had not been for the north wind we faced. It

[94] This stream is probably Hennepin River, which rises in Lake Hattie Township of Hubbard County. The other three have not been identified. Nicollet's estimate placed him at this time some 78 miles from Lake Itasca—a considerable error. According to modern measurements the distance to the mouth of the Hennepin River is 36.1 miles. Corps of Engineers, Middle and Upper Mississippi, 288.

[95] Monimin Lake, whose outlet pours immediately into the Mississippi, is fed by Grant Creek from the northeast, and the Little Mississippi River from the west. The latter rises in Daniels Lake (T146N, R36W) and flows east through a series of small lakes.

[96] This was probably the outlet of Boot Lake.

had begun to blow strongly at noon, clearing the sky that had been overcast all night and morning.

At 1:25 after another four and a half miles, a river joined us from the right bank. A little before making its entry into the Mississippi it has crossed a lake.[97] Here [*where the stream entered the river*] we left the vast, marshy prairie behind us. The countryside became more pleasant, all signs of barrenness disappeared, and the hills on either side were lower. Two kinds of oak, lime, ash, and elm brighten with the hues of their foliage the sullen, melancholy green of the coniferous trees. The latter are driven into the background, while many varieties of shrubs invade and blanket the foreground of the valley. From time to time we find a stand of pine, but the shores of the river are no longer their domain. They have surrendered to the newcomers and their appearance here and there is only tolerated. There is no doubt that the soil here is of better quality.

The river is beginning to be stocked with creatures. So far we had observed no fish, or let us say we had not seen any since Lake La Biche however closely we searched, but we found the bed of the river strewn with shells of the species anodontæ which were sometimes five inches long. The water was so clear that the speed of the current did not prevent us from distinguishing all that was on the bottom of the river. This condition of the valley improved as we approached Lake Travers [*Bemidji*].

At 4 o'clock sharp we reached the fork formed by the Mississippi and Ossawa [*Schoolcraft*] rivers. The Ossawa is wider than the Mississippi but is none the larger for that. It reaches the junction crossing flatter territory than the Mississippi; its course is slower; its bed wider but not so deep; and when its declivity and speed are equal to those of the Mississippi, as at the junction itself, the Ossawa is narrower and shallower. Furthermore, the Mississippi stems the tide of the Ossawa at the latter's mouth, thus contributing substantially to its expansion for two hundred yards upstream. All this is quite obvious as you take one look at the confluence.

After the junction we descended another mile on the Mississippi and entered Lake Irving, crossing its one-mile length to some narrow straits linking it with Lake Travers. We sailed into the latter at 4:40.

[97] Nicollet's description of the terrain indicates that this was an unnamed brook which enters the Mississippi in section 33 of T146N, R34W. It flows from Arrow Lake in Hubbard County.

Its charming appearance, a night that promised to be beautiful, and the geographical importance of the site were such that I did not hesitate to spend the night there. We pitched camp at the entrance of the Mississippi on the western shore of the lake.

THURSDAY, SEPTEMBER 1, 1836. We left our bivouac at precisely 5 o'clock. The resplendent sun had just risen and the first of its rays to shine upon the shore we were leaving skimmed over the treetops of the forest on the opposite side, illuminating the strokes of the paddles propelling our frail vessel. The night had been a chilly one. The thermometer dipped down to 36°. This morning our things were covered with a thick coat of frost and the temperature was 2° lower. The waters of the lake which the evening before read 62° only lost 2° during the twelve hours between experiments.

Lake Travers is truly a magnificent lake. As we crossed a portion of it, my soul felt the oppressive spirit of the surrounding solitudes. I wondered and pondered how it could be that these beautiful shores were not inhabited, that there were no castles, no cottages, farms, droves of animals, and those soft colors of cultivated fields that blend so beautifully with the rich tones of nature. My telescope does not even reveal the hut of a native. Near last night's camp there was a small house that served as winter quarters for an employee of the American Fur Company, and we warmed ourselves, rekindling the remains of a fire we found there.[98] The lake must be ten to twelve miles long running north and south, and four or five miles wide from east to west. The shores are of pure white sand mixed with river shells cast off by the waters. The main species are helixes, anodontæ and a small kind of an ammonite.[99] None of those large transitional stones that are so typical of the shores of lakes of lower altitude are to be seen. This lake seems to be entirely formed by the Mississippi

[98] This small wintering house of the American Fur Company was encountered by Schoolcraft and Allen in 1832. Lieutenant Allen lists it among those "subordinate, severally, to some one of the larger posts." It was probably under the post at nearby Cass Lake. See Allen, in 23 Congress, 1 session, *House Documents*, no. 323, p. 31.

[99] In his reference to a "small kind of an ammonite," Nicollet was either mistaken or he meant to describe a fossil ammonite. The latter are common in northern Minnesota. Lake Bemidji has today an area of 6,920 acres. It measures less than three miles at its widest point and is somewhat under six miles long. Minnesota Conservation Department, *An Inventory of Minnesota Lakes*, 47 (St. Paul, 1968).

which enters it at the southern tip and flows out, its volume un-
changed, from the east shore—a distance of three miles from its
entrance to its exit. My guides, Brunia and Kégouédgikâ, have not
said that there are no other tributaries than the Mississippi, but they
did say they did not know of any other. This being the case, I do not
quite know why some geographers consider Lake Travers as being
one of the sources of the Mississippi.[100]

A very few minutes after flowing out of Lake Travers, the Mississippi resumes its course over a bed of exposed rocks forming a
succession of rapids that present neither danger nor much of a handi-
cap to be cleared. The other parts of the river are wide, deep, with a
moderate current, and for nearly twenty-five miles the river flows
between high banks of sand, within whose undulations are found
good soil of the region and native trees whose wholesome and vigorous growth reflects a tranquil relation between this area and its
climatic conditions.

After this stretch of the Mississippi we cruise into a basin with
more lakes. The first to cross our path [Wolf Lake] runs longitudi-
nally northwest to southwest [sic] and is at least six miles long. We
cross it on an easterly course and take the river again at its exit. The
shape of this lake is precisely outlined on Mr. Schoolcraft's map.
However, his map does indicate it is crossed along its longer diameter
whereas one really cuts to the left near the entrance leaving the main
body of the lake to the southeast. After a few miles one comes to
another [Lake Andrusia] more round than long in its outline. We
cross it from end to end and again enter the Mississippi. The river
makes a long detour southward bringing us to Allen's Bay, which is
the west entrance into that beautiful lake known for a long time as
Red Cedar Lake, now called Cass Lake. The second lake I mentioned
above is practically tangent to the Mississippi on Mr. Schoolcraft's
map, whereas in reality the course of the river should be charted on
both ends of the lake.[101] It occurs to me that this slight error could
be the fault of the engraver, who may have reversed the way the river
is supposed to cross the first and second lakes.

The second lake, because of the detour of the river, is separated

---

[100] Nicollet was probably referring to Lieutenant Allen, who states: "Lac
Travers may well be arranged among the sources of the Mississippi." 23 Congress, 1 session, House Documents, no. 323, p. 43.

[101] Modern maps show Lake Andrusia to be more as described by Schoolcraft.

from Cass Lake by only a narrow strip of land from which one can observe both bodies of water. It was 9:30 when we arrived on this strip of land. We had barely come thirty-six miles since leaving our camp on Lake Travers.[102] During that time the wind had veered westward and the sky had clouded over but not enough to conceal the sun for observations. I took advantage of this opportunity to take astronomical bearings from this site, spending there over three hours. A good description of Cass Lake has been given by the geographers who preceded me in these parts.[103] I will therefore dispense with giving any myself.

At 1 o'clock in the afternoon we left and after fifteen miles of navigating, during which we had the pleasure of actually sailing by rigging the gummed cloth I use as a floor for my tent, we penetrated into the southern tip of Pike's [Pike] Bay, one of the most beautiful bays I have yet seen in this country. There we portaged for a third of a mile and happened on Moss Lake, which is almost round with a diameter of a quarter of a mile.[104] We portaged again after that for another two miles and then again—but much farther this time. We accomplished both portages plus the short crossing of Moss Lake in sixty-five minutes. It was 5 o'clock and looked like rain. The night was coming on and we still had far to travel, anxious as we were to reach Leech Lake. We had been out of supplies for twenty-four hours and all my clothing was going to shreds. I did not have time to verify whether Moss Lake is filled and drained by some river or other, and my guides on this point knew no more about it than I. I sacrificed this short reconnaissance that others will do later on to the desire that filled us all with ardor. If it were possible to say anything pleasant about portages, I would describe these as being good ones, over firm ground, slightly undulating with an open path and no obstacles except one swamp some fifty to sixty paces long.

The lake on which we re-embarked after the portages is also almost round and one mile in diameter [Portage Lake]. Two small

[102] According to the Corps of Engineers, 20.2 miles. See *Middle and Upper Mississippi*, 287.

[103] The earliest geographer (though not the first European) to visit Cass Lake was David Thompson, surveyor and astronomer for the North West Company, in 1798, but his report was probably unknown to Nicollet. The lake had also been visited by Pike in 1806, by Lewis Cass in 1820, by Giacomo C. Beltrami in 1823, and by Schoolcraft and Allen in 1832. See Folwell, *Minnesota*, 1:98, 104, 111, 114.

[104] Moss Lake was named by Schoolcraft for its growth of moss-like water plants. See *Narrative of an Expedition*, 74.

rivers [*unidentified*] feed it, both marked on my map. We crossed it along a chord of the circle heading southwest and made our way into the river [*unnamed*] issuing from it. This river like all those over which our boats have passed since I penetrated these regions was above its average volume. It was three to six feet deep, twelve to fifteen feet wide but very sinuous. Five miles after we left the last lake we saw a little river [*Portage Creek*] flowing in from the right, adding a volume of water nearly equal to that of the river on which we traveled. We nonetheless continued to meander for another three miles at which point we floated into a small lake [*Steamboat Bay Lake*] fed by our river, and yet another [*Steamboat River*] coming from a westerly direction.[105] This latter is of much more consequence and comes from quite far away. It springs from the highlands just to the south of Lake Travers. It crosses two lakes [*Hart and Steamboat lakes*] between which it is joined by a tributary [*unnamed*]. The second of these lakes downstream [*Steamboat Lake*] is very near the one on which we are now. We can catch a glimpse of its surface from our position; it cannot be more than a quarter of a mile away. My guides tell me it is at least five miles long. It is called *Kâbak Saghidawâg* (*saghiegun* being the English spelling), a name which in turn is given to the river crossing it.[106] The roots of this word are *kâbaké* — detour with a fork, and *saghidawâg*, entrance, that is to say, "Lake that is at the detour near the entrance."

A little beyond Lake Kabuka on the river bearing the same name, there is a portage crossing the end of the large lake [*Garfield Lake*] to the River Kâbékanâ which I described some days earlier. It is an alternate route often followed by the natives of Leech Lake when they travel west of their country. It is about as long a way as the Kâbékanâ route I took leading to the sources of the Mississippi.

River Kabukasâ [*Steamboat*] is much longer and fuller than the river we navigated from the portages of Moss Lake. The latter's name is dropped no doubt at the small lake resulting from their confluence.

[105] On modern maps the direct distance between Portage Lake and Steamboat Bay Lake is little more than half a mile. The eight miles recorded by Nicollet may be partly accounted for by the windings of the stream, which Schoolcraft described as "so tangled and wound about, in a shaking savannah, covered with sedge, that every point of the compass seemed to be alternately pursued." See *Narrative of an Expedition*, 75.

[106] Nicollet uses this name in the forms *Kabukasâ* and *Kabuka* below. It is given as *Kabuki Sagidawâ* on the 1836 map and as *Pake Sagidowa* on the 1843 map. Neither map shows the detail exactly as described here.

Five miles below Kabukasâ River, a shorter river [*unnamed*] flows in from the right bank, crossing two lakes [*Spring and Swamp lakes*] before making its entry. Finally after two more miles, we come to Leech Lake. For seven miles Kabuka River is lovely, about a hundred feet wide by six to ten feet deep. It was 7 o'clock and after dark when we entered Leech Lake. Fifteen more miles led us to Otter Tail Point where we arrived at 10:15.

SATURDAY, SEPTEMBER 10, 1836. I returned to Otter Tail Point yesterday evening after a week's rest and nourishment in the family home of the Reverend Boutwell, a Presbyterian missionary. I was hardly back when Chief Flat Mouth invited me for tea. Accompanied by Brunia, I honored his invitation and tarried there till midnight (an account of this evening will be given).[107] The chief having expressed again his wish to speak to me before his warriors begged that I postpone my departure by one day. I accepted, and today was the designated date for the delivery of his address.

This morning early the chief sent two officers or factotums to plant before my tent the flags given to him by England and the United States.[108] At about 10 o'clock, the same men came and decorated Brunia's long lodge. A long and beautiful calumet, richly ornamented with feathers, was placed horizontally on two small tree forks. The tobacco pouch, the chicory pouch, and so on, were placed above it. Until noon, the old ones and the younger generation came here one by one, well daubed with paint and beplumed. At noon Flat Mouth arrived. We all smoked and talked casually. At 1 o'clock he commenced a lengthy harangue which I shall relate later on. It was addressed to the young warriors. Immediately after, he asked if I

---

[107] In his *Report* (p. 62) Nicollet describes how he took tea with Flat Mouth "and drank it out of fine china-ware." He goes on to say: "I showed him a snuffbox . . . upon the lid of which was a full-length portrait of Napoleon at St. Helena. The chief took much notice of this portrait, and questioned me largely about this great warrior, whom he named *Naponeon*. . . . He frequently asked me for the box; and, contemplating it, would say, 'Well, it is strange, on whatever side I turn it, the figure looks at me, and seems to say "thou art my brother warrior." ' "

[108] Nothing more is said in the diary of this incident but in his *Report* (p. 62) Nicollet goes on to tell how he refused to speak to the Indians in the presence of both flags, since he was in effect traveling under the auspices of the United States and "was not provided with a *forked tongue*." Thus he forestalled Flat Mouth's intention to talk in praise of the British at the expense of the Americans, which Nicollet felt he "could not, under the circumstances, tolerate."

wished to write down, or if I wished to repeat from my heart, the subjects on which he wanted to elaborate regarding his country and my king. I answered that I wished to write down his words. Having agreed to this, he began as follows:

"Listen to what I have to say. It concerns all that has come to pass for some time. See how miserable my people look. It is indeed Providence that has brought it about that we meet here today. It is the finger of the master of our body that has guided you here. Your presence recalls to mind all that our fathers have told us and all those things that the eldest ones in our midst have witnessed of your ancestors who were the first to discover our land and the first to kindle our fire. As we look at you, we have the impression we see all those who cared for our ancestors so well, who lit for them a great fire. And all the young ones who have heard so much about them are pleased to see them in you.

"All that I have said thus far is my introduction. Now I shall speak as if I were speaking to our Father. You are our Father and we, your children, shall open our hearts to you. Do all that is in your power to send here the traders that wear a hat and place their hands upon their hips [the French]. See how the traders on Lake Superior treat your children. If you take courage for your children, so shall they take courage, for they know they shall not be ten years deprived of help, without being able to defend their soil and their lives, living only on promises, forever hunting without receiving enough to survive from the merchants on Lake Superior. See how the Americans treat us: They always say they want to help us, and yet we never see them. They abandon us to the mercy of merchants who trade at a price three times above that ever asked by the French and the English, and in return supply us only with bad merchandise, thus making the price six times higher. And these traders, well do they know the American goverment is not capable of either helping or protecting us. They do with us what they please, and if in these times when they force us to go naked and starve, we beg for justice, not charity, they threaten to leave. I end here my complaints on our poverty and on the way the Americans treat us. I shall say other things.

"Of the Americans we hear no more than of the wind that passes by without stopping, leaving but a chill in our midst. Much is said of those soldiers who will run, nay fly, to our help. But never do we see them. Blood is shed before mine eyes, I see it is not that of the beasts of the forests, but that of my young ones, and yet we cannot avenge those crimes committed against us. We are endlessly told to bury the war hatchet, and if we dig it up we are threatened with rods and ropes, or with being placed under the ground, *we* the *Missinabés*, the Eagles, the Bears (totems), free in our own forests."[109] (He repeats this last phrase three times.)

"Thus the Americans plan to treat us as they treat their black people. They do not come to see how we are in our homes, to find out about us, to help us as the French used to do, as the English used to do and still do. I know why they do not come. It is because we are poor. But when they shall be poor as we are, then they shall come to take our land, not to till it with us, but to drive us west. We shall not go west! We shall not sell! We shall not surrender our land, not until every one of the warriors you see around me has been killed.

"What shall become of us? Am I not familiar with all their actions? All the *Missinabés* in the East, do they not tell me that which takes place every summer? Have I not beheld and harkened to the Americans for the past ten years? I am not an animal. I am not like those in the East whom they call their children and whom they treat like three- or six-year-olds, a rod in their hand. They purchased their lands, and now they hold them prisoner and treat them as slaves. When they talk to me of buying our soil, I know what I have to say. But were I to give consent to the sale with the approval of my men, can our Great Father in Washington afford to pay? He may well pay for a handful of soil, and then for another; he may well pay for a tree; but our country, however small, the remains of our fathers, the blood he allows to flow daily—for all this he cannot pay.

"For ten years I have been observing what is happening; I have been listening to the American [*Taliaferro*]. He has a fine body, a fine mouth. He speaks well. He has eyes with which he sees well, but he looks askance as his mouth speaks, and when his mouth speaks, his heart is mute." (During these phrases the audience is restive.) "Never have we heard words like those pronounced by the Americans; never did the English say similar things, and we know through our fathers that never did the French speak thus. They talk of death, ropes, rods, and prisons under the ground as they settle on our soil

[109] The term *Missinabés* apparently refers to the entire tribe or people commonly called the Chippewa or Ojibway. Warren gives it as *A-wish-in-aub-ay*. See *History of the Ojibway Nation*, 37.

and take our fire, where soon one finds nought but ashes. What do they mean? We fail to understand. Do they think they can amuse us with medals and flags? What use are such medals and flags to us? Such things are for children. If these medals were dollars I would find them useful. But I cannot make dollars out of them. Hence they are useless. I do not keep them twenty-four hours. I give them to those who ask for them, and of the very many medals and flags I was given in the course of my life I have kept but two—the flags that are in front of your tent. The two medals—here they are." (An old English flag, an old American flag, an old English medal, and an old American one.)

"Be not surprised by what I say, because for the last four years, each time I have been with Americans or with agents, I have said more. I say what I think; this they know as well as you. Also I have given you my right hand but to them I give only my left hand. I tell you this before my warriors whose approval you can hear, not to burden you with repeating it to the President of the United States, but so that you can relate it to our Great Father on the other side of the Great Lake [*ocean*] so that he may know how his children are treated by the Americans. Also I have only one ear for the Americans, the left one; the right I keep to listen to others. I have heard rumors that the Americans say our country is theirs. I say the soil belongs to Him that created all things, and that a country belongs to those He placed upon it. The country on which the Americans tread is theirs. The soil we tread is ours. What do they say?

"The words I speak now are for the attention of our Great Father beyond the sea. I shall pronounce them unto you. Indeed, my Great Father, you may well call our country yours! For you were the first to discover us, to warm us, to clothe us well and brighten our feasts and ceremonies! You were the ones to enlighten us, by living and eating with us, by showing us how to use the ax and the rifle, and by lighting our fires! Yes indeed, my Great Father, it is you! You, my Father, facing me, I am pleased to confide in you. You are not the first Frenchman to whom I have opened my heart. I have been seeking them for ten years and I meet some of them to tell them my thoughts.

"The natives and all white people call me 'Chief,' but I do not consider myself a chief. If I were a good chief, I would have saved my country from the predicament in which we find ourselves. I do not know where to look. The French, you say, can no longer help us and shall never return to kindle our fires. But all those who are on the other side of the frontier with the English, whose language and actions are like those of the French, are they not French? Well, with them [*French Canadians*], as with the English we shake our right hands. But I cannot give it to the American who says my country is his. I must nonetheless pay attention. The things the Americans say worry me. I must look in the direction where there is another Great Father.

"Eight years ago, the people yonder (pointing toward Hudson Bay) suggested that I go to England. I said I would. I came back to my country to make preparations, but I am poor, and I could not gather the necessities. So I abandoned the thought. Now I am angry. The English have left me and say no more to me. Last summer I went to visit them, but the Americans at La Pointe moored my vessel and told me to wait for Mr. Cross.[110] I waited two months, then they refused to give me a canoe. It was too late. I had to return. As I left La Pointe, they fired cannon and rifle shots in my honor, but not a drop of ale was handed to me as a refreshment. And yet there was a lot of ale in the store. As I came to Sandy Lake, I heard you were in the country, and I ran to meet you. I was pleased to tell you that the fire kindled by your fathers had been well maintained by the English, that this fire still burned, but that these last years its flame had dwindled and, gathered around it, we are often very sad. This cannot go on. I must pay attention. I must change everything. I must turn the world upside down!" (Up to this paragraph, Flat Mouth had kept both medals in his hand. Now he throws one away behind him— the American one with the green ribbon—and he clutches affectionately the English one with a red ribbon. Then he continues.)

"My Father, is it our ancient Great Father and yours that chased away the English who were at St. Joseph's, at Detroit, and at Sault Ste. Marie?[111] Why are they no longer there? We used to visit them as our fathers in bygone days used to visit yours in the same place.

[110] The editor has been unable to identify "Mr. Cross."

[111] Here it would seem that Flat Mouth refers to French alignment with the Americans in the Revolutionary period and the War of 1812 and speaking through Nicollet, reproaches the French for helping to "chase away" the English. Detroit was surrendered to American control under the Jay Treaty in 1796. It fell to the English in 1812, was recaptured by the Americans in 1813, and was retained by the United States under the Treaty of Ghent (1814). Either through naïveté or diplomacy, Flat Mouth exaggerated the role played by France in these events.

We always returned satisfied with the goods obtained as we traded together, with the gifts they gave to our children. If your Great Father is responsible for this, little does he know how he has impoverished his children. Tell him this that he may allow the English to return, since he can himself no longer help us. Have pity on us, dear Father, whoever *drove away* the English, do all you can to come to our aid. We are not asking for the houses and carriages that carry the whites, their tattered clothes would suffice. Go and tell all your friends to throw theirs in our direction. See our climate, our nakedness! See to it that we be clothed, that we be free and always masters of our country. It is with this objective in mind that I beg you to carry these words beyond the sea. I add to them the emblem of our nation and of our feelings by sending to our Great Father all that you see here—a calumet, a tobacco pouch. As he sees these things, his heart will return to his children, and he shall see what he wants to do for us. As for me and my people, we never thought ill of the French, of those who wear a hat. We never hurt them, and our hands are not stained with blood. Our fathers often gave what they promised your ancestors in this country. Now our Great Father has more wealth than I; he must not abandon the children of those who supported his children.

"As for you, we are pleased to see you, we would like to have you stay longer with us. You are going to leave us, and we would like you to tell us if we shall see you again some day. All the natives who met you want to see you again, and there are several remote villages whose inhabitants did not find you when they came to visit you. They say you must return to see the land of your fathers. You are in your land. The French were the first to discover us." (Never was there the least allusion to the treaties of nations.)

When the harangue ended, Flat Mouth proceeded with the presentation of the gifts. These he leaves up to me to keep or to send to my king, provided I intercede in their favor.

First the pipe and the stem: they represent his life and soul with which he is entrusting me. The wood is that which cradled him as a baby, that which guided him at the councils and at war, that which never left him. It is the instrument that drove away the bad thoughts his head has sometimes entertained. He told me that each time I gaze at this stem, with the numerous ornaments decorating it, I must recall Flat Mouth and the things he has told me today which are the absolute truth. He then added an instrument of medicine, the tobacco pouch with some explanations, etc., etc. While he discoursed on the virtues of the pipe, implying that it is a calumet of peace and a token of affection for the Great Father, the officer holding it presented it successively to each of the cardinal points. When the ceremony was over, I was presented with the calumet; I smoked; all smoked successively after me, and I made the following speech: [*The speech is missing.*]

MONDAY, SEPTEMBER 12, 1836. At 3:30 we leave Otter Tail Point to sleep at the tip of Leech Lake where Leech Lake River flows out. The sky, rainy yesterday and last night, has improved today. A mild temperature prevails. Only five minutes after our departure we notice that the wind has become a tail wind. We hastily hoist a rig, the gummed cloth from my tent, and by 3:50 we are under way, full sail. The chiefs Flat Mouth and Little Ox, then Latrappe, Chagobay, and some other natives still staying at the village had accompanied us. As soon as they see we are under sail, they shout their farewells from the shore.

Our crew is manning two canoes. The large one that we are supposed to return to St. Peter is twenty-four feet long. I am in it with Brunia, Désiré, and the mulatto Stephen, a native half-breed.[112] It is further loaded with our luggage and my collections. The other canoe carries Brunia's brothers, three plump, big, healthy boys. They are practically savage and would be completely so had François not been fortunate enough to spend some years with the whites, hence retaining some traces of civilization of beneficial influence for the rest of the family. The second canoe is supposed to carry the four brothers back from St. Peter after they leave me there.

Since the outlet of Leech Lake is surrounded entirely by swamps, we did not try to bivouac there for the night. Instead we headed straight for the site of an old trading post of the American Fur Company situated one mile southeast of the river's entrance in the center of a pine wood half ruined by storms.[113] From this position, the lower

[112] This was probably Stephen Bonga, a member of a well-known Negro-Chippewa family that was active in the upper Mississippi fur trade throughout the mid-19th century. See Earl Spangler, *The Negro in Minnesota*, 18 (Minneapolis, 1961).

[113] The map accompanying Schoolcraft's *Narrative of an Expedition* indicates a trading post on the east shore of Leech Lake between the mouth of the Leech

MISSISSIPPI EXPEDITION 119

part of Otter Tail Point has disappeared behind the horizon because of the curvature of the earth. I estimate the distance from our point of departure to the river to be eighteen miles. The night was a beautiful one. I intended to take advantage of it, and was making preparations accordingly when I had the misfortune to lose one of the screws holding the large mirror of my sextant to its mounting. It took me so much time to repair this that I could no longer resist the temptation to sleep that was assailing me. But then it looked as if the weather was going to last, so hoping I could make up for the loss of these astronomical readings by others equally good the next morning at breakfast time, I let myself fall asleep.

TUESDAY, SEPTEMBER 13, 1836. We broke camp at 6:00 in the morning. It took us a quarter of an hour to reach the outlet of Leech Lake River, and an hour and a quarter later we came to the campsite on the left bank called *les pins clairs*, that is to say *les pins clairsemés*, [*clear pines, better described as thinly scattered pines*]. We had breakfast there, and I made some observations. The distance over water from the lake to the campsite is approximately eight miles. Halfway, a small river appears on the right shore.[114] We left our breakfast station at 10 o'clock, and soon a small river appeared on the left bank. Four miles downstream another one comes from the right bank; four miles farther another from the left; two miles later, yet another from the right. We travel two more miles, and another river flows in from the right again. Another three miles, and we find a river on the right. Ten miles beyond this another river [*Six Mile Brook*], fairly long and of more consequence, joins us from the left bank. It issues from a lake [*Six Mile Lake*] situated between Leech Lake and Lake Winnipac [*Winnibigoshish*]. As we pass by its mouth, we enter a substantial basin bordered by a nearly complete circle of wooded hills very pleasing to the eye. It spreads out like a perfect green carpet or aquatic prairie through which the river winds, making a thousand detours. The diameter of this basin is less than fifteen miles, and the prairie I just mentioned fills only a part of it. The remainder is a lake

Lake River and the Boy River. It would have been southwest of the former, not southeast, as Nicollet wrote. No other record of this post has been found.

[114] This and the other streams mentioned below (except for the last) have not been identified. None of them is named on modern maps. Six Mile Brook is the only one shown on Nicollet's 1843 map.

[*Mud Lake*] equally filled with vegetation except that blue [*pickerel weed*] and yellow lilies and reeds alone come to the surface.

We are cruising before the wind so we hoist a sail. In thirty-one minutes following a course ENE we crossed that part of the lake that is divided schematically by a line drawn between the entrance and exit of Leech Lake River. I estimate that at the rate we were traveling we covered seven miles. As we left the lake we were heading NE and therefore were still before the wind. We continued to sail until we joined the Mississippi. Since leaving the lake we have come across three rivers [*unidentified*]. The first one almost at once after the lake, coming from the left, is situated nine miles from the stream flowing into Leech Lake River from the same side before the river reaches the lake. The other two are relatively close to each other on the right bank and situated in the second half of the distance from the lake to the confluence with the Mississippi.[115] We reached the confluence a little after 2 o'clock. We stopped to take some bearings. The distance from Leech Lake to the confluence is fifty-two miles.[116] This observation site is roughly half a mile ENE below the mouth of Leech Lake River and on the left bank of the Mississippi. It was impossible to find a convenient site close to the point of the rivers' confluence itself.

Leech Lake River is a lovely, pleasing river without the least obstacle in its path. With a very moderate current, it is never less than a hundred feet wide and five to ten feet deep. Steamboats drawing three or four feet of water, with a freight of two to three hundred tons could sail over it at all times. Its bed has no rocks or boulders and has a tendency to be muddy, as is the swampy valley through which it flows. The width of the valley varies from one to four miles; it is completely flat and boggy, bordered on both sides by evergreen forests growing on sand banks, alternating with forests of hardwood trees on lower ground with a soil appropriate for intensive cultivation. These forests of hardwood are crowded with wild shrubs and bushes

[115] These streams are sketched but not named on the 1836 map. Only the first one is shown on the 1843 map, and none of them appears on modern maps.

[116] As measured by the Army Engineers, the length of Leech Lake River is approximately 29 miles. See *Reports on Examination and Survey of Mississippi River Between Winnibigoshish and Pokegama Reservoirs and from Leech Lake Dam to Mouth of Leech River, Minnesota*, 5, Chart 1 (62 Congress, 3 session, *House Documents*, no. 1223).

[117] The phrase translated above as "hardwood" is *arbres francs*. In the manuscript copy of his report, which has survived among his papers, Nicollet noted:

bearing useful fruit and berries.[117] The early frosts of the fall have waved a wand over the foliage, transforming it with magical combinations of nature's richest colors, the same colors that touch the lower reaches of the Allegheny Mountains, eastward and westward, with melancholy beauty during the months of September and October.

The confluence of Leech Lake River and the Mississippi is remarkable in that the Mississippi here totals the volumes of both rivers yet is no wider than either of the tributaries whose widths are also equal. Passing from Leech Lake River into the Mississippi one would swear that one was on the same river were it not for the sudden disappearance of the aquatic vegetation carpeting the current we are leaving and the darkening of the Mississippi waters, whose transparency dissolves into an opaque depth. Indeed, below the confluence, the depth of the Mississippi drops from fifteen to twenty feet, thirty feet quite often, while the width varies only from a hundred to a hundred and fifty feet.

Hardly three miles below the junction we come upon La Crosse [*Ball Club*] River issued from a lake of the same name [*Ball Club Lake*] in the vicinity. I do not know why Mr. Schoolcraft and Lieutenant Allen show this distance to be twenty miles on their respective maps. [*Nicollet here wrote in parentheses: "Some notes here on Mr. Allen's error with regard to the region enclosed within the punctuated lines." No such notes have been found.*] I am sure of that which I uphold here.

Once past the entrance of La Crosse River, we made all possible haste to reach before nightfall what is called the Great Point of Oaks [*White Oak Point*]. But first we had to cross an endless marshy prairie through which the Mississippi makes so many detours, each folding back one upon the other, that the distance is tripled. We cut through several points, however, and should have cut through more, but once engaged in the reeds through which one penetrates in order to make a short cut, one finds oneself in the thick of such a maze that the best of guides could not find his way out of it. Under these conditions we only progressed eight miles and stopped to camp on a prairie or a spot of solid ground, a site the natives call Swamp of the Eagles. It was a lovely night of which I availed myself for making astronomical observations. I am trying to make as many observations as possible

"Bois franc or bois forts when the growth which they constitute contains no species of conifers."

in this region, because I realize the course of the river traced on existing maps is very incorrect.

At approximately 8 o'clock I watched the prelude of an aurora borealis that lasted till dawn. There was nothing special about it other than an arch ranging northwest to northeast with a culminating point on the magnetic meridian 15° to 20° high, both ends touching the horizon. From time to time luminous columns would rise from the horizon crossing the arch vertically, lasting a few minutes and then disappearing. While they lasted, the horizon circumscribed by the luminous arch would be saturated with thick vapors, unlike clouds, and the other parts of the sky remained very clear. When the columns dissolved, there were no more vapors below the arch and the latter would stay permanently visible till erased by the break of day.

WEDNESDAY, SEPTEMBER 14, 1836. From where we camped for the night, we could see looking near north, the tip of a tree that concealed a large lake [*White Oak Lake*]. This lake, similar in size and in its swampy aspect to Muddy Lake that we saw yesterday, is crossed by Deer River. From the same camp, to the northeast, we perceived the Great Point of Oaks.[118] All this seemed no more than three or four miles away, but it took us more than three hours to make our way out of this basin, passing before each of these places and coming to the entrance of Vermillion River where I had decided to take some bearings and eat. We left at 5:30 and reached Vermillion River by 9 o'clock. I estimate the distance traveled cutting through two or three points to be sixteen miles. As the crow flies, the distance cannot be more than six or seven miles. My astronomical observations will enable us to check these distances which are difficult to estimate.

If we examine the variable nature of the marshy prairies observed since Leech Lake, as of those in general that form the level plane of the river valleys in this region, we note the borders farthest removed from the river acquire a certain degree of consistency and firmness that already supports the growth of willows and other small trees and even full-sized ones. As one proceeds farther into the marshes approaching the river, this firmness diminishes; the surface crust becomes wet and spongy; it either bears up or yields depending on

[118] Although the exact location of Nicollet's camp is not known, he could not have seen White Oak Point to the northeast. He was apparently mistaken either in identifying the landmark or in recording the direction, which would have been southeast or south.

the pressure exerted. Between the river itself and the spongy zone lie the impenetrable masses of rushes and reeds that fill the water and restrain its motion. Detritus accumulated each year eventually canalizes the water that winds its way back into the main stream.

Let us come back to the Mississippi on its course between the junction with Leech Lake River and Great Point of Oaks—or even as far as the mouth of Vermillion River. In this section its basin is confined between mere sand banks ten to fifteen feet high; they are a sterile soil indeed, sustaining evergreens at best. It is evident that the region it irrigates here was once completely flooded and that the bed of the basin rose by the process of vegetal sedimentation. This caused the water to gather finally into one main stream that maintained the original depth of the wild river of yesteryear. Last of all, it is evident the course is now harnessed by these marshes and that, in due time, it will be bordered by firm soil. Deep excavations of the latter will reveal the peat bogs presently in formation, thereby bringing evidence to future generations of the physical state of the country I am examining now which is obviously of recent formation. [*Here Nicollet wrote: "These ideas to be developed later on." See Appendix 4, p. 246–249.*]

I have charted only the four rivers [*unidentified*] that empty into the Mississippi between our last camp and Vermillion River.[119] Natives often call rivers "vermilion" if their waters are at all tinted by the washing of brown or reddish soils, as is the case here.

Where the shores of the river are higher and look like sand alone, one frequently encounters clay soils the extent of which it is difficult to determine without excavating, but, judging by comparison, I believe the clays are similar to those of Leech Lake. Of these latter I have samples to examine at leisure.

After Vermillion River, the Mississippi is less sinuous, its course is more stabilized, and it is controlled by evergreens often mixed with hardwood trees. Some of these forests, particularly those of oak, have excellent soil, but in general the region is sterile and wild. On the Great Point of Oaks there were two or three hillocks I wanted very much to go and examine. I was anxious to determine whether or not they were man-made, true to the custom of people passed away, whites or natives, who have left only such monuments to tell of their

---

[119] Only one of these streams is shown on Nicollet's maps. It flows from a small lake, probably Wininni Lake. The stream is not named on modern maps.

passage on earth.[120] But we were hurrying and lacked the proper utensils to make such diggings.

Vermillion River, *Unâmunâsibi* as it is called by the Chippewa (from *unâmunâ* meaning vermilion), crosses a lake [*Vermillion Lake*] and then [a portage] leads to Willow River. From there one descends to Duck [*Big Rice*] Lake. There starts out another portage leading to Turtle [*Thunder*] Lake. From this lake one descends Little Boy's River leading to Leech Lake. This is one of the most popular and shortest routes used for commuting between Leech Lake and the country east of the Mississippi and north of Sandy Lake.

Three or four miles below Vermillion River, a small river flows in from the right.[121] Five or six miles later we came across the first island in the Mississippi below its sources. A little later, a small river [*Rice Creek*] flows in from the right after having crossed two lakes [*Rice Lake and Little Rice Lake*]. A little farther yet a portage strikes out from the left bank. The large detour composed of a double curve traced by the Mississippi from the Great Point of Oaks to here is such that both points are more directly in contact through this portage. It is also marked on my map.[122]

Later, another river issuing from a lake very close to the Mississippi joins us. Because of the proximity of the lake and the Mississippi, the lake is called *Pakégumâg* [*Pokegama*]. There is no doubt that in earlier times it was part of the wandering waters of the Mississippi and that the beginning of a dryness has separated them by a narrow stretch of prairie. The river which flows from the lake and empties into the Mississippi crosses farther inland another lake said to be larger and certainly more beautiful than Pakégumâg. This lake bed is longitudinal and parallel to the Mississippi.[123] From the first island on the

[120] The existence of prehistoric earthworks at this point was recorded by later observers. See Newton H. Winchell, *The Aborigines of Minnesota*, 376 (St. Paul, 1911). Excavations conducted by the University of Minnesota Department of Anthropology in the 1940s and 1950s at a nearby site revealed burials and habitations ranging in age from the early to the late Woodland period (1000 B.C.– 1700 A.D.). See Carla L. Norquist, *Roster of Excavated Prehistoric Sites in Minnesota*, 14 (St. Paul, 1967).

[121] Probably the unnamed stream flowing from Leighton Lake.

[122] On both the 1836 and 1843 maps this portage is shown going by way of Wininni Lake.

[123] Damming of the Mississippi has changed the topography in this area. It is probable that the lake described by Nicollet as Pakégumâg (Pokegama) has become a part of Blackwater, Cut-off, or Joe Gould Lake. The second and larger lake referred to is almost certainly the modern Pokegama Lake.

Mississippi to Pakégumâg we traveled some sixty-five minutes or about seven miles.

One mile below Pakégumâg, a small river [*Bass Brook*] flows in from the left, the Crapet River of the half-breeds. Three miles farther downstream a waterfall suddenly appears. Its roar goes unnoticed until one is near the falls, because a bend in the river prevents the sound from traveling against the current. We camped there for the night. We made approximately a forty-mile trip today.[124]

THURSDAY, SEPTEMBER 15, 1836. The sky was cloudy all night and regretfully I was not able to pinpoint the geographical position of the waterfall. At about 3:30 in the morning the sky seemed nearly clear and I was ready. I started to take some bearings of stars but was interrupted in the process by the break of day. The sun rose majestically, and I waited for it to reach a convenient height to obtain all the bearings I needed. I had no sooner started when a cloud cover concealed it, and the weather turned to solid rain. The canoes and some of the luggage we had left at the foot of the falls were brought up to the top of the elevation bordering the left side of the river. We chopped down some dead pines, lit a big fire, and settled down to those occupations that are the lot of people who are forced to extend their bivouac. The falls of the Mississippi represent a drop of nine feet over a stretch of 260 feet or eighty-six yards of river. The falls form three tiers. The first one is a five-foot drop stretched over an incline twenty to twenty-five feet long. The other four feet divide the remaining distance into two sections, each one dropping another two feet.

These falls are a lovely prelude to the Falls of St. Anthony, five hundred miles downstream.[125] They have the additional advantage of giving the traveler the sensation one only feels in mountains, this in a region where there are none. One's imagination, dulled by a monotonous and tiring navigation over so many slow winding rivers, is

[124] The Crapet River is shown on both of Nicollet's maps and is named on the 1836 map. Pokegama Falls, three miles above the site of Grand Rapids, was dammed by the United States Corps of Engineers in 1884. See James E. Rottsolk, *Pines, Mines, and Lakes: The Story of Itasca County*, 11 (n.p., 1960); Minnesota Conservation Department, *An Inventory of Minnesota Lakes*, 186.

[125] Nicollet here speaks in very approximate terms. His *Report* (p. 122-125) shows the distance from this spot to the Falls of St. Anthony to be 427 miles. The Corps of Engineers gives the present-day mileage as 327. See *Middle and Upper Mississippi*, 287.

enlivened by the sight of the impetuous torrent. From its source to the place where we are now, the river has shown all the signs of the sluggishness and sleepiness of infancy, awakening at times to test its own strength by making sudden unruly movements. Now, all forces gathered, infancy passes away and vigorous motions of emancipation mark the arrival of childhood. This childhood grows as the river flows down to the Falls of St. Anthony. There her might and beauty are one. From St. Peter to St. Louis her power is tamed and her gracefulness enhanced by all that nature bountifully casts upon her shores in deference to her splendor and prosperity. From St. Louis to the Gulf, the river has reached maturity. Conscious of her duties, she occasionally reprimands her people, but at all times generously provides them with her wealth. Indeed, this river could very well be personified as one of the greatest beings an idealistic mind could conceive.

These falls recall the Tallulah Falls in upper Georgia. The name Pakégumâg shown on maps is hardly fitting, both because of its meaning and because of the location.[126] The falls are much more interesting from a scientific point of view. Here for the first time, from St. Peter through all the regions I have recently explored, do I encounter massive rocks fixed in place. Here one sees the bed of the river and the wall of the left bank composed of ancient transitional red sandstone. The strata exposed both above and below the surface of the water are approximately ten feet thick. They are surmounted by the sand deposit we have so often mentioned, but that in this case contains fragments of all the rocks pertaining to the transitional phyllites, shales, greenstones, syenites containing feldspar and amphibole, porphyroid syenite and syenitic porphyry; pebbles—white flint, the kind used for sharpening razors, etc. Judging by a few detached fragments I found on the edge of the river at the foot of the falls, I am inclined to think this layer of ancient sandstone rests upon transitional glossy schists.[127] There only remains for me to see the rapids of the Missis-

[126] Tallulah Falls is on the Tugaloo River near its junction with the Chattooga River in northeastern Georgia. The name Pokegama means "the water which juts off from another water" (Upham, Minnesota Geographic Names, 256) and was apparently used loosely for the whole area. See below, p. 129.
[127] According to Dr. Walter E. Parham of the Minnesota Geological Survey, Nicollet's "ancient transitional red sandstone" is Pokegama quartzite of Precambrian age. The deposit overlying the quartzite is glacial till of Pleistocene age. Nicollet was mistaken about the rock beneath the quartzite. It is Giants Range granite, also Precambrian, and not "transitional glossy schists." Letter to the editor, November 12, 1968.

sippi several miles downstream and determine the altitude of the location in relation to the level of the sea in order to assign to this rock its proper place in the geological order classification.

As far as I can predict, the rocks that are under the sand deposit of this region appear to belong to the same formation as that which characterizes the region between the Washita [Ouachita] and the Arkansas. Only what is mountainous down there is in these parts below the surface of the [level] soil which also has identical physical characteristics [to the soil in Arkansas]. If a climate change of 34° to 35° were applied here, everything would be the same, etc.[128] The height of the summit of the hill on the left side of the river measured from the water at the foot of the falls is twenty-seven feet.

It is three o'clock in the afternoon. The bad weather is persisting, but I do not really mind. All the more reason for determining more exactly the height of this observation site in relation to the level of the sea, and also for completing the readings of the geographical position of this site. And I also find time for working on my detailed maps with Brunia. The more I travel with this kind man, the more credit I give to the prodigious memory with which he is gifted and also to his profound knowledge of the land. He is always there to supplement for me the details I overlooked or forgot, supplying such extraordinary deductions and combinations of rivers, lakes, pathways, and portages that their result invariably fits into the pattern of my astronomical observations which are the foundation of the geographical research I am carrying out here.

While we are in this location under a tent—he drawing sketches with a pencil, I writing—his brothers go out hunting and looking for wild fruit. The countryside which around the falls seems to be so barren does actually have some fine spots showing signs of fertility of a sort other than game. They bring back wild plums, red, round, and as large as cherries which in no time Désiré transforms into an excellent marmalade.

It rains on into the night till 4:00 in the morning. Then the sky clears, but the wind from the south still blows, and it is hot.

FRIDAY, SEPTEMBER 16, 1836. We left the falls at exactly

[128] Nicollet was apparently looking for the old red sandstone, believing it to be the same as that which he had found in a trip through Arkansas in the spring of 1836. For a discussion of the importance of this sandstone in geological history, see Bray, in American Philosophical Society, *Proceedings*, 114:37-59.

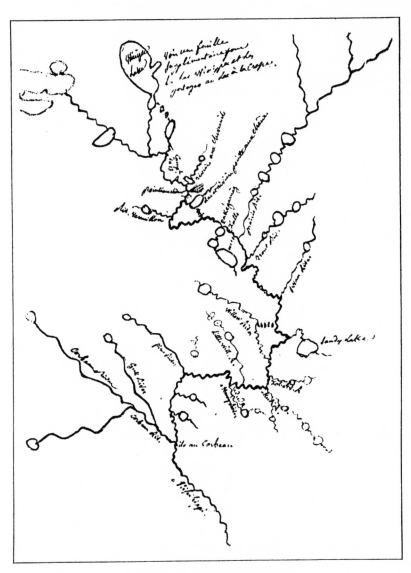

*The Mississippi between Lake Winnibigoshish and the
mouth of the Crow Wing River*

8 o'clock in the morning. The sun was shining after a night of rain without thunder and lightning. The wind from the south was still blowing and the barometer stayed low. I could not tell if the weather was going to improve. Meanwhile, before leaving, I was able to make some of the observations I needed.

The average bearing after the falls is SE. Half a mile below we discover the second island on the Mississippi, a small one with shrubs. Two miles farther away from the falls, a small river [*unidentified*] enters from the right. Next to it is a portage leading to Lake Pakég-umâg. The Indians speaking of the river or the two lakes it links [*Joe Gould and Pokegama*] always say Pakégumâg, to go to Pakégumâg, making no distinction between the three parts they are referring to, although there is a considerable distance between them.

Half a mile farther there is another river [*unnamed*] on the right coming from a lake [*Horseshoe Lake*] not far away. Between the two rivers our course veered closer to E. The ground on the right bank is covered with deciduous trees. The left bank is of sand banks covered with pines. The red sandstone rocks disappeared after the foot of the falls. Along the sandy left bank we find an abundant growth of a climbing plant that is attached to small trees. Its root is a tubercle the size of an ordinary apricot that the Indians eat and call *pomme de terre* [*ground nut or Indian potato*]. I picked up a few specimens to study them. The tubercle is full grown at about this time.[129]

Four miles below the falls we negotiate the rapids that are approximately four hundred yards long. Since the river is swollen, we can only appreciate the difference in level by observing the size of the waves and their speed. At low water, canoes can climb the rapids providing the men wade through the water. At the foot of these large rapids there appears a small river [*unnamed*] on the left; then there are more small rapids hard to see today.[130] Between the rapids there is a small island [*unidentified*] covered with hay.

At 9:25 we encounter Prairie River coming in from the left. Because of its length and the fine country it irrigates, it is a river of some importance. It crosses several lakes abounding in fish and leads

[129] See Merritt Fernald and Alfred Charles Kinsey, *Edible Wild Plants of Eastern North America*, 252 (Cornwall On The Hudson, N.Y., 1943).

[130] The town of Grand Rapids, incorporated in 1891, grew up at this site. In 1901 the large rapids was dammed to provide power for a paper mill. (See Rottsolk, *Pines, Mines, and Lakes*, 11, 43.) The small river mentioned here by Nicollet is probably the stream which flows from McKenney Lake and Hale Lake.

upstream toward Rainy Lake and Vermilion Lake. Excellent soil borders it, thickly populated, particularly by the caribou and the marten. In the days of our kings, the French used to winter on this river.[181]

Taking into account the amount of time lost from the falls to Prairie River, the distance we covered is eight miles. The bearing of the last three quarters of this distance veered from ESE, leaning more toward magnetic E. There are two perceptible errors on Allen's map here. He indicates the course of the river as being SSE and locates the rapids below Prairie River whereas they are four miles downstream from the falls.[182] So far the left bank is always higher than the right. The height of the sand banks varies between five and twelve feet and pine trees persist in crowning the tops. The right bank is garnished with deciduous trees as before.

After Prairie River, both shores level off as the sand banks improve and decline. Two miles below Prairie River there is a pretty little wooded island, the fourth island [unidentified]. Downstream, two or three miles farther we encounter three little rivers [unidentified], one on the left and two on the right, one next to the other. Half a mile farther down than the first stream, on the left again there is another river [unidentified]. (These should be classified as four creeks really.) Our mean course has been closer to E than ESE. At 10:27 we pass by Trout River issuing from a lake of the same name.[183] Distance from Prairie River is seven miles.

After this river, our course traces the following directions: SE-S-SW-W-S-SE. We stay on this detour until 10:35. Clay appears again

[181] The source of Nicollet's information on this point is not known. No confirmation has been found.

[182] Perhaps through the negligence of the engraver, a similar error occurred on Nicollet's 1843 map, which shows the rapids not only below Prairie River, but below the mouth of the stream designated Trout River. On the 1836 manuscript map two parallel marks above Prairie River were apparently meant to indicate the rapids, but they are not so labeled.

[183] This was probably Blackberry Brook, which drains Mud Lake and Blackberry Lake, flowing into the Mississippi in section 5 of T54N, R24W. Here Nicollet may have been misled by an error on Allen's map, which shows Trout River flowing from Trout Lake southwest into the Mississippi. Actually the outlet of Trout Lake flows southeast and joins the Swan River. On both of Nicollet's maps the stream labeled Trout River is shown rising in a series of small lakes and emptying into the Mississippi. It corresponds approximately to Blackberry Brook. On his 1836 map a larger lake, clearly labeled Trout Lake, is shown tributary to the Swan River. On the 1843 map the same lake is shown but not named.

above the surface of the water on either side. It forms half the height of the banks and is covered with sand. It seems to be everywhere under the sand, under the sand banks or sand deposits. When it is not to be seen above the water, it is to be found on the poles our oarsmen sometimes find hard to retrieve. After the detour there is a creek [unidentified] on the right.

At 1:05 we pass by a river of more significance than the creeks I marked on the map since Trout River. It is Little Island River [unnamed]. There one finds a small island at the mouth of the river. The distance from Trout River to Little Island River is approximately fifteen miles. In the course of those fifteen miles, every time the ridges or elevations come closer to the river thus forming its banks, we observe that they are composed of various kinds of clay—dark red, brown, gray-brown—topped with sand. I also note that since the falls these sand deposits covering the layers of clay no longer contain rolled stones.

We smoke a pipe for about ten minutes. At 1:15 we find a small river [unidentified] on the left, half a mile below Little Island River. At 2:15 or fifteen miles beyond the last river we can see a path on our right. It is a portage leading to Cut Hand River [Splithand Creek]. This river crosses a pretty lake [Splithand Lake] and its waters enter the Mississippi at 2:57 or four to five miles downstream.

A little after the junction with Cut Hand River, the Mississippi makes a large bend to the north which we bypass by making a portage on the right bank. At 5:47 we pass Swan River, twenty miles below Cut Hand River. Distance traveled during the day, from the falls to Swan River, is about sixty-two miles.[134]

Usually the point of confluence of rivers is rendered pleasing to the eye and mind of the traveler by the contrast he finds in a different view or new landscape. The entrance of Swan River into the Mississippi, however, is as ugly and sad as one can possibly imagine. Here the Mississippi is narrow; it makes an angle and its current is so slow, in spite of these two circumstances, that there is not the slightest murmur to be heard. Then, at the corner of the angle slowly but more quietly yet arrives Swan River issuing from the ugliest of ambushes

[134] This is given by the Corps of Engineers as 55 miles (Middle and Upper Mississippi, 287). Here and throughout the rest of his course on the Mississippi Nicollet's estimates of distance are not greatly at variance with more modern measurements, especially if one allows for changes in the channel over a period of more than a century.

composed of brushwood, toppled trees, reeds, and mud. Some day, the hatchet will embellish this site, but nothing is going to give it life or movement. Those who come here after me will perhaps think I am hard to please. A poet in love, let us say, might see here an allegorical representation of a bride who for the first time abandons herself with apprehension and timidity into the arms of the spouse of her choice! And although I was witness to this encounter in a sparkling sunset followed by magnificent moonlight (I even made some observations during part of the evening on a little green carpet very close to the nuptial bed), I heard no sighs, no whisperings, and, however much I tried to coax my imagination toward the muse of the poets, the most this union could inspire me with was the allegory of a sulking couple who, united without love, had nothing to say and dared not even complain of their mutual misery under the strain of myriads of mosquitoes humming in their alcove.

But if Swan River does not have an entrance worthy of the attention of landscape artists, it does have advantages that will prove to be of great value to trade. Navigable, it winds through rich land deserving the finest crops and forms with Prairie River an important waterway that will link the region with the neighboring country. Swan River flows from a lake located in the highlands that divide the waters of the Mississippi and St. Louis rivers. It is said the lake actually straddles the divide and that it sends waters on both sides!!![135]

The countryside irrigated by Prairie and Swan rivers is inhabited by a small band of Chippewa called *Bois Forts* because of their predilection for living in thick forests, far away from others. The band is now led by a chief called the Little Frenchman, a half-breed tossed at random into the forests by a Canadian who happened to meet his mother, who was of the Bois Forts band. It never occurred to him that he had fathered the little king of a small tribe renowned for its courage, intelligence, kindness, honesty, and great spirit of hospitality.[136]

[135] Nicollet does not show such a lake on either map. However, he shows a West Swan River flowing into the Mississippi from a large lake which is "Great Swan Lake" on the 1836 map and a much smaller "Swan Lake" on the 1843 map. The latter is closer to reality. He also shows on both maps an East Swan River, rising close to Swan Lake and flowing via the St. Louis River to Lake Superior.

[136] The Bois Forts band were generally said to live somewhere farther north than Nicollet locates them. Warren (*History of the Ojibways*, 39) places them on the North Shore of Lake Superior. Under the Treaty of 1854 they received permission to reside on an undefined reservation in the vicinity of Vermilion

SATURDAY, SEPTEMBER 17, 1836. The south wind which prevailed yesterday with fine sunshine threatens to affect us differently today. The sky is overcast, it is hot, and the mosquitoes are very hostile. We leave Swan River at 5:37 in the morning. At 9:30 we are forced to stop in an uncomfortable resting place, driven there by rain and hunger. So far we have traveled nineteen to twenty miles. Small rivers and creeks flowing into the Mississippi have been so abundant since Swan River that I have given up entering them into my journal and am limiting myself to marking them down on my sketched maps.[137]

The countryside since Trout River became finer and lovelier as we advanced. Indeed, a great change took place after we discovered clay strata under the sand. These clayey soils surmounted by sand forming the banks along the Mississippi are part of another formation and do not appear to have anything in common with the sands mixed with pebbles that characterize the western part of the river I have just explored. This geognostic change produces yet another great change in the nature of the soil and its products. Nature's mechanical forces exerting themselves upon the layers of clay and sand are accelerating the dehydration process of the savannas that in other times bordered the Mississippi here as they still do in those regions we have recently examined. We see, on both sides of the river, the points of land formed by elevations following one upon another, constantly changing, eaten away by the current. Detached clays and collapsed sands are carried off and fill the hollows little by little at the expense of the heights. Every recess between the points is stuffed with alluviums brought by the surging river.

This is an example of the well-known formation process of banks and shores along rivers winding through plains. Therefore, since clay made its appearance, we have observed banks identical to those we saw much farther south between the Arkansas River and the Gulf of Mexico, banks higher than their submerged backgrounds that are either lakes, muddy swamps, or marshy prairies depending on the soil.

Lake, and in 1866 they were moved to the present reservation at Nett Lake. Kappler, comp. and ed., *Indian Affairs*, 2:650–652, 916–918; Folwell, *Minnesota*, 4:192. No mention of the Little Frenchman has been found. A man of the same name was head chief at White Oak Point in the 1880s. See Folwell, *Minnesota*, 4:214.

[137] The detailed sketch maps referred to here and on p. 137 were apparently lost.

However, these lowlands dry up more rapidly than other regions, and it is the surging river itself that facilitates and hastens the process by the very nature of the plants that come to grow in it. Here, as we approach Sandy Lake [*Big Sandy Lake*], I note the shores of the river are identical to the dikes built by man in lower Louisiana and to those accumulated by nature farther upstream as far north as Red River. Canebrakes [*probably reeds and cattails*] have invaded these dikes as well as the shallows and are disputing their right to more ground from the native forest trees and from the marshy prairies. They invade the latter, fastening, thickening and weaving the plants, composing a crust, consolidating it with clay, sand, vegetation, and trees which are dragged away and deposited by the river in the recessed coves. Thus, once more the geologist and botanist can witness the great phenomenon of vegetation in full development which I demonstrated elsewhere as having taken place in the South and West, but also as having disappeared following the arrival of civilization.[138] This is the great struggle between the canebrake reeds, the prairies, and the forests to determine which one of the rivals shall master the soil, subject of their dispute. However, in these parts, the phenomenon does not reach the grand scale which it does in the South, because the climate checks the mighty upheavals of vegetation.

I am scattering these thoughts at random so as not to lose their train as the countryside inspiring them rolls by and will continue to roll by for several hours more, perhaps for days.

It has rained constantly since this morning. It is a light and warm rain, falling through mists and fog. Sometimes it is just a drizzle. Our camp is so uncomfortable that after waiting in vain for nearly six hours for a pause in the rain we decide to embark without it. So we leave, and after three hours we find ourselves only one mile away from Sandy Lake. We disembark necessarily because of the rain and falling darkness, and also because we are afraid we might not find firewood at Sandy Lake if we try to make it there tonight. It rained all night. Adding up the distance covered in the afternoon to that of the forenoon I cannot figure it to be more than thirty-eight to forty miles.

SUNDAY, SEPTEMBER 18, 1836. It is raining so much this morning that we cannot go to Sandy Lake which is no farther away

[138] In a number of scattered essays in his papers Nicollet discusses the building of such natural dikes along the Mississippi in Louisiana.

from us at the end of the river than twice the range of a gunshot. At about 10 o'clock there is a change. A peal of thunder we have just heard brings along a fine shower of rain. At last we are going to be able to leave this quagmire, our host since last evening.

We reached Sandy Lake around noon. There I found Mr. W[illiam A.] Aitken, manager of this territory for the American Fur Company.[139] He had returned only yesterday from a trip to Lake Superior. He was most polite and thoughtful toward me and urged me to stay a few days with him. I would have accepted willingly had the season not been so far advanced. He is a well-informed man whose easy and communicative conversation was of great help to me. His long experience of the country and its people adds substance of the utmost authority to his opinions. I showed him my geographical findings. He seemed to find them satisfactory and proved it by making some observations on his sector of the land which I immediately used, making some corrections under his very eyes and supervision. We then talked about several other things related to my research program, and I was pleased to find confirmation of my ideas in his long experience. The twenty-four hours I spent in his company went by all too quickly.

The surroundings of Sandy Lake are of an agreeable aspect. The ground, particularly on the left shore, is of sand and pebbles surmounting a formation of clay. This new encounter with pebbly sand which I was convinced did not exist in this region tends to make me believe that the current which brought it came from the northeast. I have not formulated an opinion as yet; I am merely observing the facts in order to describe this great geological phenomenon separately. The stones here do confirm an opinion I have evolved since we were at Leech Lake, but which up to now I dared not bring forth. When I designated these stones as "rolled stones," "boulders," I was referring to a

---

[139] Big Sandy Lake, located on the main route from Lake Superior to the upper Mississippi, was an important point in both the British and American fur trade. A North West Company post was established there in 1794 and was succeeded in the 1820s by the American Fur Company post built near the outlet of the lake. Aitken (1787?–1851) went to the country about 1802 as an employee of the North West Company and later transferred his allegiance to the American Fur Company. He traded at a number of posts in northern Minnesota and was for many years in charge of the company's Fond du Lac department, with headquarters at Sandy Lake. He was "noted for his urbanity and geniality." W. H. C. Folsom, *Fifty Years in the Northwest*, 483 (St. Paul, 1888); Upham and Dunlap, *Minnesota Biographies*, 6; Nute, in *Minnesota History*, 11:371.

given idea I had gathered from American books. Actually, my own observations point out to me that they are not "rolled stones." All these pebbles and stones that one finds on the shores of the lakes, in river rapids, or buried in sand are sitting on an irregular surface on which they seem to be permanently based. Of their angles and sharp edges, only those exposed to the action of scouring waters are battered and rounded off. But as long as they maintain a size that enables them to resist the force of the currents, one finds them planted on a firm base, showing all the characteristics of stones that have not moved.[140] Their usual volume is one to two cubic feet. Very occasionally one finds some as large as three to four cubic feet in the water, but buried in the hills of sand one sees enormous ones, some of their edges jutting forth.

Of those stones that are truly rolled, however, one seldom finds any of a volume greater than a few cubic inches. They are the direct result of the present forces bearing upon them after water dug them out of the sand and reduced them to their present dimensions. They continue to roll each time the river swells, and their travels can be estimated by their decrease in volume since their point of origin. This does not hold true where large stones from sand, lakes, and rivers are concerned. Wherever I found them, I was never able to detect the slightest progressive alteration in their volume, and they are more or less the same with regard to their volume and with regard to the nature of their formation. It will be of importance to examine whether the beds of these sands and stones are subject to a system related to their altitude above sea level. This can only be investigated, however, after I have finished the map of the territory where they are located. I shall have to compute their heights, trace the chains of hills, and plot the lakes, rivers, and sand deposits—both those where one finds these beds as well as those where they are not to be found.

I am adding a few words on the land stretching from Pakégama to here, particularly from Swan River. The river's annual rises and the deposits it carries raise the level of the marshy prairies situated in the coves between the points, thus causing the channel to meander and improving the soil. It is in such places that one may see the richest

---

[140] This discussion of the phenomenon now recognized as glacial drift shows Nicollet's ignorance at this time of forces in geology which he later came to recognize. His reliance upon American books shows that he did not arrive in the United States with any previous knowledge of geological theories current in his day. His later development as a geologist is significant against this background.

vegetation the climate has to offer, growing in luxury. The canebrakes first do the foundation work, consolidating the shallows, and last of all the forest trees invade and conquer the land. From Swan River on down there are few notable rivers, but an infinity of rivulets flow into the river supplying it with the accumulated water of the marshes. This ground formation is quickly accomplished, particularly once the clay strata appear. The water mixes the clay with the sand and vegetation, creating a soil which tends to make the country very fertile. Soil improvement will be accelerated when the country is occupied by farmers who will supplement nature's will with their toil and their animals. The latter will help further by trampling the ground and destroying the canebrakes, whose heads and young shoots they are wont to consume.

From its junction with the Missouri on down to the Gulf of Mexico, the water of the Mississippi enjoys the reputation of being very wholesome and of being heavy and hard from the Missouri upstream. I can now add that in the section of the river crossing the clay formation starting below Pakégama Falls the water is once more very drinkable and wholesome. The soil it dissolves eliminates the transparency that was so typical of the river below this section downstream as far as the Missouri and upstream all the way to the sources. It is light, salty, and has a slight laxative effect on those tasting it for the first time. Mr. Aitken, answering my questions on the subject, told me that each time he makes his annual business trip he is inconvenienced by the water of the places he visits and that only on his return to the water of the Mississippi at Sandy Lake does he recover.

The annual rise of the Mississippi in the clayey sections presents little danger of flooding. The course of the river is fixed, its bed forever established between the numerous points of land elevations rising as high as eight to fifteen feet by the shore and by the natural embankments built up in the low spots between points. When the river water is high, the flooding of the marshes behind the embankments is funneled through the many little channels mentioned before, and the drainage is brought about in the same way—the currents taking the opposite direction as the level of the Mississippi drops. I have indicated on my map as best I could all these channels, not so much to show how meticulous my observations are, but rather to enable the farmers and geologists to determine someday how much change takes place in these parts.

Only one extraordinary rise of the Mississippi is remembered here, that in the spring of 1826. It was caused by heavy rains and the sudden melting of snow and ice. Mr. Aitken tells me that the water rose above the sand point that separates the Mississippi from Sandy Lake River on which are built the facilities of the fur company. The water maintained this level for more than a month and then drained off down the river. Here the Mississippi current, because of the many points causing it to meander and the slight level differential of the bed, is almost slow. [*Here Nicollet wrote in the text:* "Climate, public health, longevity, etc." *He apparently meant to remind himself to continue discussion at this point.*]

Sandy Lake is the main camping site of the Chippewa tribe called Strong Ground.[141] I find no Indians there, for they are reaping wild rice in the marshes and rivers of the interior. Trade, hunting, and fishing are the industries of Sandy Lake.

It rained for the remainder of the day and also during the night. It was cold and uncomfortable with a southwest wind blowing strongly. It was quite impossible to carry out the astronomical observations I needed badly to chart this important geographical site.

MONDAY, SEPTEMBER 19, 1836. The weather was abominable during the first hours of the morning. I was upset while Mr. Aitken was kind enough to rejoice at the thought that I might be obliged to spend more time with him. Toward 9 o'clock there was a change. From time to time the sun would pierce the clouds and I would make the most of it. By noon I was not able to finish my readings, but the observations I had gathered were sufficient. We left Sandy Lake and thirty-two miles of canoeing brought us, by nightfall, to the mouth of Willow River. The sky was completely clear now, but the atmosphere rarefied by three days of rain had brought about a wave of exaggerated cold for the season. While I was making observations to determine the geographical position of the entrance of the river, the thermometer dropped down to 28°. The night was beautiful. I stayed up until 11 o'clock waiting for the moon to climb over the tops of the trees so as to measure its respective distance from the stars. Meanwhile to keep warm, my men sang and danced as Indians do. The thermom-

[141] See above, p. 45n. Apparently Nicollet mistook the name of the chief for that of the band, which other sources refer to simply as the Sandy Lake band of the Mississippi Chippewa.

eter dipped down to 25° and all the luggage we had not found time to dry out was covered with frost. Fortunately the sky became overcast and the cold less intense. We were able to soften our blankets as well as our bear and buffalo skins, and we went to sleep at about midnight. Unfortunately, however, I could make no astronomical observations other than those made earlier in the evening.

The countryside of today's travels is of the same character as the regions we have crossed since Swan River. If there is any difference at all, today's travels were an improvement.

TUESDAY, SEPTEMBER 20, 1836. We broke camp at 6:24. Course WSW.

6:27. SSW ½ SW
6:30. SW
6:34. SSW
6:37. SW
6:38. Willow River

We left the mouth of Willow River at 6:42. There is a long swamp on the right bank of Willow River entering the Mississippi at the same time. It resembles a river so much you would swear two rivers were entering the Mississippi.

I noticed yesterday, though too late, that the course of the Mississippi as it is charted on the most recent maps, is wrong from Sandy Lake downstream.[142] I am making the necessary preparations to plot the section of the river that is yet to come.

The small canals are diminishing in number while rivers of greater importance are being formed. Thirteen miles below Willow River, Wild Rice [Rice] River flows in from the left bank.

Twelve miles farther on the same side Muddy [Ripple] River appears. Ten miles farther on the right bank we see Little Willow River. Six miles more downstream from the left bank comes Red Cedar Lake River [Cedar Creek].

We could have covered several more miles today but the weather that had been lovely and cold this morning was now cloudy and turning to rain. We had to make the best of a site on a point of land separating the Mississippi from Muddy River to spend the night.[143] Hardly

[142] Allen's map shows the Mississippi from Sandy Lake flowing SSW, while Nicollet and modern maps show a more SW direction.
[143] This was near the present site of the town of Aitkin, founded in 1870.

had we settled down when an autumn fog accompanied by drizzle and mosquitoes decided to spend the night with us. We nevertheless enjoyed a cheerful evening thanks to the exotic behavior of my half-wild men around the fire and a calumet dance marvelously executed by one of the Brunia brothers—enough to make one die of laughter.

WEDNESDAY, SEPTEMBER 21, 1836. What a sad equinox day! The same weather as last night prevails this morning without any sign of oncoming change. But we do have a lovely fire, a tent over our heads, paper, pens, and pencils and plenty to do. All this is enough to make one forget the things a dull day might awaken in a soul saddened by our predicament. I feel well; I am working hard and am satisfied. My men are patient, cheerful, and happy. What does it matter if the autumn leaves are falling! What if winter does come. God is great; He is good. I am more indebted to Him for the good things He brings me than I owe Him prayers for the things I am deprived of. May His will be done elsewhere as it is done on this desert, my abode for today, and as it shall be done on the desert that perhaps I shall cross tomorrow.

[*Here the manuscript diary ends. Four days later, on September 25, Nicollet and his party had reached the mouth of the Swan River. There they encountered Flat Mouth and a group of his braves from Leech Lake. Another day was spent in speechmaking, the outcome of which was a resolution by the Indians to accompany Nicollet to Fort Snelling and confer with Taliaferro. The entire party arrived at the fort on September 28, 1836.*[144]]

[144] Nicollet to Taliaferro, September 27, 1836, Taliaferro Papers.

St. Croix River Journey

AUGUST 2–11, 1837

WEDNESDAY, AUGUST 2, 1837. I left St. Peter at 9 o'clock in the morning with Mr. Aitken and Reverend Boutwell.[1] The canoe and crew are Mr. A[itken]'s. We entered the St. Croix at 3 o'clock sharp. We traveled forty-two miles in six hours.

The two- or three-mile section in the middle of the lake [St. Croix] is twice as wide as the preceding section. The lake veers NW and NE. The average bearing is N. The hillsides are covered with red cedar mingled with birch and double-needled pine of a pitiful appearance.

Mr. Warren and Mr. Dubé are in another canoe with a crew roughly the same size as ours.

It is a lovely night, fresh and without mosquitoes.

THURSDAY, AUGUST 3, 1837. We come out of the lake in three and a half hours after covering fifteen miles. So we have traveled a good thirty-two miles in seven hours. We take breakfast two miles upstream among islands. The banks are of parallel layers of sandstone.

---

[1] In addition to Aitken and Boutwell the party included, as indicated below, Lyman M. Warren and Jean-Baptiste Dubé. Warren was a partner of the American Fur Company with headquarters at La Pointe. He and Aitken had attended the treaty negotiations with the Chippewa at Fort Snelling—a profitable event for both traders, since the treaty gave Aitken $28,000 and Warren $25,000 in payment of the tribe's alleged debts. Boutwell, who had also witnessed the treaty sessions, was on his way to join his family at La Pointe and seek a more satisfactory mission site than Leech Lake. Dubé (or Du Bay) was an interpreter and trader from Lac du Flambeau, Wisconsin. Folwell, *Minnesota*, 1: 173, 177; Kappler, comp. and ed., *Indian Affairs*, 2: 364; Taliaferro, in *Minnesota Historical Collections*, 6: 214–220, 250–252; *Dictionary of Wisconsin Biography*, 109 (Madison, Wis., 1960).

We camped halfway up the lake, sixteen miles beyond the entrance, the distance we covered in three and a half hours. The shores are rugged and steep, interrupted by lovely, sheltering coves. The shallows are plentiful. It is indeed a picturesque river.

At 9:45 we are four miles beyond our breakfast stop, or thirty-eight miles from the Mississippi; reached the junction of the Wabizipinikan River emerging from the left bank. *Wabizipin* is a kind of fruit produced by a very prolific aquatic plant on the Mississippi. This fruit is very useful to the Indians who eat it and call it swan potato.[2] *Wabizipinak* indicates the region where the fruit is to be found, hence *Wabizipinakan Sibi*, the river [*Apple River*].

We are making good progress — up to four miles per hour until 6 o'clock. We camped at the rocks situated just before St. Croix Falls. The distance covered from breakfast time till we reached the rocks is thirty-two miles. We did not notice any river on the right bank of the St. Croix from its mouth to the falls.[3]

FRIDAY, AUGUST 4, 1837. We left at daybreak. The three miles from the rocks to the falls were difficult ones. We then had breakfast and visited the surroundings. I made some astronomical observations. The distance from the Mississippi to St. Croix Falls is seventy-six miles.[4] The river beyond the lake is almost as wide as the lake itself but it loses the characteristics of a lake because of its shallowness and the presence in it of numerous islands which divide it into channels. We left the falls at 9 o'clock. For five or six miles there is a succession of rapids. Navigating is slow and arduous. After the rapids we advance more easily, using paddles or poles as the river bottom is of rocks or pebbles mixed with sand.

On the right bank enters the *Mokiginowish* [*Dry Creek*]. The natives say it is the first river since the Mississippi to come from that shore. Later on, the *Attanwa Sibi* [*Trade River*] flows in from the left bank. It is a lovely river. Its high banks recede into the distance,

---

[2] This is also known as arrowhead, arrow-leaf, or duck potato. See Fernald and Kinsey, *Edible Wild Plants*, 86.

[3] Nicollet missed no rivers of importance, but contrary to his impression and the information given him by the Indians (see below) a number of streams do flow into the St. Croix from the west. Among them are Bolles Creek at Afton, Browns Creek at Stillwater, and Lawrence Creek at Franconia, Minnesota.

[4] Nicollet's own estimates of the various distances to this point total 69 miles. According to the Corps of Engineers (*Middle and Upper Mississippi*, 167) the distance is 52.5 miles.

forming a valley of gentle slopes covered with woods. Ash and oak trees are the predominant species, pine trees appear sporadically. Greenstones or hornblende form the base of the hills bordering the valley that rise three hundred feet above the level of the river.[5] At 6 o'clock we float by Sunrise River on the west end of the large bend which the St. Croix traces. The distance from the falls to Sunrise River is thirty-two miles. Sunrise River, or *Memokage Sibi*, emerges from the right bank. We camped a little beyond this river. The night was cool and beautiful.

SATURDAY, AUGUST 5, 1837. We left Sunrise River at daybreak. It was raining and the weather was on the sultry side. At 9 o'clock or fifteen miles farther we have breakfast. We passed three streams, all on the right bank. The first is the small Red Cedar River [*Goose Creek*]; the second, Reed River [*Rush Creek*]; the third, Little Rock River [*Rock Creek*]. Near this last one, sandstone reappears in parallel formation along the right bank.

We resume our travels at 10 o'clock. At noon, or six miles after breakfast, we pass by Whitewood or Basswood [*Wood*] River on the left bank. At 1:30 we reach Snake River five miles beyond the preceding tributary. The last avenue leading to it runs NNW and finally NW. The banks of the St. Croix are still covered with black alder, sumac five or six feet tall, white and red oak, soft maple and [*one word illegible*], ash and poplar, elm, hawthorn, white birch, some walnut or oil nut or shagnut trees. White pines are mixed with deciduous trees, and there are wild plum trees on the ridges.

The bottom and edges of the river are filled with masses of greenstones. Large blocks of them are to be found in the rapids. The valley is still formed by the base of the hills.

Toward the mouth of Snake River one also sees, mixed with the vegetation mentioned above, red cedar, spruce, spruce fir, and red pine trees.

After Snake River, pine woods are abundant. They crown the peaks of hills and mix with the other species which border the St. Croix. There is a bare island at the mouth of Snake River. A Chippewa village rises upon it, composed of several lodges. It is a very attractive

[5] If this sentence is taken to refer to the mouth of the Trade River, the stones were not bedrock but rather glacial debris. The nearest bedrock exposures are the basaltic cliffs to the south of the falls.

site. On Snake River, twenty-five miles upstream from the mouth, is located *Pakagâma* [*Pokegama*] Village.[6]

A few miles before Snake River we found a fine lodge and a bark canoe, both abandoned. A piece of bark hanging on the door informs us that the family has moved to Lac Court Oreilles, that the family is composed of the father and mother, two boys and three girls. The father is of the bear, the mother of the eelpout totem.[7] The lodge and canoe being useless, the Indians of all ages who were escorting us thoroughly enjoyed demolishing them, displaying the enthusiasm of a group of runaway schoolboys. They were not satisfied till the canoe was perched on top of a tree. All this was accompanied by shrieks of youthful mirth. One or two miles beyond Snake River another series of rapids begins, but they are not as difficult to conquer as yesterday's. There is much water, so we are only confronted with the current, there being no other obstacles to overcome.

Three miles from Snake River, another river, the *Chaudière* or Kettle, appears on the right shore. It enters directly into the rapids.

The St. Croix continues its course in long stretches without noticeable bends, bearing between NE and NW.

We camp at the head of the rapids, nine miles past Snake River. I make some astronomical observations.

Snake River passes by Mille Lacs and, farther north, Kettle River winds its way toward its sources on the left of Lake Superior.

SUNDAY, AUGUST 6, 1837. We left at the break of day. At 3:45, three miles beyond the beginning of the rapids or twelve miles from Snake River, we find a stream on the right. It is Sandy [*Sand*] River, probably Schoolcraft's Foule River. Five miles farther Clam River flows in from the left bank. Another seven miles bring us to Everflowing River [*Crooked Creek*]. Two miles upstream the Sioux Portage is to be found. It has six resting stops and leads from the St. Croix to Yellow Lake near the mouth of Yellow River. At 1:15

[6] This village, on the Pine County lake of the same name, had become in 1836 the site of a mission directed by the Reverend Frederick Ayer for the American Board. In 1838 Boutwell was to take charge at Pokegama. See Folwell, *Minnesota*, 1:174, 177.

[7] The eelpout or spineless catfish, more correctly known as the eastern burbot, is widely found in the waters of Minnesota and neighboring states, according to Samuel Eddy and Thaddeus Surber, *Northern Fishes With Reference to the Upper Mississippi Valley*, 258–260 (Minneapolis, 1947). The woman may have been of the catfish totem. See Warren, *History of the Ojibways*, 44.

or three miles beyond Sioux Portage, a river called *Eninandigo Sibi* or *Rivière aux Épinettes* or Fir Spruce River [*Lower Tamarack River*] enters from the right bank. Its name is derived from *Eninawdigokâ*, meaning fir spruce growth, a word not to be mistaken for *Eninatigoka*, meaning maple growth.

Three miles beyond this river that winds far away toward Lake Superior, Yellow River appears on the left bank. A hill rises at its mouth on which the Chippewa establish their villages at certain times of the year. Yellow River is named after a lake with yellowish waters, three miles from the mouth. The surrounding hillocks, similar to those I have had occasion to observe since we left St. Peter, display the same primitive deposit. When it forms chains of hills the deposit is covered with pine forests, etc.

We halt and later move on from Yellow River at 3 o'clock. At 5 o'clock, after advancing another six miles, Upper Fir Spruce [*Upper Tamarack*] River appears, as wide at its mouth as the other [*Lower Tamarack*] but shorter.

MONDAY, AUGUST 7, 1837. We camped one mile beyond Upper Fir Spruce River. At 4 o'clock we embarked and at 4:15 or three miles after Upper Fir Spruce River we encountered the River Where Canoes Are Made, or *Attonowining* [*Chase Creek*] from *attono*, he that makes canoes. There are some powerful rapids [*State Line Rapids*] below Attonowining. Six miles farther, the beautiful and long river named Namekagon joins us from the left bank. It passes by Lac Court Oreilles with which it is linked by a portage. Its complete course is navigable, and it is the one most used by the Chippewa. Half a mile below Namekagon are some long and strong rapids [*Big Island Rapids*]. After the rapids the river is flat, and beyond the Namekagon it is shallower but of equal width. Since there is far less water, the men take to wading and propel the canoe by hand.

According to the experience of Mr. Warren, who spent several winters in these parts, the distance from Yellow River to Namekagon is sixteen miles.

From the Namekagon to the last fish dam, it is quite a day, nothing but a series of rapids.[8] The strongest and longest of them is called Cobblestone Rapids.

[8] These are still known as the Fish Trap Rapids. The origin of the name is obscure. Possibly some natural obstructions found in the river at this point were

Seven miles after the Namekagon there is a portage used to avoid the obstacles presented by the St. Croix. It is called Women's Portage. It skirts the river and is only a quarter of a mile long, but at the same place a route starts out which leads straight to La Pointe village on Lake Superior. The natives make the trip in two to two and a half days' time. The route overland is two or three days shorter than the route on water by the way of the St. Croix and Bois Brulés [Brule] rivers. Mr. Warren and Mr. Boutwell take this road, guided by the natives of Lake Superior who have accompanied us thus far.

TUESDAY, AUGUST 8, 1837. Last night we camped some twelve miles up from Women's Portage. This morning we move on before 4:00 A.M., resuming our ascent of the rapids. The worst ones are behind us now and among those ahead there is one stretch of very steep rapids, one-fifth mile long. It is called Sheldrak[e] Rapids.[9] It presents no danger but it is particularly trying for the crew. At 6 o'clock we reach the last fish dam, six miles beyond last night's camping site, eighteen miles upstream from Women's Portage, or twenty-five miles after Namekagon River. At 7:30 we come to the Indian village ruled by Kabemappe, whose name means He That Sits to One Side.[10] The camp is situated three miles above the last fish dam I just mentioned. There is yet another fish dam, this one for sturgeons, a quarter of a mile before the village at the terminus of the rapids, where the river is three times wider. However, it should not be mistaken for the preceding one. The Indians call the sturgeon dam Namekawagon. The expansion of the river here, similar to a lake, is what Schoolcraft calls Wild Rice.[11] We left Kabemappe's village at 9 o'clock after

extended by the Indians in order to improve fishing. James Taylor Dunn, *The St. Croix: Midwest Border River*, 271–273 (New York, 1965).

[9] This rapids is not named on modern maps. The name Sheldrake may have been suggested by the reddish cliffs in the area, similar in color to the plumage of the ruddy sheldrake of southern Europe. Dunn, *The St. Croix*, 271.

[10] Schoolcraft met this chief in 1832 and described him as a peacemaker "who has become respectable for his influence in this part of the country." The chief signed the 1837 treaty, where he is listed as "Ka-be-ma-be, or the Wet Month." Schoolcraft, *Narrative of an Expedition*, 139; Kappler, comp. and ed., *Indian Affairs*, 2:492. Other sources refer to the chief as Kabamappa or Wet-mouth. See Dunn, *The St. Croix*, 45.

[11] This body of water was created by the natural obstruction known as the sturgeon dam. Schoolcraft calls it only "Namai Kowagon." Its size has been increased by the erection of a dam, and it is now known as the St. Croix Flowage, or sometimes as the Gordon Flowage. Schoolcraft, *Narrative of an Expedition*, 138; Dunn, *The St. Croix*, 268.

breakfast, and after having repaired our canoes that had been so badly damaged by the rapids. There is a potato field at the village, as well as a scalp dance pole. The soil of the location is poor and sandy.

At noon we pass by Clear Water [*Eau Claire*] River on our left. We are ten and a half miles from the village where we had breakfast.

At 1 o'clock we pass Buffalo River [*Ox Creek*], three and a half miles beyond the preceding river, on the same side. At 2:45, or six miles away, we make our entry into the Upper Lake of the St. Croix. It is six miles long. We cross it from end to end and start out at once on the two-mile portage over the height of land. I make some barometric observations on the summit and at the beginning of the portage on the northern end of Upper St. Croix Lake. [*Here Nicollet recorded the following barometric readings: "4:30* P.M. *— 28, 775–69, 5–69, 5".*]Cloudy sky and threatening rain.

We make the portage and by nightfall we camp on the place where one embarks on Bois Brulés River.

WEDNESDAY, AUGUST 9, 1837. The sky is cloudy for the third day in a row. It rained a little last night and there is no chance of a clear sky. [*Barometric readings: "4:30* A.M. *— 28, 820 — 51, 5 — 51, 5. Foggy sky."*] According to the natives and voyageurs the St. Croix and Bois Brulés rivers both have their sources in a little lake at the bottom of the valley which we can see below the ridges followed by our portage. Schoolcraft confirms this in his book. It is too extraordinary to believe without making sure. The valley followed by the St. Croix before it enters the large lake is wide and deep, oriented northwest. The Bois Brulés River comes from a vale which is beside the St. Croix valley and its springs originate in a little transversal branch which separates the valley from the vale.

To convince me that the two rivers have common springs, one of our fellow travelers assures me that the natives told him they had ascended the Bois Brulés in a small canoe up to the lake. To verify this I ascended the Bois Brulés from the place where we embark (at the end of the portage) to descend it. There the river is only six to eight feet wide and one foot deep. Barely a hundred yards upstream, I found it reduced to the size of a brook a foot wide and a foot deep briskly furrowing its way through thick brush surrounded by muskegs that form the bottom of the vale. [*Here Nicollet noted: "The temperature of the brook is 45.4°, that of the atmosphere 68°."*] It would therefore have been impossible for canoes to have penetrated any farther. I could not even walk farther myself because of the swampy waters and impenetrable brush.

Judging by what I saw I do not doubt that the St. Croix flows through the wide valley that opens before and embraces the large lake for a small number of miles, running parallel but in an opposite direction to the Bois Brulés. However, because of the dense forest that obstructs its edges and slopes, this valley is also impenetrable.

A quarter of a mile beyond Upper St. Croix Lake as one follows the portage on the height of land, he observes a pretty little lake [*Lake of the Woods*] cradled by hills to the right on a plateau. It flows into the Bois Brulés two or three miles below the portage. All the tall hills are covered with pines mixed with fir spruce. For the first two miles downstream the Bois Brulés is no more than a brook six to ten feet wide. Its shores are so cluttered with willows, alders, and boulders of greenstone that the men must constantly take to the water to pull the canoe through or even lift it in some shallow spots. I shall draw an outline of the sources as I believe I saw them. Mr. Aitken is as skeptical as I about the local stories told of lakes supplying water to rivers flowing in opposite directions in a region crisscrossed by valleys and hills.[12]

There are no trout in the St. Croix, but there are some small salmon-trout from Lake Superior in Bois Brulés River, even at the place where we embarked to descend it.[13]

We stop at 8 o'clock for breakfast. We are eight miles away from the portage. The river is flat, there is no current to speak of; it is perhaps slightly over one mile per hour. The whole crew noticed that. Two rivers on our left, one on our right [*Wilson, Angel, and Jerseth creeks*]. We move on at 9:48. The current is still weak, the river flat, fifteen to twenty feet wide and three feet deep. After leaving our breakfast site we pass by a river [*unidentified*] emerging from the left with all the appearances of being as wide at the mouth as the river we are on. Our course is a very sinuous one, and our mean bearing is NNE. Little by little the river widens to forty or fifty feet and straight

[12] For a further discussion of this much-debated point, see Dunn, *The St. Croix*, 42.

[13] Contrary to Nicollet's impression, there are trout in the St. Croix. By "salmon-trout" he apparently meant the common lake trout which in Lake Superior reaches a large size and is sometimes incorrectly called "landlocked salmon." See Eddy and Surber, *Northern Fishes*, 112.

stretches increase in length. The bed is of sand sometimes mixed with large pieces of greenstone endangering our canoes and calling for constant vigilance. Three miles after breakfast the river bed becomes flatter yet, and its width reaches sixty feet. Vegetation begins to bedeck the surface, and the bubbles of air mixed within appear to be almost motionless. Five miles farther there are straight stretches of river up to a quarter of a mile long deviating a little to the right or to the left of the magnetic NE.

From the portage to here there are no signs of hills on either shore. However, from time to time, first to our left, then later on, to our right, small elevations draw in as close as a quarter of a mile, retreating almost immediately afterward. The valley of the Bois Brulés seems to me to be four to six miles wide. Its bottom is composed of an immense savanna stocked with larch and fir spruce trees. Pines appear only on the ridges of the forty- to fifty-foot hills enclosing the valley and gently corrugating the savanna plateau we are crossing. It is therefore very difficult for us to see the rivers that constantly feed Bois Brulés over the seven or eight miles following our breakfast stop. One can see waters reaching the river on both shores but they seem so still that one dares not classify them as tributaries. The fact is, the valley is all water and savanna. Right now, at 11:15, we are only seven or eight miles away from the place where we had breakfast, at a spot where the hill on the right ends close by the river, which is two to three hundred feet wide studded with beautiful islands. There is much similarity between this valley and the one descending from La Biche [*Itasca*] and Travers [*Bemidji*] lakes, toward the latter part of that section of the Mississippi.

The geographic language of the Chippewa is richer than ours. Places where there are islands covered with hay mixed with bushes and trees dividing up the savanna and places where a river resembles a lake are called by them *pakwayanwan*. At noon we found ourselves in such a *pakwayanwan*, and it was difficult for us to find the main stream of the river again. As we emerged from the *pakwayanwan*, we discovered the first rapids. They are therefore approximately eleven miles beyond our breakfast site, or nineteen miles away from the portage. Salmon-trout abound here. These rapids are short ones. Their rocks are of the same nature as those in the rapids of the St. Croix. Here, it would seem, begins the decided incline facing Lake Superior, and our speed that I estimated to be five miles per hour since breakfast is going to increase. Five minutes later the second rapids appear, the Vassal [*Falls*] Rapids. I shall no longer outline the rapids that are going to follow in succession. Our course remains the same: NNE.

The Vassal Rapids are short, but travelers who descend them for the first time are obliged to make a portage.

The height of the water in the river seems to be in equal proportion in the rapids and in the flat sections that preceded them — an indication that it is approximately the average annual height of the water, averaging high and low water.

It is 12:30. As we leave the third rapids, short ones but difficult to descend because of the trees on the shores and the rocks in the bed, we enter a beautiful mile-long basin. The river is large. At the end the hill on the right side closes in, forming a wall of green — pine trees that lend to this portion of the river a new expression of pleasing beauty in comparison with the flat sections we have just left. The larch trees bordering the river are in their prime: no more shaggy ones. If the river were deeper and no rocks protruded we could call this a lake as was the case with Lake Pepin on the Mississippi and Lake St. Croix at the mouth of the St. Croix. The direction of this lake is magnetic N. From 12:47 to 12:50 we made our descent of the fourth rapids. Then comes another lake, or expansion of the river, identical to the preceding one and also one mile long, bearing NNW magnetic. We leave this lake at 1:00. At 1:10, or three-fourths of a mile farther, a portage starts out on the right bank, used by those who wish to avoid the rapids ahead, an overland route which provides a resting place for some of our men who take it.[14]

We move on at 1:17. After the second lake, the hills withdraw. We are now in a region similar to that of the sources of the Mississippi: sand, pebbles, pine trees on the heights and savannas, larch trees, reeds, and bushes in the hollows and bottoms. There are traces of primitive deposits all over the heights, but only small quantities of granite; stones are generally smaller. Small siliceous stones, coarse agates and carnelians, quartz, and bloodstones lie in the river. Our mean bearing since the second lake is slightly W of N.

At 1:40 we face the fifth rapids with obstructions. We have covered two miles since 1:17. At 2:10 we meet Sleeping Bear River also called *Nibegomowin* [*Nebegamon Creek*], on the left bank. We are

[14] Apparently the canoes were lightened but not portaged over this stretch.

still among the rapids which are very swift at times. We are progressing at a true six miles per hour. Our average course is still NNW veering toward NNE and W. We lost three minutes bailing out water from the canoes. We left the rapids at 3 o'clock. We have covered eight miles on a magnetic NNW course. The last two miles of this distance present elms on the right bank and this portion of the rapids is called Elm Rapids. The left bank of the same portion of the river has banks thirty-five to forty feet high, and near the end of the rapids the elevations pass on to the right bank. There are banks of sand and brown pebbles, an accumulation of local disintegrated rocks.

We pause to pick up our men and resume our trip at 3:05. At 3:30, after three miles, a small river flows in from the right bank [*Rocky Run*]. The elms are still with us, and the bank on the right has disappeared. The river's bends are short and veer from the magnetic E toward the magnetic W. Although the current is slower and the water high, our men paddle hard and we are clocking six miles per hour.

At 4:05 after another six miles, the river is divided by a large wooded island into two narrow navigable channels forming a right angle, one heading east, the other north. The section we have traveled since leaving the rapids was sometimes very much obstructed by fallen elms.

5:40. After ten more miles, a new series of rapids.

At 6:10. Two more miles and we pitch camp.

THURSDAY, AUGUST 10, 1837. At 4:20 we resume our journey. It rained during the night, and it is still raining as we continue to descend the rapids. At 6:30, after twelve more miles, we execute three portages one after the other. The first one is half a mile long, the second a third of a mile, the third spans three hundred yards. Taking the intervals into account, the total distance is three miles. We reach the terminus of the last portage at 8:00 and have breakfast. The unfortunate combination of difficult rapids, portages to carry out, and rain, caused great fatigue among our men, ruined our gear, and made this morning's progress a painful chore. We move on again at 9:15. By 10:30 we are five miles farther; by 12:30 we have journeyed another eight miles. Here, the last portage begins. It is a short one. The distance to Lake Superior is twelve miles.[15]

---

[15] The entire passage about the rapids of the Brule River is written in a very uneven hand, unlike Nicollet's usual small, neat script. This and the use of the

FRIDAY, AUGUST 11, 1837. Lake Superior. The weather is still bad at dawn. Later the wind dies down. Mr. Aitken, pressed by his business affairs, leaves first in his canoe with a crew of six. Soon I follow him in another canoe manned by three. The weather is fine but we face a head wind. We pass by the following rivers: *Piwâbiku Sibi Wisens* (Little Iron River), *Piwâbikû Sibi* (Iron River), *Pak-waika Sibi* (Rush River), *Mashkigi Minikani Sibi* (Cranberry River), *Shishkaweka Sibi* (Fish River), and *Sibi Wisens* (Little Fish River).[16]

At 4:00 in the evening we passed by and visited the *NenaboJû* Rocks, one of the greatest natural curiosities one can see in America.[17]

The sky is favorable to us and we continue to travel during the night. At 11:00 our canoe collides with a rock near a point we were passing too closely. No damage; we were merely badly frightened. We pass several points enclosing bays. At the bottom of some of these bays, rivers flow in.

At 2:30 in the morning we reach La Pointe where Mr. Aitken had preceded us by only four hours.

La Pointe. Stayed there Saturday, Sunday, and Monday.[18] A meeting of the partners of the American [Fur] Company is held.

Mr. Simon [*Lyman M.*] Warren — manager of La Pointe territory.

Mr. Aitken — manager of the Sandy Lake, Leech Lake, etc. territory.

present tense throughout indicate that the diary was kept under conditions of haste and exhaustion.

[16] The names of these streams are given here as translated by Nicollet (see Appendix 6, p. 265). The modern names of the streams entering Lake Superior between the Brule River and present-day Bayfield are, from west to east: Fish Creek, Reefer Creek, Iron River, Flag River, Cranberry River, Bark River, Lost Creek, Siskiwit River, Sand River, Raspberry River, Red Cliff Creek, and Chicago Creek.

[17] These were probably wave-sculptured cliffs, caves, and arches of sandstone found at the end of the Bayfield peninsula. Another traveler, who passed them in 1842, was as impressed as Nicollet, describing them as "some of the most stupendous of God's works." See Grace Lee Nute, *Lake Superior*, 274 (New York, 1944). NenaboJû, now usually spelled Nanabozho, was a heroic figure of Chippewa legend to whom mighty feats were commonly attributed. See below, Appendix 6, p. 264.

[18] In 1837 La Pointe was a thriving community of Indians, traders, voyageurs, fishermen, and missionaries — the most important village on the south shore of Lake Superior. Its population in 1840 numbered 458. See Hamilton Nelson Ross, *La Pointe — Village Outpost*, 91–99, 114n. (St. Paul, 1960).

Mr. Eustache Rouss[a]in — Kiwewina (the bend) [*Keweenaw*] territory.

Mr. Gabriel Franchet [*Franchère*] — Sault Ste. Marie territory.

Mr. John Holyday [*Holiday*] (nearly blind) — Sault Ste. Marie also.

Customs of Warfare
Among the Chippewa

NATIVES WAGE WAR without making any preliminary declaration, without revealing beforehand their motives or requesting a redress of their grievances. If an outrage has been committed against a nation, a tribe, a band, a village, or against any single individual, it must be avenged. Any man in the nation capable of bearing arms and of mustering a party may take the initiative in proposing means by which such vengeance can be inflicted. Depending on the gravity and the extent of the outrage, and also on the rank and influence of those taking this initiative, the war which is the means of vengeance will be either national, partially national, or simply that of a chief and his party. In every case, when war has been decided upon, it is the duty of all the nation to see to it that absolute secrecy shrouds the preparations from the enemy. Should the natives act otherwise they would deprive themselves of the strongest weapons they can wield: surprise attacks and stratagems of war.

The preparations for war are the same with all the native nations of North America.[1] The same order of ideas, identical opinions and superstitions prevail everywhere. The only variations are dictated by local circumstances, which entail modifications in costume, in the means of survival and travel, and in weaponry. From my own preference, I shall relate the events that take place under such circumstances among the Chippewa of the upper Mississippi lakes. The intelligence and taste which distinguish them from their neighbors as well as their particular environment as a people of rivers and lakes lend to their ceremonies a certain character which is as new as it is striking.

[1] Here and elsewhere Nicollet refers sweepingly to "all the native nations of North America." His observations were in fact limited to tribes of the eastern and southern woodlands.

A Chippewa who has decided to wage war prepares two deerskins. One must be that of a buck, the other of a doe. On the first he paints in red the form of the sun and of the eagle of war, the male eagle called *kiliou*, and on the other, the shape of the moon and of the female bird of the same species.[2] He hands both hides to an *oshkabewis*[3] who goes and hangs them in the most conspicuous place in the village. When the people see the two announcements, they know that something is afoot and that a council will be held to give further information and to deliberate on the proposals that will follow. Sometimes the individual who had the signs posted anonymously will not convene the council for several days, several weeks, even several months. In the meantime everybody keeps guessing. The signs do indicate that there will be invocations to the manitos who bestow the necessary light for guidance by night or day, and also that the spirits of valor shall participate; these are indeed signs of war! Yet nobody jumps to conclusions, for the hieroglyphics could have an entirely different meaning if the manitos invoked happened to be the very spirit of the person calling on them. This person apparently did not see fit to be more specific for the present; hence the enigma prevails and everyone waits with reserve and patience.

When the day finally arrives the *oshkabewis* scours the village and surroundings delivering a little stick of white cedar to each man designated to attend the council. These particular sticks are never painted or colored like those used to summon to the medicine ceremonies and supposed to be brought back by the guests when they appear for the ceremony. Women and children must not come anywhere near the meeting place. In the morning of this day, the *oshkabewis* has prepared a circular lodge eight to ten feet high, open at the top. This enclosure is made out of bark and hay and differs from the vaulted and girded structures the Chippewa build for their dwellings and medicine lodges. The guests arrive as soon as they receive the little stick. As they step into the lodge they can see a pipestem suspended horizontally between two forks of wood planted into the ground. Underneath it is placed the gular pouch of a pelican (*Chedewigondashkwaï* — from *chede* — pelican — and *gondashkwï* — the throat of an animal) that is still held

[2] Baraga (2:189) gives the spelling as *kiniw*.
[3] Nicollet's spelling of this word varies. The editor has chosen the present form as closest to that given by Baraga (2:335), who defines *oshkabewiss* as "Waiter or attendant of an Indian Chief." See also Warren, *History of the Ojibways*, 318.

by the two bones forming the lower part of the beak of the animal. The pouch contains smoking tobacco, and next to it is to be found the *oshkanzhiwôg;*[4] instruments made out of a great number of deer hooves fastened on the end of a handle. They use it to accompany war chants and also, in some instances, as a symbol indicating a chief is present.

At the sight of these three objects the members arriving know for certain that war is going to be the subject of the council. They move to their places in silence and wait. He who brought them together speaks sitting down as if engaged in ordinary conversation. The pomp they usually display in councils held on other occasions, either among themselves or with whites, is left out here. The speaker sets forth his intention of going to war against such and such a nation to avenge an outrage or offense committed against the nation, village, himself, or somebody dear to him and whom he feels it is his duty to protect. He then implies that he needs help and that he must make up a fighting force matching the gravity of the case. While he speaks, an *oshkabewis* lights the pipe he presented beforehand to the manitos of the skies and of the earth and also successively to the manitos of the four cardinal points beginning with the east and going round by the south.

This first ceremony of the pipe is reserved for the male spirits, those represented on the sign or poster of the order of the males, superior in every way to that of the order of the females. The *oshkabewis*, having accomplished this, presents the pipe to the members of the council, each in turn, starting on the left side of the lodge in relation to the entrance. At this point the speaker can evaluate his worth among his fellows, yet his scrutinizing gaze follows the movements of the *oshkabewis* as if he were quite indifferent. Each time the *oshkabewis* presents the pipe to a member, a yes or no is to be expected. He who agrees to wage war manifests his consent by accepting the calumet presented to him; he who refuses turns it away with a wave of the hand.

Thus ends the first part of the ceremony. A recess follows. Individ-

---

[4] The plural of an animate substantive is formed by adding a syllable of which the last letter is invariably "g." The letters which precede the final "g" are "so various that we distinguish not less than twelve different terminations." See Baraga, *A Theoretical and Practical Grammar of the Otchipwe Language,* 38 (Montreal, 1878). In this word Nicollet chose the "o" and elsewhere marked it with the phonetic symbol (ô), which the editor has added here.

ual pipes are smoked, and groups begin to converse about indifferent subjects, making no allusions to the purpose of the council.

He who convoked the council makes another oration and tells the *oshkabewis* to smoke the female spirits symbolized by the second poster. He speaks more softly, inviting those who still hesitate or refuse to follow him in his adventure to meditate till the next day, which is dedicated to the enrollment. The natives never say "go now" or "withdraw now," not even "let us retire"; this would be an offense, a violation of one's free will. Under the circumstances the speaker says "*kidazhiwitamin*"—let us clear the lodge—as if he were saying "I have nothing else to add." When the *oshkabewis* has finished smoking the spirits and has passed around the pipe to the others who are thus given a second chance to accept or refuse war, the day is done. Everyone retires peacefully excepting the *oshkabewissug* who watch over the council lodge. This lodge of war has become a sanctuary that may not be profaned by the presence of women or children.

During the remainder of the day and night, private meetings are held in the lodges of the elders where the propositions made in the morning's council are discussed. Obviously the *oshkabewissug* and he that placed himself at the head of the war party are not invited to these intimate gatherings in which everyone should feel free to expound on his reasons for consenting or refusing to go to war. The *oshkabewis* is replaced by the *mizhinâweg*[5] who temporarily perform their functions. A final selection is brought about in the course of these private meetings. Those who do not wish to go to war leave one after the other as they finish exposing the grounds for their refusal. Those who remain immediately begin to work up their excitement. Each one prepares a pledge which consists in engraving on a piece of bark the symbol of the totem to which he belongs.[6] Pipes are emptied and refilled, the drum rumbles, and part of the night is filled with war chants.

The next day, at sunrise the *oshkabewissug* prepare the lodge of war for the ceremony of enrolling the warriors. The pipe duly filled is suspended across the two forks, the pelican pouch and the *oshkanzhiwôg* are set in their places, and in addition to what was there yesterday, there is a piece of red cloth spread out on the ground. The

[5] Nicollet later defines this word as "the appointed waiter." See below, p. 183. The present form is plural.

[6] The editor has used the common spelling of the word "totem," or clan. As with "manito," Nicollet substituted a "d" for the second "t." For a full discussion of its meaning see Hodge, ed., *Handbook of American Indians*, 2: 787–794.

partisan who is now war chief arrives. The *oshkabewis* who passed the calumet around twice in yesterday's ceremony has already informed him of the number of warriors having demonstrated their approval of his cause; his friends will not have failed to convince others during the intimate gatherings of the night; some may have withdrawn. This interesting matter will now be made quite clear.

The *oshkabewissug* step out of the lodge and announce four times over that the enrollment ceremony is about to begin. A few minutes later soldiers appear, one by one or in groups of two. They march into the lodge, moving along the left side, which with the Chippewa is always the side of the rising sun. Each lays on the red cloth the piece of bark marked with his totem. They go round the lodge and place themselves to the right of the entrance in such a way that when all the places are filled, the first who came in will be the first on the right as you go in and will be the first to leave, while the last to enter will be the farthest to the left and last to leave as he follows the others making their round of the lodge. This is a formality which is regularly carried out in meetings related to war or medicine ceremonies. They refer to this as going round following the movement of the sun. The youngsters who are enlisting for the first time and who have never fought must present themselves with blackened faces. (A certain number of women enlist also. Later on we shall see the part they play at war.)

The enlisting operation ends quite naturally when no one else arrives. Then the war chief picks up the pieces of bark that were laid on the red cloth and arranges them according to their totems—so many of the eagle family, so many of the bear family, so many of the marten family, etc. He now knows the number of soldiers composing his army. These are his pledged volunteers and he is their appointed chief; but when the expedition is over, their mutual engagement automatically dissolves—they are no longer as soldiers or chief to one another. It now remains for the chief to evaluate the strength of his army versus the forces he must fight, and he must carefully weigh all the odds of his enterprise.

At this point and before going any further, certain matters should be stressed. I assumed the initiative of war had been taken by the chief of a party or by a noble warrior who wished to increase his prestige among his countrymen. Had the initiative been taken by the legitimate chief, the proceedings would have been exactly the same. However, it is probable that the motives for war would have embraced greater public interests than those that move a partisan who often drinks only a personal cup of vengeance.

In a case where the legitimate chief does not appoint himself war chief and the initiative is seized by an individual, the former does not nurse any jealousy for this. He attends the deliberations of the council as an individual; he also attends the private meetings following the council and gives his reasons for approving or disapproving the war. Should he be opposed, he will definitely abstain from giving advice to the others. He will limit himself to giving his opinion on how the matter should be viewed in the light of the interests of his country, or he will quite simply put it on the grounds of his personal interests. He will peacefully withdraw from all interference and will not on this account lose the influence he possesses or the consideration he enjoys. However, on such occasions his example will have more influence than anything he might say. If, on the other hand, he did intervene, his very authority would be in jeopardy in the minds of the natives whose basic principle it is to act of their own accord and to reject all advice providing it does not originate with their closest parents.[7]

If the chief does ratify the war proposed by the partisan, he enlists as a soldier bringing also his piece of bark with the other men. If the party chief is motivated more by nationalistic feelings than by personal ambition, it occasionally happens that he will beg the lawful chief to take his place and direct the campaign as he sees fit, with no condition laid upon him to follow the strategy of the partisan. The lawful chief may accept this proposal or he may decline and carry on as a simple soldier.

The last somewhat significant campaign waged by the Chippewa of Leech Lake against the Sioux took place some five or six years ago. The expedition was raised by an elder brother, and it was approved by Chief Flat Mouth. This leader fought as a soldier, but his elder brother remained chief of operations.[8] There are also occasions when two chiefs of war rise together. Both of them have painted deer hides posted up, announcing that a council will be held at which further news will be communicated. When the partisans have stated their intentions and it is acknowledged that their objectives are identical,

[7] Nicollet apparently means the individual's natural parents. In many tribes aunts and uncles were referred to as "stepmother" or "stepfather." See, for example, Quimby, *Indian Life in the Upper Great Lakes*, 130.

[8] For Elder Brother see above, p. 8on. The editor has not been able to identify positively the significant campaign referred to by Nicollet.

the two men confer, and one relinquishes his rank in favor of the other who then assumes all responsibilities.

Whatever conflicts may arise as a result of these aspirations, everything is straightened out on the day of the enrollment. The war chief checks whether or not his troops are sufficient. If he feels they should be increased, he calls on other tribes, bands, or villages of the nation, and this is how he proceeds: Suppose that the initiative of belligerency originates at Leech Lake. The war chief dispatches an *oshkabewis* to the Chippewa bands living by the lakes of the surrounding country. The *oshkabewis* carries off with him the pelican pouch, a calumet, the *oshkanzhiwôg*, and a chain of two or more strings of cylindrical ceramic beads as the mark or symbol of the message he bears. He marches off to Red Cedar Lake, which is nearest, and heads directly for the chief of the village to whom he unfolds the purpose of his mission. The lodge is cleaned out at once, the calumet is placed between the cut tree forks with the pelican pouch underneath, and the *oshkanzhiwôg* is planted into the ground symbolizing the person of the chief who sends the message.

Meanwhile the rumor of the arrival of an envoy has already spread around the village. The messenger steps out of the lodge and cries: "*He . . . he, he-he, he . . . he,*" and closes these three shouts with the words: "*Inakâmigod ninibidon*—I bring news." Everybody flocks around, and the men take up their places in the lodge, rotating around the lodge as the sun moves in the sky. The messenger fills the pipe, lights it, and gives it to the chief to pass down from hand to hand while he speaks. Then he stands and, holding up the ceramic necklace, he tells what came to pass at Leech Lake, announces there will be an enrollment the next morning, and fixes the place, day, or moon where all units are to rendezvous. He abstains from making any comments or giving any particular details. The gathering is broken up and private conferences are held. The next day those in favor bring their pieces of bark showing their totem. The *oshkabewis* registers so many eagles, so many bears, martens, etc., and goes on to perform the same ceremonies at Sandy Lake, Red Lake, Lake Winnipeg [*Winnibigoshish*], etc. Later he returns to Leech Lake to make known the number of warriors from various bands by which the army will be increased.

While the *oshkabewis* is busy making his rounds, back at Leech Lake the enlisted men are drilling away, and the chief does everything possible to enliven the spirits and zeal of his men. The women prepare the footwear of their husbands and relatives, make provisions, and help to assemble the costumes. Men manufacture their weapons and the mysterious ornaments they will wear and provide themselves with munitions.

The very evening of the enrollment the troops perform a military parade designed to awaken the martial spirits of the languid, to lure the waverers, and to embarrass the obstinate. Bravadoes, songs of war, and abuse are appropriate under the circumstances, and they are discriminatingly applied to the individuals who remain quietly in their lodges as the troops pass by. The expressions they use in such cases are curious and typical of the independent and vainglorious spirit of the Indians. Since a native does not recognize the right of anybody on earth to command him, it is only by appealing to his pride that one can win him over. From time to time the troops halt and proffer allusions such as these: "This one is an old woman. He would rather eat sugar and wild oats than defend his country!"—"Such a one would do well to wear his wife's petticoat and give her his breeches; she has more courage than he!"—"Observe him, in front of his lodge! What is he doing there? He is waiting till his wife tells him he can sit beside her. Show him the banners of war and he will take cover under her skirts! And what about those beribboned youngsters over there, all dolled up in red? They would rather flirt than take up their arms and smear themselves with black!" etc.

Such remarks uttered in a natural style difficult to imitate, also sung and accompanied by gestures emphasizing the contempt expressed by the words, do not fail to have some impact, and the shame they inspire does contribute toward increasing the strength of the army.

After this tour, the soldiers deposit their medicine bags and war bonnets in the lodge of war, whence they cannot be withdrawn until the army goes to battle. Their weapons and costumes are brought to their dwellings. From then on, the lodge of war is a meeting place much used by the warriors. Within it they smoke, talk, sing war songs and keep up their bellicose fervor.

Until the time comes for all units engaged in this war to meet, specific days are reserved for maneuvers, for learning the tactics and stratagems of war, and for the basic drilling of the recruits who have never been in action. These exercises have exactly the same purpose as our tactical maneuvers in Europe, but before launching into a description of them, it is necessary to introduce the weapons and costumes of the warriors, as well as the beliefs and superstitions that give rise to them.

Their war costumes incorporate the advantages of appearance, safety, and also lightness for the sake of maneuverability. Shoes are made of *makizinum*,[9] a skin footwear. Several pairs are attached to their belts or strapped around like cartridge boxes. Their *mitasses*[10] (leggings) made out of blue or red cloth, or from deerskins, are to the Indians what pants are to the whites. They are attached to a belt by strings, and a tail, composed of ribbons, bird feathers, and pieces of furry animal skins, dangles from the belt behind. Garters contour the legs; and the exterior signs of man, which the leggings do not cover, are concealed by brief supports. Also attached to the belt apart from knives in their sheaths are: a tobacco pouch, the *påkåmagón* [*round-headed club*], a mirror with scissors, and a little pocket containing red and other colorings and thousands of little knickknacks to which the natives are as enslaved as whites are to theirs. The rest of the body is naked though sometimes covered with a light and short calico shirt. The spear is inseparable from the rifle, which it supplements when the rifle cannot be triggered. A pretty little bag containing plants prepared as remedies for all ills also hangs on the left, next to the shot pouch. It is called the *pinjigoossånens* and contains the sacred relics of the native, tokens of his faith that instill courage, strength, and life. This bag is not to be confused with the one they call *pinjigoosån* or *midai-wåyån*, both of which I shall describe in the chapter dealing with the institution of medicine among the Indians.[11] The *pinjigoossånens* is their little campaign pharmacy.

The Chippewa of the Mississippi lakes gave up using bows and arrows long ago, also the club made out of hard stone and several other lethal weapons generally used by all peoples of North America in bygone days which are described in so many books. To find these

[9] The French of Louisiana did not use the standard French word *mocassin* derived from the Indian through the English. See William A. Read, *Louisiana French*, 63 (Baton Rouge, 1931). Hereafter the editor has substituted moccasin for Nicollet's Louisiana French word *soulier*. Baraga (2:208) gives the Ojibway singular form as *makisin*.

[10] Baraga (2:233) spells this word *midåss*. See also Read, *Louisiana French*, 97. Hereafter the term leggings will be used.

[11] See below, p. 196, 201–208. The form *pinjigoossånens* is plural. For another description see Walter J. Hoffman, "The Midéwiwin or 'Grand Medicine Society,'" in Bureau of Ethnology, *Seventh Annual Report*, 1885–86, p. 215 (Washington, 1891). Hoffman spells the word *bin-ji-gu-san*.

instruments today, one must visit the Sioux of the prairies and all the other nations farther west and northwest as far as the Pacific. The Chippewa without exception have adopted the rifle, and the only ancient weapons they have kept are the spear and the elegant but lethal *pâkâmagôn* shown in the drawing.[12] Both of these weapons are still of a sacred character and are classified as objects which women, children, and strangers may not profane by their touch. Those Chippewa who do not carry two rifles possess at least one, and they take care of this weapon above all others, replacing it whenever they can by a better and more beautiful one. It is the weapon they absolutely need for fighting and hunting and on which their safety and existence depend. Of all the objects they can offer as presents that are not considered sacred, it is the greatest. A rifle, a powder horn and shot pouch, the spear, the *pâkâmagôn*, and two belt knives—such are their weapons of today.[13]

 . . . in hunting or in war. It contains mainly those remedies that heal wounds, that give flexibility to the limbs, and that prevent bullets from penetrating the body. This particular kind they grind and chew, spitting out the resulting froth onto the parts of the body they wish to soften and preserve. The Chippewa trim and fashion these various articles that compose their weapons and costumes with taste. Multicolored ceramic beads, ribbons, animal skins and bird feathers are the basic accessories they use to dress up in as many different ways as their fantasy and imagination dictate.

Fantasy is also their only guide in the ways they color their faces and bodies. But there is one part of their attire that follows an unvarying custom—the arrangement of their headwear, the war bonnet. The sacred skin of a bird is its foundation. They attach it to the top of their heads letting the beak bounce up and down on their foreheads. All kinds of accessories trim it so as to produce a general effect of hideousness likely to terrify the enemy. This skin or plumage is for them a guardian, a genius, a spirit, a manito of war which strangely

[12] The drawing has been lost. Apparently Nicollet distinguished between the ordinary stone-headed club and the round-headed weapon he called the *pâkâmagôn*. For the former he used the French term *casse-tête*. See Read, *Louisiana French*, 109.

[13] Apparently Nicollet failed to write a few words necessary to the meaning of the text as the next page is in sequence, numbered in his own hand. There he is describing bags of healing herbs and remedies, or *pinjigoossânens*.

enough will not inspire courage, bravery, or fighting skill, but will inspire them in what they should do, how they must operate to avoid death.

This belief or superstition is yet another falsely applied interpretation of the experience of the native. It originates in the particular order of their sensory concepts, brought about by their observations. While hunting they noticed how the audacity and high flight of the eagles, falcons, and hawks kept these birds beyond the reach of rifle shots; how the suspicious crow is difficult to shoot on the wing because of its sudden acrobatics in the air (in case of danger it takes an undulating course and tumbles, thus defying the sharpest shot); how all species of night birds have the marvelous faculty of being able to lead their lives unnoticed on the very grounds of their enemies; how tiny species like the hummingbirds are gifted with minuteness and skill enabling them to escape and hide in bushes. Therefore, concludes the native, if I place upon my head a sacred bonnet made out of the skin of an eagle, crow, owl, or hummingbird, if I mimic the instincts and habits of the bird caught in the same predicament, and if I beget his favors through worship and nourishment, the bird will protect me. Then, when I am facing an enemy who is in a better position than I, this good manito will make me seem too far away, or too swift in my zigzag contortions, or as if the night has obscured me, or as if I were too small for the bullet. Thus does my enemy lose his advantage, etc. The time it takes for him to react gives me time to kill him first.

No wonder that in the wake of these concepts it is so important for the natives to be under the protection of a war spirit. Also, a native does not select such a manito at random, nor according to his fancy. Inspiration guides him in the recognition of his particular god, and we shall observe how this inspiration is stimulated in the chapter on dreams and fasting.[14]

The birds I just mentioned are considered sacred by all native nations of North America. They invoke them in their ceremonies and they are a part of all their war songs. These are the birds the natives call *pinêssi* (in the singular) and *pinêssiwug* (in the plural).[15] Their skins serve to make war bonnets and also as bags in which the natives place their herbs, thus increasing the power of the manito. Bearing

[14] This chapter was never written. It was apparently intended to be part of the section on "Stages in the Life of the Indian." See below, p. 192n.

[15] Baraga (2:86) spells this word *binêssi* and defines it as "a large bird."

this in mind, the war bonnet does effectively become in peacetime a bag consecrated in medicine ceremonies.

These birds are the most appropriate spirits for the general circumstances of native warfare. But there are many other gods apt to protect warriors in all the mishaps of battle: climbing birds that shun the hunter by creeping around tree limbs as they are being pursued; aquatic birds famous for their ability to dive and hide under the waters; quadrupeds that escape their enemies by fleeing down burrows. All of them are so many manitos that confer upon warriors under their safekeeping not the power to do what the manitos do according to their instincts but the faculty of appearing to the enemy as these animals appear to theirs.

The bear is a great manito of war, especially the grizzly bear. The furor it makes and the strength it deploys against its enemies have made it an object of awesome terror and profound superstition. This we shall witness in the chapter on medicine ceremonies. In the eyes of the natives of North America, who have no knowledge of the tiger and lion, it is the most ferocious of all animals. They say that its life is supernatural and that it can be shot twice without dying. To be able to survive one or two bullets is so mighty a feat for an animal that a native cannot neglect to seek its favors. Although the native finds it impractical to use the skin of this animal as a costume—it would be too cumbersome on the battlefield—he is content with wearing a necklace composed of its claws or a helmet he makes out of the skin of its head.

A young man going to battle for the first time should always have his face blackened and may only wear a fancy suit composed of insignificant ornaments that are not sacred. I do not think he can even carry the spear or *pâkâmagôn*. Only after his first campaign, and after having been subjected to the dream and fasting ceremonies that reveal his manito to him, is the young man promoted to the rank of warrior with all the prerogatives thereof. This privilege is his whether or not he saw the enemy and whether the campaign was a success or not.

Those women who join the ranks of the warriors bear no arms other than the knife and the common hatchet, and the only distinctive feature of their costume is an empty bag made out of skin or cloth. They tie it to their backs like a burden, symbol of their domestic duties, indicating they are not entitled to any more dignity or consideration at war than in their huts at home. Their co-operation on the battlefield is limited to dressing wounds and a task to be performed on the enemy's dead that will be mentioned later.

On the day set for maneuvers the soldiers, duly equipped and armed, head for the lodge of war, where they are divided into two camps. The camp that represents the enemy, composed of rank-and-file warriors, makes for a neighboring forest, occupies it, and prepares an attack on the lodge of war defended by the other camp under the command of the war chief. The members of the latter smoke, talk, sing, and simulate a disastrous sense of security—the result of a fatalistic lack of prudence—that invariably keeps the natives off their guard in their camps.

(And how could they avoid the misfortunes brought about by this fatalistic lack of prudence?[16] In the three concepts that preoccupy the mind of the native—to eat so as to survive, to recover from ills so as to live, and to defend himself in order to go on living—has he not placed his fate in the hands of the gods of his Olympus? Does he not benefit by manitos that bring him the animals he can kill should he need food or clothing — manitos who also guide him to the plants that heal, and other spirits that protect him from his enemies, and still more spirits who think for him on every occasion of his life? Why then should he take care? Foresight implies that the faculties of intelligence are active and developed, that they exert alertness, comparison, and evaluation of the sensations of pain and joy. The native has not reached this point. He is passive in all the mechanisms of his comprehension; he knows only the good or the evil use of his physical faculties, and he acts as if he were fatally spellbound or hypnotized by the spirits with which he fills the universe and which he discovers in every type of phenomenon presented to him by nature.[)]

[(]Christians face a century of work to enlighten the Indian and guide him over the threshold he must pass in making the transition from a mass of sensory concepts to the faculties of abstraction and moral sense. If there is any further delay in the study of the conditions and needs of this child-man—study which may lead to the ways by which he may be brought into the bosom of Him who died to save mankind—a century of extermination and an aftermath of darkness await us. One-tenth of the earth's habitable lands will be covered with graves.)

[16] The parentheses around this and the following paragraph are Nicollet's. He may have intended not to include these reflections in the published work.

The camp in the forest practices for a long time before attacking. The rank and file are taught to fight in a wood from tree to tree; they are shown what stratagems to employ on open ground, how to lie in wait for the enemy, letting him gain an apparent superiority while they are exposed to his fire in order to win the real advantage and make a killing.

Wearing the bonnet of a manito is not all; one must also imitate his cry and flight behavior if one wishes to benefit from the gifts possessed by the manito bird fleeing his enemy. He that wears crow's plumage must mimic the cry of the crow, jump, dance, and perform the best contortions he can to convince himself that he is similar to his manito. Thus he will escape the enemy's fire, using the same tricks employed by the animal to outwit his enemy. All warriors must behave accordingly with the war manito of their choice, and this is what the maneuvers are about in these camps, both in the forest and in the lodge, before they come to blows.

Soon, short whistles from swan bones blown softly so as to be heard from only within a short radius echo back and forth from several points. All is ready. An outburst of shrieks announcing the attack fills the air, and shots fired on the lodge of war trigger the defensive action of those within. They pour out of the lodge from all sides, scrambling through the walls of hay with which it was built.

I shall not go into every detail of a contest such as this, nor of native battles in general — they have been described so often and so well in nearly all modern languages. My objective is to clarify the ideas that dominate such events, and I shall therefore pass on to matters that serve this purpose.

One can observe that the natives have essentially two types of war cries. One is used to sound the alarm or start an attack, also to announce a victory or to express the triumph that follows a small conquest or a complete victory. It is made by vibrating the hand softly over the mouth while the voice pitches high shrieks, either intermittent or prolonged in full and amplified tones. It is the *sasakwewin* of the Chippewa, the "hurrah" that is universal among all the native nations of North America. The other cry is the one uttered in battle. Since every warrior must mimic the cry of the animal bedecking his head, there are as many kinds of these cries as there are manitos of war represented on the battleground. It is called the *nanawâjimoowin*.[17]

---

[17] Baraga (2:17) gives *nind aiajikwe* to mean "I cry loud."

This cry, which is a composite of all the diverse cries, is strange, impressive, awesome when heard from a distance, but when each cry is heard separately, its origin remaining unknown, the impression is bizarre, almost ludicrous, and one would be tempted to laugh if the spectacle of battle were a laughing matter. Since the youngsters in action for the first time are not allowed to dress their heads with the skin of a sacred animal, they are not allowed to mimic either. The only cry they can shout is that represented by the sound of *hihi, hihi, hihi.*

When the war chief notes that the maneuvers are well on their way, he throws into the midst of the melee a dummy, or some kind of ball representing a human head made out of skins or a blanket or hay that he prepared ahead of time. The purpose of this provocation is to enable the troops to practice all the moves related to the act of scalping the enemy. Since this act is the most powerful of warriors, since its realization calms hatred, appeases vengeance, and determines victory, I shall describe its main points.

Natives do not wage war to make conquests. Their restive and turbulent minds, a reputation they wish to acquire, an affront to be avenged—these, as far as they are concerned, are grounds for war. If their motives are often very flimsy, the reparation they claim to put a stop to war is not very important either; a handful of hair taken from an enemy is ample justification for several weeks' celebration of a victory obtained at the expense of several months' preparation. By their standards an open battle, scoring twenty or thirty dead, counting the losses on both sides, is worthy of being classified as a historical event. I am not here referring to cases where a native nation takes part in a war between two civilized nations or fights alone one of the latter, nor to those frequent instances when native parties on a hunting expedition stumble across camps of other nations and exterminate the women, children, and aged in the absence of those capable of defending them. I am referring to war as a matter of principle, based on the opinions, prejudices, and superstitions of the natives uncontaminated by outside influences.

History shows that such a war can neither be long nor murderous. Its outcome depends entirely on the first minute of the encounter. Whether both parties are searching for each other, or whether one is sought unsuspectingly by the other, as soon as the assault takes place and the *sasakwewin* has filled the air, both parties size each other up in a wink. If one feels it is weaker than the other, it flees en masse and from then on it is "save himself who can." Then begins a war of pursuit that will soon end at the expense of those whose legs are feeble or hampered by rough terrain. If both parties judge that they are an acceptable match, there follows a head-on clash, chaos presiding! There are no directives, no tactics; there is a total absence of strategy. Everyone looks out for himself and charges for his trophy. The most eager soon confront each other, while the experienced warriors whose popularity could arouse envy among their fellow warriors shun the center of action and phlegmatically go about ducking and dealing decisive blows.

Then a strange scene takes place. The *nanawâjimoowin* replaces the *sasakwewin*. The first-rate champions are within rifle shot; they eye each other, dance, jump, and shriek. The first to be caught in the sights of a gun stays on the same spot, jumps higher, shrieks louder, waits for the shot, never flees, and even appears to ignore the person holding him between life and death. A whizzing bullet puts an end to this pantomime, and the jumping target whether struck or not falls to the ground. The ring of the rifle shot as well as the fallen man attracts the warriors from both camps close by, some scrambling for the scalp, others to save him. He that fired the shot, uncertain of his success, no sooner hesitates to confirm his victory than he is outrun by men transported by a blind fury.

But lo! one of these rash ones collapses! The fallen man has risen and fled, and the potential victory has now changed sides. The site is now being disputed for the sake of a corpse. The first to lay enemy hands on it will grasp a lock of hair from the top of the head and cut out the skin holding it by the roots. In the few seconds that remain before the arrival of an onslaught of other morbid trophy-seekers, he has time to decapitate the victim and throw the head to his rivals, who wrangle for it shouting with madness as they would wrangle for a ball in a game. A second lock of hair is cut off, then a third, and when the head has nothing left to be ripped off as a trophy or symbol of glory, the band runs toward another site of action. As they go by the mutilated body still lying complete on the ground, each warrior appeases his wrath by discharging his gun into it, or piercing it with his spear, or cutting off the flesh and shattering the bones with his *pâkâmagôn*. Then, with foaming mouths, women enter the scene. Having no right to scalp, they clamorously cut from the victim the marks of man, which by tradition they are entitled to prepare as ornaments for their triumphal crowns.

These atrocities often take place at several points on the battlefield at the same time. But before long they die down. As each side loses several men and gains possession of as many pieces of scalps, warriors begin to desert their ranks, opponents break away and disperse, and for lack of men the battle comes to an end.

The stratagem which gives rise to the scene described above never fails to astonish the whites who happen to witness it. It has been the cause of many a victim among the civilized nations engaged in battle with natives. I should also add that it has made many more victims among the superstitious natives themselves whom the manitos of war do not always effectively protect from bullets fired by their brave and skillful enemies. Stories and reports related by travelers often present these facts as proof of the courage and composure of the natives in the face of death. I have heard others support a different interpretation, considering the facts as proof of the stupidity of these people. A man poised before the barrel of a gun aimed at him, shrieking odd utterances, bouncing up and down on the same spot thereby making a more conspicuous target of himself is indeed an extraordinary sight. I think we can now weigh the value of these opinions: the native in such moments is so entranced by the belief that he is acting under the influence of a spirit who will protect him that his reasoning is completely obscured, his coolness doubtful, and his courage more doubtful yet. Thus our feelings toward him should be inspired by pity rather than by admiration or respect.

This now leads me to speak of the criterion used by the natives to determine the valor and glory of their warriors. He that fells an enemy with a gunshot in no way contributes toward his own prestige if he does not also succeed in taking the scalp of his victim. If he fired from a certain distance, he did not expose himself any more than those fighting at his side and hence is not entitled to any more honor than they. The real danger, the danger that confers glory to him that overcomes it, lies in the act of scalping an enemy believed to be dead but who may be only wounded or pretending to be dead in order to trap the first to come close. The danger is further increased by the efforts made by the adversaries to save their comrade should he be merely wounded, or to prevent the scalping of his head should he be dead. This demonstration of courage and the successful accomplishment of the operation lead to the greatest award conferred by the natives for military glory. The outward sign of this distinction consists in adorning the top of one's head with a tail feather of an imperial eagle (the *kiliou*) on which two marks have been painted with vermilion.

In war, because of the immediate danger surrounding the warriors, scalping is carried out in such an expeditious manner that the operator is satisfied with the piece that remains in his hand after the first slice of his knife. Moreover, should he take time to carry out a full scalping operation, there would be no extra glory attached to it. He has but to be the first and to have the proof in hand. Thus there often remains enough hair on the victim to tempt the courage of other warriors who may follow after him. In this case, the rules take into account two additional scalpings performed on the same subject. The warrior that takes the second bunch of hair is entitled to a *kiliou* feather with only one red mark; the third warrior, the last, may wear an identical feather but with no red mark at all. As for him who shot the victim, his merit ranks after the three who did the scalping. The only distinction he is entitled to is . . . [*unfinished sentence*]

The grades of merit awarded for the scalping of a woman at war are subject to the same rules. However, since a woman is merely armed with a small hatchet, the danger is not so great, and the outward token of distinction is accordingly less striking. Instead of a *kiliou* feather, a feather from any other kind of eagle is used, with two red marks, or only one, or none at all. Women at war do not have the right to touch the hair of a slain enemy warrior even if they reach the corpse before the warriors of their own side. I have already indicated what their trophy is should they succeed in going through all the motions. They may also wear the feather of an . . . [*space left here by Nicollet*] which they tie to their hair on the back of their heads letting it fall along their braids, in contrast to the *kiliou* feathers of the warriors arranged with as much elegance as taste on the top and around the top of their heads.[18]

This method of appraising bravery as well as the symbols used to identify the various degrees of merit are the same among all Indian nations of North America. The different echelons one encounters on

[18] The editor was unable to discover in sources contemporary with Nicollet or later what these other feathers might have been. For a thorough discussion of the awards system among the Chippewa, see Hodge, ed., *Handbook of American Indians*, 1: 354, 409; 2: 914.

the various scales of merit do not invalidate the generally accepted principle. The Sioux, for example, take into account four successive scalping operations on an enemy killed in action. The first to do it wears the feather with two red marks standing straight on the top of his head. The other three follow the rules quoted above except that the feather is worn inclined on the head.

I have read in several books and have heard several people maintain that scalping is always performed on people alive.[19] Some distinctions should be underlined here. The operation as I described it, in addition to the fact that it involves so much danger, demonstrates that this is quite impossible among natives. A brave dashing toward an enemy who has just collapsed makes a point of moderating his impetuosity as he nears the body, and if he is fortunate enough not to have had his temerity chastised by a bullet coming from the body lying on the grass, he will only close in after ensuring his own life with a rifle shot triggered by the slightest convulsive quiver. And the apprehension inspired by the body is still so great as he is about to touch it, that before pulling his knife for scalping he prods it several times with his spear or *pâkâmagôn*.

Therefore it is presupposed that the operation of scalping can be carried out without any danger. Since in the minds of the natives there is no idea associating itself with this total absence of danger other than that of acquiring a mark or concrete token of their triumph or successful revenge on their enemy, they are apt to scalp harmless women wherever they come across them and also white people that are only wounded. This is evidenced by their tales of war with the French, English, and Americans. These peoples, waging war as an art based on principles, do not use guile en masse any more than they suspect their enemy of using it on an individual basis. But to my knowledge there is no evidence of natives plotting to capture and attack an enemy, white or red, for the cruel sport of scalping him alive. Such an act would not increase their prestige in the first place, and, to be sure, the chasing of one person by several others is a victory they consider to be already too flimsy to warrant any additional degradation

[19] See, for example, John Long, *Voyages and Travels of an Indian Interpreter and Trader*, 58–60 (London, 1791); Jean-Bernard Bossu, *Travels in the Interior of North America, 1751–1762*, translated and edited by Seymour Feiler, 65 (Norman, Oklahoma, 1962). Those who maintained in Nicollet's day that Indians always scalped people alive were not among the serious students of Indian life and culture.

by a useless act of cowardice. Hence, between them, the challenge consists in being the first to fell this enemy with a rifle shot and then in being the first to scalp him.

It is the enormous importance attributed to scalps as an emblem of heroism that explains the absence of mercy and the cold-blooded cruelty with which they conduct themselves toward an enemy reduced to powerlessness by the odds surrounding him. For him to drop his weapons and plead for mercy would be all in vain. The massacre continues. A concentration of executioners bring their hideous faces so close together towering over him that all else is blotted out. There will be no prisoners taken, unless, as sometimes happens, an individual raises his voice to say that he will keep some under his protection or will see to it that some be put under the disposition of families that might have sustained losses at war. History tells us of the fate reserved formerly for prisoners taken by the Iroquois and other nations. It also relates to what extremes of grief certain generous men would venture in order to save those they had decided to adopt from the fury of warriors still deprived of tokens of valor and last to reach the scene of triumph. Today these last obstacles still exist, but such prisoners are no longer destined to fire and torture. If their protectors succeed in keeping them safe all the way home, their fate no longer calls for pity. There are Sioux prisoners among the Chippewa and Chippewa prisoners among the Sioux. Either way, men, women, and children seem to be happy enough to decline the possibilities of repatriation following prisoner exchange agreements linked to pacification parleys between the two nations. There are also women on either side who have been scalped some time or other and who do not appear to be any the worse for it other than having part of their skulls deprived of natural protection against the wrath of the elements!

On my return to St. Peter from the sources of the Mississippi, I learned that toward the end of July [1836], seven or eight Sioux from the Lake Pepin band paid a visit to some twenty Chippewa women of the St. Croix River picking blueberries. On their return, these gallant neighbors told how they had contented themselves with killing and scalping one of these women and scalping four others.[20] The chief of this band, who reported the event to the agent at St. Peter [*Taliaferro*], added for the sake of conversation, "My young men could

[20] According to Taliaferro's journal, August 6, 1836, the incident occurred near the Chippewa River, not the St. Croix.

have killed and scalped all of them, but they limited themselves to the exact revenge we owed the Chippewa of St. Croix these last four years. There was a man among these women who fired and fled. It was lucky for him and the women that he missed, for had he shot someone I don't know if my warriors would have been satisfied with the life of a fifth woman to offset the loss of their comrade."

In this case, the Chippewa of the St. Croix appear to have been the instigators of the trouble. In 1831, they indeed cut the hair of four young Sioux from Lake Pepin, and in 1832, they killed and scalped a woman from the same band. It would seem that the two nations have now settled their dispute on the frontiers of their territories. Time will tell whether or not the Chippewa themselves were not settling an account for an outrage endured beforehand and if all this is not a direct consequence of the law of retaliation that inflames the hostile disposition of these nations as far back as one can remember, furthering its cause first in one direction, then in another.[21]

To bring this chapter to a close I shall emphasize:

1. The arrival of various war parties on the rendezvous site — their songs and the order of battle observed by each squadron when it comes into view of those waiting, the welcoming musket fire, the shots fired into the waters of the lake.

2. The last military parade in the village, performed by all bands united — the young men that go to war for the first time, painted in black, concealed under their blankets, dispersed in the ranks without showing their faces. The purpose of this parade is to attract the reluctant ones who could still increase the ranks. They march into the war lodge where arms and costumes are laid down. The farewell of the warriors to their families that very night: their sorrow, their mutual anguish; they even weep, these men we consider to be so indifferent; they weep, but only in their families, never before strangers; they give advice to their wives in case they should die — "If I do not return don't think about me, give me something to eat sometimes; you know I like tobacco and sugar, etc.; give me some whenever you can."

3. Departure of the whole party the next morning at the crack of dawn. Women, children, and the elderly sit sadly in their canoes on

[21] Warfare between the Sioux and Chippewa continued in a series of retaliations until as late as 1863, when the Sioux were removed from Minnesota. See Folwell, *Minnesota*, 1: 150–155; Warren, *History of the Ojibways*, 485–493, 499, 501–503; *St. Paul Pioneer*, August 19, 1863.

the river or lake, gloomily awaiting the separation. The *oshkabewis*, assisted by the soldiers, assembles the canoes of the war party, gathers them in a column, several rows attached together, the number of files being in proportion to the width of the river or lake which they must follow until they are out of sight of the village. On this particular morning the warriors are no longer permitted to speak to their families, neither can the latter come within close range of the warriors. The warriors leave the lodge of war, begin to sing songs of war, and file down to the point of embarkation. Everyone moves into his position, two, three, or four per canoe. The young ones going into action for the first time lie down flat in the canoes so as not to be able to see or be seen. This is prescribed so that their resolve may not be weakened at the sight of the anguish that overcomes the families returning to the village; also to avoid their leaving with impressions and memories that might deprive them of the courage and composure of which they will be in dire need. All the other warriors remain standing for the departure. The canoe transporting the *oshkabewis* is in the middle of the column, all banners deployed, the war branch hoisted with the calumet attached to it. The mouthpiece of the calumet is oriented in the direction of their destination so that the manitos of war may smoke and be favorable to their cause. The same canoe displays the flags of the war chief; it carries the various devices he will use in the ceremonies he will celebrate in order to see into the future. The column begins to move and the singing grows louder. Only the extreme left and right sides paddle, while the back row steers. As the column slowly gets under way in the midst of shouts and chants, a multitude of canoes carrying the people who will remain in the village silently crisscross each other in all directions, moving toward the head of the column, paddling and splashing away water behind them, simulating obstacles and handicaps to be overcome by the warriors, and also expressing their sorrow by gestures that seem to indicate that the warriors should not leave them. All these canoes seem to be searching for some detour or other, some small passage through which they can slip and block the way. The column solemnly advances, dispelling the vain obstacles. When it is no longer within sight of the village and the people have withdrawn, the formation breaks up and the vessels sail at will toward the place where they will abandon the river or lake to travel overland or to negotiate a portage leading them to another lake or river.

4. This embarkation scene, as well as the ceremonies and manifestations surrounding it, are the cause of solemn and dismal reactions, and one can well imagine the profound impression that seizes those who leave as well as those who remain home. The only place left where one can hope to witness such a solemn scene is among the Chippewa of the lakes and sources of the Mississippi, for only there can one find the right geographic conditions.

Before leaving the scene of embarkation the war chief reviews his campaign plan and makes a positive indication of the route and direction he will follow, of the place where he will halt, and where the campaign will end by itself, if up to this point the enemy has not been encountered. This is an essential duty the chief must perform, for the warriors pledged themselves to follow this plan exclusively and any deviation from it would disengage them from their word and expose the chief to massive desertion. After this briefing, the chief still hopes some belated warriors, impressed by the ceremonies, will have changed their minds and decided to catch up with the party. In order to pass information on to them, he draws the route they will follow on a piece of bark and fixes it on a pole stuck into the ground. (See chapter on figurative writing used by the Chippewa.)[22]

5. The war party continues its journey by portage from river to river, river to lake, etc., until they feel they have reached land where they might meet their foe. The canoes are left in a safe place, the soldiers leave the things that are not indispensable with the intention of picking them up on their return trip. Every night as they camp, the chief will perform, beyond the campsite, some conjuring rites in order to divine the whereabouts of the enemy, their number, etc. He invokes the birds of war. Here also one is inclined to think his implorations are solemn, that he is praying, that there is in him something of a man invoking God. But his incantations that seem to be so religious, that so greatly impress those who do not comprehend their meaning, are mere words making little sense, or boastful puerilities such as: "The birds listen unto me, I can imitate them, I can do just what they can do." The chief thinks he is a manito himself. And if perchance he foretells more or less the truth and is successful in his enterprise, then he is a great man!

6. Then they leave the canoes in a safe place, and the soldiers unburden themselves of what is not absolutely necessary, to be picked

[22] Only a fragment of this chapter was completed. See p. 266–275.

up on their return. On this journey one must survive, and each man brought only a few handfuls of flour or wild rice. During an expedition that may last weeks, sometimes months, one must count on food from hunting. To provide for this and yet maintain security, the chief has detached several men familiar with the land to go one or two days' march ahead. This *avant-garde* scouts the land, and when they observe something that should be reported, they retrace their steps until they find the party. Since the latter is scattered hunting and since they will only be reunited in the evening at the campsite selected in the morning, it is necessary to have conventional signs permitting them to recognize each other from a distance before they can actually distinguish each other. The Chippewa on such occasions use signals made with the blanket each one of them carries. The first man to notice another man holds up his blanket straight in front of him thus revealing it to the other man who sees it. If the latter answers with the same signal, he is a friend, if not, then one must be careful.

The signal they use to indicate that one must hide, either to avoid the enemy or to ambush him, consists in lifting up the blanket as before and then letting it drop. To indicate that one can show oneself and approach, they throw the blanket in the air holding it only by one end. If these warnings as well as others are not judged sufficient to bring in the scouts, pieces of bark on which a caution has been registered are simply left in places where someone from the party may pass, more caution is exercised, and the hunters stay closer to the meeting place.

The chief does not hunt; he follows the route stipulated in his plan. He is supplied by his troop as far as his subsistence is concerned, and, in return, if a certain warrior lacks tobacco, moccasins, etc., he will supply some, either from his own reserves or by intervening with those who have an ample supply of such articles.

6[*sic*]. When the enemy is believed to be only one or two days away, the party selects a secluded spot in a wood or somewhere else, where they unload some of their burdens, lay down their blankets and some of their clothes, provisions, etc. They then strip off practically all their clothes, besmear their bodies, keeping on only the manito war bird which is the fundamental headwear of the warrior. This depository is by the same token the place where they will meet again in case of a disorderly and precipitate retreat. One of their military tactics consists in trying to discover the place selected by the enemy for such a depository. When they do, men are detached to detour around the enemy while both armies march ahead and then clash. These men hide, and if theirs is the winning army and the enemy withdraws frantically toward the rendezvous depository, they kill the retreating warriors as they arrive. The retreat is then made in another direction, each man for himself, and the tardy are captured by the victors. Formerly they selected depository sites closer to the battlefield, a few hours before the parties actually met, but experience has taught them to choose locations somewhat more circumspectly.

7. According to the superstitious beliefs of the natives, all these details of precautions, ceremonies, customs, and observances related to preparations for war and campaign preliminaries are indispensable if their enterprise is to be crowned with success. The slightest oversight on the part of the chief displeases the manitos and gives the men a perfect right to denounce their pledge to him and to abandon him, even in danger, without drawing upon themselves the contempt befitting cowards.

The Chippewa of the Mississippi tell of an event that took place in the preceding generation, one which in their minds justifies the necessity of not deviating from the rules passed down by tradition on this subject. The Sioux had murdered an isolated woman, and the circumstances surrounding this crime were such that the tribe of Leech Lake was stirred to the point of rage. This woman's brother refused to let a single hour pass by without carrying out the vengeance to which his affection for his sister entitled him. In less than three days he was on the warpath accompanied by twenty men, all volunteers. They happened to lose track of their foe but came across four other lodges belonging to Sioux families on a hunting trip and wiped them out. Dazzled by this first success, they went looking for more and this time stumbled on an encampment of forty lodges of the same nation. The latter made them pay dearly for their temerity, for only one man returned from this expedition, and the Chippewa maintain the manitos had made them mad for not having performed the preliminary ceremonies of war prescribed by the rites.[23]

All this explains why the natives talk so much of war and are so long in preparing for it. Their rules compete with the necessities of

[23] No incident clearly resembling this one has been met with in other accounts.

hunting at certain seasons to feed the family and to collect enough supplies for their absence. For this reason also most projected wars fail even to develop.

To these causes one must add still another: the right of each warrior member of the medicine society to perform his own conjuring ceremonies, to dream, and to see into the future. To be quite specific, drafting men is of no avail to the chief, brings no security, for their performance remains subject to the powers of their personal manitos. If such a warrior happens to dream that the enemy will not be met, or that the odds are hopeless, he will simply withdraw of his own accord; his withdrawal will involve others, and the campaign will either be a fiasco or a defeat. The records of the French, English, Americans, etc. are filled with such examples. Tanner, in the narration of his adventures, repeatedly adds more, taken from his own experience.[24]

All these considerations tend to invalidate the reputation of virtuous courage acquired by the natives. The more I observe them and think about it, the more I am convinced that their institutions are contrived to justify or motivate their cowardice — all this in spite of a great number of extraordinary men they have had and still have, but whom I consider as being exceptions. There is too much bragging and blustering among them. A mediocre warrior is held in such high esteem that cowardice has to be the criterion they are reduced to, or has to be their common denominator. I am referring to natives as they are described in three centuries of history and as my own experience for the last four years has shown them to me. Their disposition toward vengeance, so often mentioned, that cold-blooded cruelty that characterizes them so, etc. — these are not inner drives or part of their constitution but proceed from their institutions and from their educations.

8. Describe the improvised fortifications built when encampments of hunting expeditions are attacked by surprise; the redoubts surrounding the trenches within the lodges themselves where women and children hide when they find time enough to build such fortifications; the redoubts at the mouth of the St. Francis [*Elk River*]; and those on the rivers that flow into Red River where the Chippewa and Sioux fight most often.

[24] John Tanner, *A Narrative of the Captivity and Adventures of John Tanner*, 87, 125, 141 (New York, 1830).

9. Signal used when returning = 2 quick strokes — 1 stroke — 2 quick strokes.

Signals when one is lost [*one word illegible*]

Fire signals set in specific points — forest and prairie fires.

10. See chapter on death, for details supplementing this chapter concerning warriors dying on the battlefield.[25] Warriors prefer to have their bones spread out over the prairie rather than to be buried in a place where women can trample their remains. They consider it an honor to be scalped. Not to be scalped is a sign of contempt. That is why they decorate their heads so. When a warrior is slain, they dress him with their most precious things, place him against two stakes, put a pipe in his mouth, a rifle in his hand, and turn his head toward the enemy.

The Sioux and the Chippewa sometimes open up the body of an enemy slain in battle, draw a few drops of blood with their hands and swallow them. Most individuals then spit them out, but the bravest swallow them.

Men of the same nation fighting among themselves do not scalp one another.

[25] This chapter has not been found.

Stages in the Life
of the Indian

BIRTH AND ITS CEREMONIES: *WINDAWABOWIN*

Toward the end of her pregnancy, a mother prepares a crib with its linings and trimmings.[1] She prepares two other articles, both symbols of the hope that is soon to be realized one way or the other. These articles are a little pair of leggings, and a small skirt, both to become the outward signs of the sex of her offspring. If she gives birth to a boy, the little leggings are attached to an arch of wood forming a sort of guard over the crib above the baby's head. If it is a girl, the leggings are put aside and the skirt is attached. Natives do not ask one another if the child in the crib is a boy or a girl; one look at the object attached to the arch and they know.

In the chapter dedicated to medicine I shall explain how deliveries take place.[2]

The newborn is washed with cold water. The umbilical cord is knotted. Some cut off the part now useless, others leave it till it falls off of its own accord. In both cases, a pretty little pouch made out of skin, trimmed with beads by the Chippewa, with porcupine quills by the Sioux, is manufactured beforehand as a receptacle for it. This little pouch becomes a relic, and it is also attached to the canopy next to the leggings or skirt. Other trinkets are added and the lot composes the ornaments of the crib, later to become playthings for the child.

When a child is born in a place where there is a substantial population, the event leads to a practice seldom observed by strangers. If the newborn is a boy, the men of the village take up their arms and

---

[1] For further description, see below, p. 188; Appendix 5, p. 255.
[2] This chapter was never written or was lost.

go to sing and dance around the family's lodge, firing shots. The band enters, and one of its leaders offers the child a small rifle carved out of wood and delivers an oration that implies more or less the following: "I found your rifle. It seems you did not take good care of it. We bring it back to you. Here it is. Indeed you must hunt to survive and you must defend yourself when the enemy strikes. Keep it safely."

If the newborn is a girl, congratulations are proffered by the women of the village. They all take up the domestic hatchet, singing and dancing around the lodge and making gestures of women busy chopping wood. Then they enter and offer the baby a little hatchet made from wood saying: "We found your hatchet. It appears you did not take good care of it. We bring it back to you. Here it is. Indeed you must chop wood to stay warm, and chop more wood to fortify your lodge should the enemy attack. Keep it safely."

The songs appropriate for such a congratulatory visit are the following for the women: "*Kidabakite, kidabakite, kidabakite* — You shall strike, you shall strike, you shall strike. *Hen! hen! hen!* — Yes! yes! yes!" They pretend the baby girl answers "yes" to their utterance, "you shall strike." The men sing: "*Ayabe obikwôd, ayabe obikwôd, ayabe obikwôd. He-hen! he-hen!* etc." They pretend the baby answers "oh yes!" to their chanting "*ayabe obikwôd*," an equivocal phrase referring indirectly to the organ characterizing the male. Both songs can be heard far away announcing the event that has just taken place to all the families around. Needless to say, the family treat the visitors as best they can, giving them something to eat.

When the anxieties of the delivery and its consequences are over for the family, the father prepares a banquet which the baby is supposed to be offering. If it is a son, the father invites one or two of his male parents or friends and says to them, "He that you see in the crib is happy to have come to earth, happy to see that which he has never seen. He shall stay with us as long as he shall live; it is his pleasure to hold a feast and here is that which he has to offer; he gives it unto you; do with it what you will." These first two guests, after having estimated the quantity of things offered to eat, go and invite other friends, limiting the number to the amount of food available. But all must be men.

If it is a girl, the father invites one or two female parents or friends and talks to them in the same way. These persons proceed with the organization of a banquet to be attended exclusively by women.

When the feast is ready and the guests are gathered, one of the two first guests who conveyed the other invitations speaks and sets forth the object of the banquet, the feelings of the newborn who is offering the feast. He brings his oration to a close by saying *"Eshiwikomigoy-ang* — That is why we were invited," and they all answer with the exclamation of gratitude so well known among the natives, "Ho! Ho!" When all has been eaten, the orator says, "You may go when you wish." A similar ceremony is performed by the women.

During the entire ceremony, the father and family remain neutral and do not take part in the banquet. Only in a time of grief, when it is presumed the family has little or nothing left, does the manager of the banquet tell the *mizhinâwe* (the appointed waiter) to give them something.

I was never able to discover, in spite of all the information I gathered, anything leading me to believe the natives had superstitions like those inherited by Europe from the Orient, superstitions related to such things as predictions and predestination which in turn lead to necromancy and astrology. They do not link the birth of a child with any particular natural phenomenon, neither with any disposition of the skies or the moon, nor with the seasons of the year. Nevertheless, a few respectable writers have given considerable credence to a contrary opinion.[3] I am inclined to believe they were mistaken in their interpretation of certain predictions sometimes made by medicine men with regard to some patient or other — predictions inspired by envy, jealousy, or some other cause of dissatisfaction leading them to condemn their patient. I shall point out in my chapter on medicine what circumstances drive these impostors into taking the liberty of making such predictions in order to appease the passions which guide them.[4]

I could detect only one superstition connected with birth: the one that dictates the date when names should be given to the newborn. These names are given only in spring or summer. While these seasons prevail, all the spirits are supposed to be about, and they are more willing to extend their protection. In the fall, however, they seek a

[3] The editor has been unable to determine what writers he referred to.
[4] Nicollet apparently did not develop this subject as fully as he had intended. See, however, below, p. 185, 217.

hiding place, and in winter they are completely concealed. Hence, if a child is born in the fall or winter, it will not be named until spring. Meanwhile, the mother will give the child a name reflecting her heart's sentiments and hopes. It will be a nickname which will either be forgotten or will stay with the people of the village, if by any chance these very people have not already given the baby a nickname of their own inspiration. Indeed, all Indians have such nicknames.

The name ceremony or *windawâbowin* (from the verb, *windon*, to name) is occasion for a banquet. If the child is a male, the father selects a godparent who must be a man. If it is a girl, the mother chooses a godmother. A boy has no godmother, a girl no godfather. A boy is named by a man chosen by the father, a girl by a woman chosen by the mother. That a man should never interfere with the education and destiny of a girl, and that a woman should never interfere with the education and destiny of a boy after he has left his mother's breast is a universal and constant principle among the natives of North America.

From then on, the notions and conceptions of the natives are involved. As these convictions combine with other concepts passed on at the various stages marking youth, adolescence, and manhood, their influence encompasses the whole life of the newborn. The father chooses a godfather among the other parents. This is *de rigueur*. He selects the one who has the most power (the actual expression used) — in other words, a man whose power is considered to be equal to that of the spirits in the arts of warfare, hunting, and healing. It is imperative that the manito godfather extend to the child not only his own influence, but also that of his manitos, and for this reason a godfather invariably starts out by giving to the child the name he received from his own godfather. Then he gives another name, one that is in harmony with his thinking. And these names should always recall the names of certain spirits or something suggesting power. The family and the village adopt one of these names and use it for the child. Such a name is called by the Chippewa *ôgitshizhinikazoowin* — his big name, the name that corresponds to our family name.[5] Here are some examples: *Mâkôdepiness* — Big Black Bird; *Kabibonoke* — He That

---

[5] Elsewhere (p. 187) Nicollet gives this as two words: *ôgitshi izhinikazoowin*. Edward F. Wilson, *The Ojebway Language*, 297 (Toronto, 1874), gives *ezhenekawsoowin* as meaning simply "name." Baraga (2: 196) defines *kitchiwawinikasowin* as "glorious name; holy name."

Makes Winter; *Ozhawash Kogizhik* — Blue Sky, etc. Sometimes the
father chooses two godfathers. In this case, one of them gives his
family name to the child and the other a name suggesting his way
of thinking.

The same notions transpire where girls are concerned. The name
must always refer to something having power or good qualities. But
it is also imperative that these names be inferior in power and in quality to the names of men. Thus Blue Sky, which is considered the
purest state of the sky, will be a man's name and cannot be given to a
girl. But a girl can be called: *Omiskwâkwâdokwe* — Red Cloud, or,
Sessegânokwe — Hail, or, *Mâwinas* — She That Weeps, or *Papikwe* —
She That Laughs. To demonstrate how serious they are about names,
let me mention that if a child is constantly ailing or unfortunate and
the family decides to consult a medicine man about it, the impostor
will conceal his ignorance or his vengeful motives with regard to the
godfather by recommending a change of name because the one the
child now has is that of an evil or weak spirit.[6]

As far as the banquet is concerned, the formula for the invitations
is the one adopted for all kinds of feasts. In the case of naming rites,
the father says to the godfather he chose, "My son gives himself unto
you, he wishes to become your roots and to perpetuate your name.
Here is that which he giveth unto you (pointing to the kettle and
dishes prepared). Do with these things as you will." The godfather
invites some men who quickly gather around the food. He makes a
speech revealing the object of the banquet: "This child gave himself
unto me, he wishes to be my roots and perpetuate my name. I give
myself unto him and the other children who like him shall be called
Mizhâkwôd — Clear Weather — *Mizhâkwôd Ôgaizhiwi inigon Wiga-
binojiyun.*" He adds a few more words about the event and closes by
pronouncing the words, "*Miyû ekeweyân* — It is the last sound from
my mouth," or, in other words, "I have spoken; I have finished my
speech." The participants answer, "*Hohô! Hohô!*"

Then they eat. The banquet is usually plentiful. The guests must
eat all they are given even if they should be inconvenienced. If, however, the helping was too large, there is a way to avoid indigestion.
It consists in presenting the remainder of the food to the child, pretending that he accepts it and keeps it. When one is hungry again one

[6] For an example in relation to the ceremony of the *jisakan*, see p. 217.

comes and finishes it. As the guests finish their meal, they turn over their plates and put the remaining bones in the kettle in which the meat was cooked. These feasts are enlivened by jokes and conversation. The godfather starts it with a song that precedes his oration. It is the only song allowed by tradition.

The father and mother are part of the festivity and, when all has been eaten, they proceed with the naming ceremony. The godfather takes the child from the arms of its mother and says to it, *"Niawê Mizhakwôdkadezhinikaz"* — My namesake, you shall be called *"Mizhâkwôd."* He then kisses the child and hands it to the neighbor on his right. The latter takes the child and says, *"Mizhâkwôdkadezhinikaz tshianimajikômigâg* — You shall be called *Mizhâkwôd* as long as the earth shall thrive." He kisses the child and hands it to his neighbor who pronounces the same words and so on until the child reaches the last guest, from whom the mother takes it.

This terminates the banquet and the participants leave at will. The bones of the banquet are rolled into bundles of hay and thrown into a river or lake, or for want of the latter, they are suspended from a tree in the forest so as to be out of the reach of animals. Since it is imperative that nothing resulting from this pure and simple ceremony be soiled, all that is edible must be consumed and the leftovers that are not edible must be put into the trust of the spirits of the air and water.

A custom observed by all the natives is never to pronounce the name of a person in his own presence. If it is necessary to mention an individual while the latter is not part of the conversation, terms describing him without ambiguity must be used. If such a person is part of the conversation and this person's name is brought up, mentioning it is avoided by giving a twist to the sentence. Such twists are proper to the nature of the language. Calling a person by his or her name is disrespectful; it is what we would call lack of manners, sheer rudeness. When they are with white people on the occasion of a council, nothing can cause more embarrassment than for the interpreter to find himself reduced to calling a name in order to make plainly understood the statements he is asked to translate. When there are native guests in the dwelling of a family, quite often children forget themselves on this point of Indian *savoir-faire*. One will notice at once the reaction of the father or mother, who will tell the child to keep quiet.

Or the children are warned to be careful and told that if they pronounce their own name they will not grow up.

This explains the strange reserve displayed by natives when they are asked their name. Travelers have interpreted this restraint in many different ways but always in a way derogatory to the character of these peoples. The name, or family name, that has been given to them and that they call *ôgitshi izhinikazoowin* is to them something sacred that they did not bestow upon themselves but that was imposed upon them. Hence they do not feel they have the right to tell it to anyone who happens to come along. Unless you are very close to an Indian he will not say to you, *"Mizhâkwôd nindizhinikaz* — I am called *Mizhâkwôd."* But after much embarrassment and confusion brought about by your question he will say halfheartedly, *"Mizhâkwôd izhinikazoowug* — They call me *Mizhâkwôd."*

Things are different where their nickname is concerned. This name can be pronounced when mentioning somebody even in the actual presence of this person. But this does imply that jest and familiarity are the common denominators of such a departure from the rules. Suppose an Indian pays you a visit and you give him something to eat. Should some sarcastic joker on the premises notice that your guest is eating greedily he might say to him, *"Windigong kidizhiwissin* — You eat like a giant."* Such an epithet could be adopted by women and children alike, who from then on will only call him *windigong ezhiwissinid* — he that eats like a giant. Such a name will stay in the neighborhood, and the same man may even acquire similar names in other places. But do not be afraid that this man will admit having such names if you ask what his name is or what they call him.

Their totem name is the only one they disclose without hesitation or reserve. It is not a sacred name, neither is it connected with any favors of the spirits. There is no mystery attached to it. The totem being an institution of a purely civic nature, they are inclined to quote with pride the name of the great family to which they belong. It is simply a collective name. To find out this name you should not say, "What is your totem?" You should ask instead, "Who is your totem — *Awenengin kitodem?"* He will answer, *"Mâkawâ* — the bear."

The given name and the totem name are those used indifferently to designate a respectable person who is absent. The nicknames are for the other cases, etc.

EDUCATION AND CARE OF THE CHILDREN

Of all the cribs I have seen in my life among civilized peoples or natives, I do not know of a kind that better fills the requirements of baby care and the reassurance of the mother's heart than the shape of the crib used by the Chippewa. I shall give a complete description of it and add drawings, showing how its very conception combines elegance and taste with the security and comfort of the child, how its practical aspects benefit the mother, while satisfying the pride of the whole family.[7] The materials used for the bed in the crib are wood rot, a particular kind of moss, and the down drawn from cattails gathered by mothers in the autumn and then treated in a special way.

A mother will not consent to weaning a child the first year unless she is compelled to do so for a good reason. She will feed it for two, three, or four years. One often sees a little boy leave the playground with his bow and arrow, find and unveil his mother's breast, suckle a few moments, then return to his game with his little friends. The mother is "queen" on this point. She cannot be overruled and, in fact, neither her husband nor anybody else will try to give her any advice. It is only during this period of time that she has any authority over her sons, that she can scold or spank them. However, she will not do so in the presence of the father. Only as long as the child cannot follow his father on his errands and hunting tours may she exert this authority.

Her authority over her daughter is a perpetual right that cannot ever be opposed. Never will the father interfere. In reference to matters of education, advice, scoldings, punishment, permissions, etc., the father is in charge of the sons, the mother of the daughters. If the father wishes to inform his daughter of something that might be to her benefit, he will only do it through the intercession of the mother and vice versa. It is a matter of tradition, of separation of duties in the family, and not a matter of one sex having power over the other.

As soon as a son is able to follow his father, you will never see the latter travel without the former. Hiring an Indian with children as a guide or hunter while omitting to tell him he can bring his son along is exposing oneself to being deserted by this Indian a few days later, or to having on one's hands an Indian so depressed and so numb that he

[7] Nicollet's complete description and drawings (if he made them) have not survived.

will fall sick. Take care of the son and be gentle to him while paying no attention to the father and you will have two beings devoted to you to the point of death. Do not neglect, either, to place father and son side by side. In the canoe and in camp, should the child inconvenience you or should he be troublesome, look into the eyes of the father, and, henceforth, however long a time you remain together, you will encounter nothing but good reasons for being affectionately close to both these beings. The same applies to the mother. There is no example of a father traveling with his daughter while the mother stays at camp or in the village, and vice versa.

As soon as a boy is able to walk on his own, he takes possession of a bow and arrows, even in the midst of nations where this weapon was abandoned long ago. The day he can venture alone several hundred yards from the village, he hunts birds, and his arrows are tipped with wide and blunt heads, capable of wounding only small animals while preserving the eyes of children. From this time onward the child always remains active. Observe him even as he lies flat on his stomach in the forest or on the grass. Should he notice an acorn or some fruit or other, right away he will plant two little twigs into it and there you have a body with two legs! Add another piece of wood, some grass or a piece of feather and now you have a man. In no time at all he assembles another man. A little red coloring, some sap squeezed from grass on some diluted soil, will differentiate them and the mock battle starts.

He makes his own bows, spears, his *pâkâmagôn;* he carves and sculpts bark, engraves with his knife. The day a little girl can stand on her own two feet, she begins to play with a doll, she weaves mats, baskets, makes little dishes out of birch bark, and helps her mother with the chores.

These young creatures have hardly reached the age of five when their minds are exposed to notions of hardship, endurance, and physical pain, the burdens they are apt to encounter in the course of their lives. They are told about fasting: "Go for a walk, run, hunt, cut down wood, stretch nets for catching fish, leave early in the morning and come back at night." The tradition is to blacken their faces before they leave. When they return in the evening they wash and eat the plentiful supper prepared for them by the father and mother. Such drills take place more and more often; they become longer and longer as the child grows stronger and older. The father conducts the fasts of the son, the mother those of the daughter. Once the instructions have been given, further directives are reduced to simple descriptive gestures that make a far greater impression upon natives than all the speeches one can possibly deliver. In the morning, the father takes a piece of coal, hands it to his son who smears his face with it and leaves on an empty stomach, armed with his bow and arrows, without being tempted by the breakfast that is being prepared. Should he not feel disposed toward carrying out a drill on that particular day, he will refuse the piece of coal. Nothing more will be said, and the father will await another day before repeating his symbolic gesture.

The mother's attitude toward the daughter is the same. The latter does not go hunting, but she spends the day cutting wood in the neighborhood, sewing outside the lodge, or, if she feels she can overcome the temptation of eating, she may stay at her mother's side. This sort of fasting recommended to the children of both sexes is called *kiigwishimowin*.

The purpose of blackening their faces in these cases is probably to conceal from others expressions of pain. The tradition is interpreted as a sort of physical exercise, because the parents tell their children to remain constantly busy and enterprising. They must learn not to falter under the strain of hardships, for during periods of misery they shall have recourse to the stoic virtues which alone can save them. They are also told that their fast will be a time for visitations from the spirits, that they shall learn to distinguish the one which will give himself unto them to be their manito.

They are taught early to endure physical pain without complaining, without revealing the slightest emotion. Tattoos impressed with needles stuck into pieces of wood are among the lesser pains they inflict upon themselves voluntarily. Such practices are not prescribed by parents; they are simply a matter of course among children of both sexes. They take small cylinder-shaped pieces of resinous wood and holding them against their hand, forearm, shoulders, etc. they put them on fire and let them turn into ashes in the very wound left gaping by the burning cylinder. The boy who can resist this pain *will be a man*, the girl, *a good woman* [italics Nicollet's]. If, on the contrary, the pain is not endured, faults contrary to these qualities are to be expected. There is more tattooing as the children grow, but neither among the Chippewa nor among the Sioux is it practiced to disfigure or render ugly. Girls tattoo two or three vertical lines on their chins.

Men tattoo the backs of their hands and their wrists. Chippewa some-times mark their totem between their shoulders.

Children know those games of dexterity played in our schools, such as the one that consists in disengaging a ring passed through a cord, and many others I am familiar with but that I cannot name without giving a description which would be a waste of time. I was taken aback one day when I ventured to teach them a few, for they started laughing at my expense as soon as my first movements indi-cated I was about to play one of their own games. Their skill at it showed how rusty I was! Their recreation games are the moccasin game, *makizinâtadiwin*; the dish game, *pâgeswin*; the little cone game, *pipinjigânadwin*. The latter is usually played by little girls and women. There are others for evening entertainment — guessing games for ex-ample, even or uneven numbers played with a certain number of pieces of wood. Men also take part in such games, but they also take more interest in them and display passion to the point of ruining themselves. They are always good sports, however, gay and forever in a happy mood.

The moccasin game is the merriest of them all because it is accom-panied by a song and often lends itself to laughter.[8] The quickest for winning or losing is the dish game. You may include among these games that of the ball or club: *paga adôwewin*, also some card games: *kwekiwebinibewin*, which though played with our cards, are different from our games.[9]

Here is a description of the game *makizinâtadiwin*, the game of the four moccasins. There can be any number of players. They are divided into two teams. There are four balls. One of these balls bears an inscription of sorts. The score is forty-four and the points are counted using little sticks. The person to start the game is selected by tossing a knife as we do a coin. This person takes the four [*one of which is marked*] balls and hides them under the four moccasins any way he wants, one in one, two under two etc. He sings and passes his hands above the moccasins over and over again so as to deceive the onlookers. His opponent lifts up the moccasins trying to guess under which one the balls have been placed. If he says, "I don't want it," as

---

[8] See Frances Densmore, *Chippewa Customs*, 114 (Bureau of American Eth-nology, *Bulletins*, no. 86 — Washington, 1929).

[9] Nicollet noted at this point, "Describe these two" but never returned to complete the section.

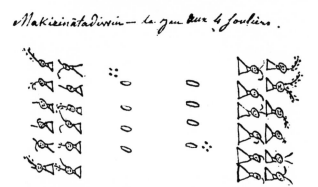

The makizinâtadiwin *or game of four moccasins*

he lifts the first moccasin, and the marked ball happens to be there, he gives up eight points. If the ball is not there he gives no points because he said he did not want it. If, as he lifts the second moccasin, he says again he does not want it, and the ball is there, he gives four points. If it is not — no points. The odds in his favor are now increasing because he has reached the third moccasin which he turns up declaring, "It is there." If it is not he pays six points. If it is, he takes the game and next time he hides the balls. The fourth moccasin is never lifted, because if the marked ball has not yet been discovered after the third, the person who did the hiding is entitled to another turn. It is therefore to one's advantage to be the hider as often as possible.

A child's first hunting success is marked by two feasts, one for the first bird killed, the other for the first four-footed or furry animal slain. This is the *oshkinittagewin*, from *oshki* — new, and *nittage* — a verb meaning to kill. They proceed with the celebration by sending invitations in the usual manner, but there is no particular ceremonial. The circumstances leading to the event are emphasized. The animal killed is placed in a dish of sugar or corn, etc., and the beak or head is left exposed. The bow and arrow are hung up nearby, and that is all. These symbols tell the whole story.

ADOLESCENCE [10]

During early youth the heart of the child has been trained to endure hardships and physical pain. The mind of a boy has been turned

[10] In the manuscript, this subheading reads "Adolescence, The Great Fast,

toward hunting and warfare so that he may become a man capable of supporting and defending a family, a man worthy of those marks of distinction that are the very motivation of the natives' ambition and pride. The girl has been oriented toward concepts of reserve, bashfulness, and modesty to a degree that defies civilized societies, and she fulfills the role allotted to women of good character.

However, this primary education was not proffered positively, dogmatically, *ex professo*. The teaching methods of the Indians are neither repressive nor preventive. They proceed by elimination and one learns what to do by dint of learning what should not be done. Their craving for liberty and individual independence is so great that from the day a child can stand on his own legs not a soul on earth would dare to give him an order. If he is sometimes spanked, it is only when he still depends on his mother's milk for food, because he cannot yet speak and can only comprehend the language of corporal punishment. Perhaps this temporary authority exercised by mothers explains their opposition to weaning their children early for fear of having to give it up. Corrections inflicted later on are alien to the customs and do not take place without the community calling the violator such names as brute or scoundrel.

The child that can speak and walk is free. He only needs physical strength to complete his separation from the family. Experience is his only master. If you spend an hour with a native family you will observe the children enjoying the wildest of frolics while their parents watch over them anxiously, never saying more than "*Kegu, kegu* — Don't do that, don't do that." They never caution to the point of telling the children what they should do. Should they have something important to prescribe or to recommend (please note I do not say to command) custom has provided a symbolic language to this effect and words are dispensed with. For example, note the way they present a piece of coal to children as an indication that they should fast. If a child misbehaves among his comrades, the law of retaliation, the fundamental principle preserving native society, applies, keeping the child on the straight and narrow. If he strikes someone, he is struck in return. If he steals, something is stolen from him. If he kills the dog of another family, the dog of his own family is killed. Only when

Marriage." Nicollet completed only the first section. Other notes relating to courtship and marriage are included in Appendix 5, p. 256–258, and Appendix 6, p. 265.

the parents catch the children in the act do they pronounce the only word they dare say: *"Kigimajidodôm* — You have done wrong," or *"Kigiminododôm* — You have done well." However, the law of retaliation only applies between parties of equal strength. Anyone who believes he can punish a young native for a prank makes a serious mistake. This to them is an act of cowardice, as it is with us, and a member of the family would consider it his duty to step into the balance and equalize the forces engaged.

In the course of their self emancipation, the children quickly realize that there is no better way to learn than to follow the example and listen to the conversation of their elders. Hence their respect for tradition, also for the things their fathers have to say. Natives do not argue; they do not reason; they always refer to what they heard in the course of the conversations of their fathers and grandfathers.

Indian Medicine Ceremonies

MADODISWŌN – THE VAPOR BATH LODGE

Among the Indians of North America, steam baths are not a matter of luxury and sensuality. Their usage is a sacred one, pertaining to medicinal rites.[1] The common man is banned from it, and it is authorized only in appointed cases and in accordance with prescribed forms from which there can be no deviations.

Let us first of all consider the construction of the lodge according to these rites. However many people are supposed to enter into the vapor lodge, its vault cannot have more than four or eight arched supports. Mark on the ground a square or octahedron. Plant a flexible branch from a young tree at each angle and fold these branches toward the center of the lodge making them converge at the pole of the base of the polygon. Tie the arcs together at their converging point so as to form a vault not exceeding a height of three or four feet. Form a noose halfway up the vault from thongs encircling the arched supports and tighten it to consolidate the whole frame. Cover with woolen blankets, leaving room for an entrance through which one can slip in and out, and the lodge is completed. A bed of sand is laid out at its center on which are placed some round stones, four or eight of them, according to the number of arched buttresses forming the lodge. These stones are heated outside and then brought in where their surface is sprinkled with water which vaporizes and fills the lodge with steam. Branches are laid out to serve as seats for the *midé*,

[1] The writers who preceded Nicollet generally failed to note the relationship between the vapor bath and the medicine rites. See, for example, Louis Hennepin, *Description of Louisiana*, translated by Marion Cross, 146 (Minneapolis, 1938); Alexander Henry, *Travels and Adventures in Canada and the Indian Territories*, edited by James Bain, 307 (Boston, 1901); Marc Lescarbot, *History of New France*, translated by W. L. Grant, 3: 185 (Toronto, 1907). The significance of the vapor bath is fully covered in Densmore, *Chippewa Customs*, 94.

or bathers.[2] Add a vessel containing water and two sticks tipped by sprinkling brushes for dipping and spraying water and you have a complete *madodiswōn,* built and ready to serve.[3]

Here are the circumstances for which the *madodiswōn* ceremony is prescribed:

1. The doctors who hold one another in high esteem and who adhere to the rites very rigorously must never open the *pinjigoosân* — a bag containing their drugs and their herbs — nor visit or inspect the plants without previously performing the steam bath ceremony.[4] If a native has been away for a long time, and if in the course of his travels his bag was exposed to humidity or to anything that might lead him to think the herbs had undergone a change, he builds a lodge and enters it. His wife heats the stones, brings them in, and makes sure the vapor stays inside. There the man smokes, sings, says some prayers, and comes out. He then prepares a feast for that evening or the next day. First he invites another doctor whose plants he declares he wishes to visit and to whom he also says he is offering a banquet. He asks the doctor to bring to the banquet any others he might care to invite. The latter goes about the business of the invitations using his own judgment, making no particular distinction between individuals, doctors or otherwise, but excluding women. The guests enter, rotate around the lodge following the direction of the sun, and sit down. Each man places before him an empty dish he has brought. Pipes are prepared and the signal to smoke is awaited. The man offering the feast says, "*Kanagakana.*" Everyone repeats, "*Kanagakana,*" lights his pipe and smokes. During the smoking session the man whose responsibility it was to make the invitations takes the kettle and passes around filling the dishes. The host gives a short address on the subject of the inspection of his medicine bag and ends by pronouncing, "*Kanagakana,*" which everyone repeats. Then they begin to eat. But before the first mouthful is swallowed, each places a morsel of food on the ground in front of him for the spirits. The dishes are turned over and everybody withdraws in a customary and prescribed order. He that

[2] Nicollet gives this word throughout as *midais,* the French phonetic spelling for the generally accepted *midé,* which Baraga (2:233) defines as an "Indian of the Grand Medicine."

[3] Baraga (2:204) gives this as *madôdisson.*

[4] For description and pictures of the medicine bag, see Densmore, *Chippewa Customs,* 93; Ruth Landes, *Ojibwa Religion and the Midewewin,* Plate 8 (Madison, Wisconsin, 1968).

The madodiswōn *or vapor bath lodge*

conveyed the invitations for the banquet stays with the host. Both
men inspect the medicine bag, mysteriously, assuring themselves that
there are no witnesses, not even a member of the family.

2. You wish to consult a doctor with regard to an important matter, such as a remedy or a secret, perhaps to inspire the love of a girl,
or maybe about a disease you do not wish to reveal. You prepare a
madodiswōn and invite the doctor in whom you place your trust.
You assist him in his ceremony, and, when he has entered the lodge,
you lie flat on your face to speak to him under the blankets. You give
him an account of your affair while making him offerings of tobacco,
fabric for making leggings, etc. "My grandfather," you say, "I wish,"
etc. You then withdraw while he smokes, prays, and sings. Meanwhile
you smoke to the divinities, especially the sun — this ceremony pre-
scribes it. He then goes on to a feast, as in the former case, where he
declares that a grandson has asked him for medicine of which he has
only a little left — he does not say for whom nor for what purpose.
The feast is held at your expense. The following day you go and fetch
the doctor again, not forgetting to bring more tobacco, sugar, and so
on, for the feast has consumed much of what you already gave.

When you have neither much time nor wealth to invest in such
consultations, there is a quicker way that is commensurate with one's
means. The institution of Indian medicine is accommodating. Always
divide your presents into two categories, one edible, the other useful.
Visit the doctor in the evening, tell him your trouble, and however
late the hour of the night, he will rapidly gather several colleagues
with whom to devour your small offerings, and he will say to them
he is sorry he disturbed them but that his grandson is pressed. They
will then withdraw, and those mysterious secrets that will make you

agreeable to the eyes of the cruel ones, or that will cure you of the love of those that were much too yielding, are bequeathed to you.

3. The *madodiswŏn* is sometimes practiced by a chief who has something to ask of his nation but who, deprived of some authority or power as a chief, seeks the sponsorship of the medicinal rites to impose his views. First of all he invites four *midé* for a steam bath. He expresses his views to them, and they in turn, guided by the chief's recommendations, invite scores of others. They dispatch the *oshka-bewis* all over the land, bearing small sticks, a foot long, painted in different colors. One is delivered to each person invited and a date is set. Those sticks that could not be transmitted because of the absence of the persons for whom they were intended are brought back to the lodge. The sticks are the instruments used to accompany and beat the rhythm of the chants sung under these circumstances, at which time drums are not allowed. On the appointed day, the guests arrive and enter the steam lodge in which they hear the message. They then deliberate on it among themselves, without the intervention of the petitioner.

The baths are followed by a banquet, a great feast, *wikondiwin*. Everyone withdraws. The lodge stands empty and around the stones from which arose the steam are arranged the little sticks of those who could not honor their host. The sticks bear witness to the fact that the absent ones were invited and are held as the consent of those for whom they had been intended. When I arrived at Leech Lake, Chief Flat Mouth had been away for two months visiting English trading posts where he requested ammunition for those schemes he had not yet given up.[5] Before his departure, he had held such a feast. I saw the *madodiswŏn* he built and about thirty to forty sticks, proof of the absence of some of the guests. In spite of this, a vast number of natives had attended the celebration, for the ceremonies had lasted nearly a week.

[4.] A person may also use the *madodiswŏn* to call upon his manito, his divinity. Here again, a steam bath is followed by a banquet held in honor of the divinity of the celebrant. It is he who takes the bath. As for the guests, they consume the banquet. In a case like this the lodge has an exalted purpose, and it takes the form of a temple dedicated to the individual's God.[6] Instead of eight arches and eight

[5] See above, p. 84n.
[6] Here Nicollet wrote: *"au Dieu de l'individe"* — to the God of the indi-

stones to heat, the lodge is composed of ninety arches and there are ninety stones. They do their best to build the lodge to the image of the manito.

Majigabo was calling on the bear, his manito, in this fashion when I passed Leech Lake the second time.[7] The celebration took place on the summit of the hill called Otter Tail Point. The population of the lake as a whole attended. In his prayer he declared, "You are sick, you are on the verge of death, and I bring you care. You shall be charitable unto me. You shall have pity on me if you do not perish. You have been a great spirit, etc."

5. The *madodiswōn* ceremonies are indispensable to those who wish to enter the society of medicine men. The request for initiation and the instructions to be received beforehand are subject to this ceremony.

THE *MIDÉWIWIN* [8]

The initiative of designating an individual to the pursuit of medical knowledge is not the privilege of the person having such a vocation. That is why all Indians are not *midé* as they would all like to be. No, such an initiative is the privilege of parents or friends influenced by a dream which revealed to them that such and such a person, a son, a daughter, or friend was not well, that something was opposing his or her existence, etc. Formerly a single person revealing such a dream about another person was justification enough for designating this person. This led to much abuse, and anyone could easily become a member of the *midé* society. There has been a reform of this abuse, and it is said that Flat Mouth was one of those who contributed most toward it. It is now necessary that two persons at least dream that so and so is going to die, in order that he may be nominated.[9]

visible. He probably meant to write: *"au Dieu de l'individu"* – to the God of the individual.

[7] For Majigabo, or Matchigabo, see above, p. 77–80.

[8] Nicollet spelled this word *midewin*. The editor will use the generally accepted form, *midéwiwin*. Logically this section begins here, and it is so arranged for the sake of clarity. In the manuscript Nicollet placed the heading seven paragraphs later, before the words "On the day of initiation . . ." For the most complete description of this ceremony, see Hoffman, in Bureau of Ethnology, *Seventh Annual Report*, 164–197.

[9] How lasting or widespread this reform was is open to question. See Hoffman, in Bureau of Ethnology, *Seventh Annual Report*, 163.

The candidate having made up his own mind, prepares a feast, invites four *midé* and tells them what his parents suggested, following their dream. He then states plainly he wishes to become a doctor. On the second day the candidate builds a *madodiswōn* for the four *midé*. Within it they decide upon another group of four *midé* who are necessary to complete a faculty of eight. This preliminary ceremony of the *madodiswōn* does not call for a banquet. On the third day, the candidate gives the eight *midé* another steam bath. He waits upon them and gives them what they need to smoke. At this point, the *midé* conferring among themselves decide how they will act upon the request. On the fourth day, there is another steam bath for the eight *midé* and they reveal to the candidate that they have agreed upon his initiation. They inform him it will be held at a certain date, usually a few months hence if the candidate's condition is not serious. For they believe that the revelation of great medicine saves the life of the person to whom it is revealed, and therefore the delay proposed varies with the amount of danger perceived in the candidate's ailment.

On the fifth day, in the evening, the candidate prepares a banquet. He invites the eight *midé* to it and the latter invite eight more, each one inviting another. However, these last guests can be either men or women, and they are selected in such a way that if the candidate is a male the number of men is greater than that of women, or vice versa if the candidate is a woman.

Before bringing in the last eight *midé*, the original ones who compose the regular faculty of eight have a secret ceremony with the candidate. When the new group of eight has been presented, a declaration is made to the effect that medicine shall be revealed to the candidate. A banquet is held. Each *midé* sings one or two songs, mixing in some dances. The ceremony ends late at night. To be described here: what I observed at the presentation of the Chief of the Land's daughter. The *midé* ceremonies are called *midekondiwin*.[10]

Nothing else is done until the time specified for the great initiation, a time such as the period when the natives returning from their hunting expeditions are gathered in large numbers. Spring is usually the season preferred. The candidate builds a new *madodiswōn* for the eight *midé* and the ceremony is followed by a feast. The number of

[10] The description suggested here was either never completed or has been lost. For Chief of the Land, see above, p. 8on. Tanner calls the ceremony *metai-we-koon-de-win*. See *Captivity and Adventures of John Tanner*, 285.

invitations for the feast is determined by the faculty. The faculty gives the candidate a number of sticks equal to the number of people invited, to be delivered one per guest, as a token of invitation. Two feathers of different colors are to be found among the sticks. The candidate has been told to whom they should be given. The two feathers designate the two "managers" who will conduct all the ceremonies on the day of the great initiation, making sure that everything is carried out according to the rites. Those that receive the feathers are fully aware of the honor the faculty is extending to them.

At the feast of that day, the faculty proclaims that the time has come that such and such a person shall become a *midé*, and that, conforming to the traditions and recommendations of their fathers and forefathers, it is imperative that the great day be preceded by three nights of medicine chants to the spirits. The feast takes place, and the congregation dissolves. The three following days are dedicated to chants sung individually at home. During the day, those who have private ceremonies to perform, such as the visitation or consecration of plants, make the most of this lapse of time. At night they sing in their lodges till the late hours. Certain departures from the rules have infiltrated these practices, and custom has given its blessing to a habit whereby those who are not doctors are allowed to share the widespread joy marking the preparations for the great event. Men, women, and youngsters go from lodge to lodge, dance and make merry. Food is handed to them.

On the fourth night, the eve of the ceremony, this merrymaking becomes, as they put it, respectable again. *Ómanajitonawâ* – they are observing moments of holiness so to speak. Those who are not doctors abstain from all disturbance. All the *midé* whose intention it is to attend the ceremony of the next day make for their respective homes and, according to the rites, open or seek out their *midewayanug* [11] bags, their costumes, and their instruments. The faculty is gathered in the lodge with the candidate who has brought all the spoils he is expected to furnish. Here the faculty informs him of all the tests he must pass the next day and the part he will have to play. He is being conditioned, trained, moulded, etc.

On the day of initiation the whole village is in a trance and beginning at dawn natives arrive from all directions. The *mizhinaweg*, the

[11] Plural of *midaiwâyân*. See above, p. 162.

two who received the colored feathers, proceed with the building of a large enclosure with two doors, or entrances, one facing east, the other facing the setting sun. Meanwhile, the faculty and the candidate are gathered before the lodge in which they spent part of the night, prolonging the instructions of the candidate. *Ôkagikimawân* — they give him advice. The gifts offered by the candidate are composed of blankets, fabric, kettles, rifles, traps, etc. in quantities large enough to make eight packages for the eight members of the faculty. Furthermore, there is a dish containing eight mouthfuls of something to eat called the *mideonagôn* — the dish of the medicine ceremony. The gifts are called *pâgijigônun*.

When the large enclosure or *midewigomik* [12] is completed, all the *midé*, men and women, gather within it and occupy their appointed seats. At this point, the way the ceremony begins varies among the nations. But these variations, which do not alter the basic principle of the celebration, are a mere consequence of local circumstances. I shall point out how the Chippewa proceed, and later on I shall indicate the modifications brought about by the Sioux.

When all is ready, the *mizhinaweg* notify the faculty, and its members make an exit, walking solemnly one at a time. The first to come out is the candidate. He carries a stick on which the gifts are suspended. (The presents that are not edible are called in the singular, *sasagiwijigôn*, in the plural, *sasagiwijigônun*.) The last to come out carries the *mideonagôn*. All are singing. The candidate says: *"Wâbâmishin, wâbâmishin, wâbâmishin,* etc. — Look at me, look at me, look at me, etc.; *ezhinagwiôyân,* etc. — behold the state I am in, etc."

They enter the lodge by the east entrance, the side of the rising sun, go around by the south, west, and north, and place themselves along the east side of the lodge, facing the center. The *mizhinaweg* take the gifts from the hands of the candidate and hang them up on two cords at a certain height.[13] The faculty makes another revolution, following the same direction, singing another tune to the following words: *"Anendayânine, anendayânine"* (repeated). *"Wemittigoshiwug omadindaganiwan nindayamoowan* — I have them, the goods from the whites."

[12] Densmore gives *midewigan* for the lodge in which the *midéwiwin* was held. See *Chippewa Customs,* 14.

[13] Here and at several other points in the description Nicollet refers to a drawing or diagram which has been lost.

When the song is finished after their round, the candidate and the eight pronounce loudly so that all can hear, "*Kanagakana*," and the audience answers in chorus, "*Na.*" The faculty rises, moves over to [another position] and sings a song: "*Nabek ôwibian manito ninda-nissa*—I could kill a spirit with my medicine bag made out of the skin of the male bear." (*Nabek ôwibian: ôwibian*, from *nib*, that with which he strikes in medicine, the granule of ceramics.) "*Nabek ôwibian*—My medicine bag from the bear, with which I kill, strike, blow the ceramics that strike you ill."[14]

The candidate kneels down on a spread-out blanket. The eight rotate around the lodge passing south and saying, "*Nikanug, nikanug*—My colleagues, my colleagues," hailing with their hands until they settle on the west side. Then they turn around and face the candidate. From this point, the eight start a series of eight revolutions around the lodge passing south, west, etc. They follow each other in line, but the eight revolutions are performed especially to demonstrate the power of the medicine to kill through testing it on the candidate. The leader, as he starts the first round, holds his medicine bag like a rifle, marches forward threatening the candidate with a shot he is about to fire with his bag shouting, "*Hohohoho! hohohoho — hoho! hoho! — ho!*" The candidate trembles, but he is only wounded by this blow. Whereupon the faculty moves over to the north end, at its appointed place, and the candidate sits down before the faculty.

[There] are two hearths where fires are kindled for no reason other than to light pipes during the intervals, or to have a source of heat should these events take place during a cold season.

[There is] a post called *midewatig*. It has a base of several inches and a height of three to four feet. It is painted to suit the fancy of the *mizhinaweg*.

Looking south and vis-à-vis the faculty are the singers with the drum *mittigwâkik*, and the *shishigwân*[15] for accompaniment, and a little mallet for beating the drum called *pagaâkookwân*. One of the eight delivers an oration on the power of the manitos, their power to

[14] In this and later references to a "granule of ceramics," Nicollet apparently meant the *migis*, a white shell of sacred significance used in the rite. See Hoffman, in Bureau of Ethnology, *Seventh Annual Report*, 167, 191, 234.

[15] *Shishigwân*, sometimes spelled *shissigwân* by Nicollet, is a rattle. Baraga (2:174) spells it *jishigwan*; Henry, *shishiquoi* (*Travels and Adventures*, 115); and Tanner, *she-zhe-gwun* (*Captivity and Adventures of John Tanner*, 135).

heal or to weaken, power passed down to the *midé* after having been transmitted from generation to generation.

After the address, the candidate rises and walks around the lodge, making a stop in front of each member of the faculty. To each one in turn he addresses a word of greeting, emphasizing this by a gesture of the hand as if he were counting them, or giving them his blessing. White people watching the ceremony are unusually fascinated by this part of the ritual. Yet it is nothing more than a family word of greeting expressed to each member of the faculty depending on his age or sex in relation to the candidate's own, such as, "My father, my uncle, my cousin," or "My aunt, my cousin, sister." And he says to each one, "*Shawinimishim* — Have mercy on me, pity me, be charitable unto me."

The eight file off again and complete their first round. Then they start another, but this time the leader is the one who was second the first time, while the one who struck the candidate just now is at the end of the line. So in the course of this second revolution, the second member of the faculty will be the one to strike with his medicine bag as he passes by the candidate also threatening with the words, "*Hohohoho! hohohoho! hoho! hoho! ho!*"

The third round is headed by the third member of the faculty who will follow the same ritual, and so on, until it is time for the eighth round. This one will be more impressive and more conclusive. Through the seventh round the candidate was merely wounded. Now he must be killed! And this is the task of the last of the members of the faculty who is holding the medicine bag made out of a bear's skin, the power of which was praised in the preceding song. This song would have been different had they used a different kind of bag.[16]

The one who is to kill the candidate makes an oration before starting the eighth round: "Here is a medicine bag handed down to me from my grandfather by my father. My father said unto me that I could never miss my mark when using it. But I am old, my colleagues, help me that I may find the strength to blow, to fire upon this man over there on his knees! There is a red mark upon his heart. I shall strike there and my medicine bag shall not fail me." And he begins to threaten, '*Hohohoho! Hohohoho!*'" He moves gradually toward the

---

[16] Bags might be made of many things, including weasel skin, mink skin, wildcat paw, and rattlesnake skin. See Densmore, *Chippewa Customs*, 93.

candidate, followed by the other seven members. As soon as he is within reach, he fires saying, "*Ho!*" and the candidate falls dead.

From time to time, they add some artful tricks to this particular part of the ritual. For example, they trace a red mark on the spot where they decide to strike the candidate. Sometimes they place on that spot a little drum with a mark in the center, and the drum is pierced when the *midé* fires, or rather, the candidate pierces it as he falls dead.

Now has come the time to prove by the candidate, that if the medicine has the power to weaken and kill, it can also heal and resuscitate. When the candidate collapses, a frenzy seizes the assembly and the people. The singers move over to the pole and dance around it playing the *shishigwânun* and the drum. Every assistant of the *midé* rises to beat the rhythm, and the members of the faculty stand around the dead one covering his body with their medicine bags. A few moments later, they try to lift his body carefully, hoisting it on its feet, punctuating its gradual return to life with shouts, "*Ya-ha! Ya-ha!*" The candidate is now up on his feet—revived! So they give him some medicine to drink, and there he stands, in perfect health. He is now initiated. He has the power of medicine, a fact the remainder of the ceremony is about to prove.

His first act consists in acknowledging every member of the *midéwiwin* as his colleague. Thus far he called them father, brother, cousin, son, mother, aunt, sister, etc. Now he will greet them with the title, *nikanug* (my colleagues). He walks around the lodge pronouncing this title, and moves closer to the faculty where his diploma is handed to him by the member who gave him the *coup de grâce*. The diploma is in the form of a medicine bag that confers the power of medicine practice and a granule of ceramics, symbol of disease that one can either communicate or heal. He walks around the lodge again, with the gifts this time, saluting the assembly with the title, *nikanug*. He then moves over to the west side where he sings the following song (the singers sing it for him if he cannot sing): "*Migayenin endiyân midewug endowad*—I also am as the *midé* are."

He will now demonstrate that he can make himself ill and then cure himself. He moves in front of the faculty and swallows a granule of ceramics—a disease, that is. He goes farther around, returning to the west side, shouting, "*Nikanug, nikanug.*" There he is stricken and falls. He is seized by convulsions, the disease smothers him, but he has the power and he shall vanquish it; he drags himself toward the faculty and, making a last convulsive effort, he restores the granule of ceramics. The faculty assists him in his efforts, saying, "*Yâ aaa! Yâ aaa! Yâ aaa!*" over and over. He picks up the ceramic granule and places it in the head of the medicine bag to use when the opportunity arises.

The candidate sits down. He is about to be granted the right to attend the *midé* banquets. This ceremony consists in his consuming the eight mouthfuls in the *mideônagôn*. They are fed to him one by one, each member of the faculty administering a mouthful. He has but to open his mouth, the food is introduced, and he gulps it down assisted by such cries as, "*Yâ! Yâ aaa! Yâ Ho! Hohoho.*" (I took particular note of all these interjections because they are as amusing as they are suggestive of the gestures they emphasize.) The mouthfuls are called *midewissiniwin*—the food of the *midé*.

When this initiation repast is over, the choir sings to its heart's content. Meanwhile, the initiate or novice goes to take the gifts that had been suspended. As he passes the pole he says to it, "*Migwetch kâshâwenimiyun*—I thank you, for you had pity on me." He then distributes the gifts to the eight, saying to each one, "*Migwetch kâshâwenimiyun,*" adding to these utterances of gratitude the title of father or brother, etc., depending on the age of the person he addresses in relation to his own. Thus he says, "My brother, I am grateful unto you for you had pity on me."

He will now test the power of his own medicine, and he begins on those who are reputed to be the strongest—the members of the faculty. He will go around the lodge eight times and each time he passes before the faculty he will *blow out* [*as a candle*] or *strike* one of its members with his medicine bag. The latter collapses; he is ailing, but he is cured instantly and rises again. It is enough that the victim make a face, thereby proving that the blow had an impact. The words used to describe this act, *to blow*, or *to shoot* with the medicine bag are the same ones used to describe the shooting of an arrow with a bow, the verb *pimowen* (imperative=*pimowe, pimowem*).[17]

After having made these experiments with the faculty, he will do likewise with the singers. They hand over their instruments to the faculty, who continue the singing while the novice makes another eight rounds on each one blowing out a singer. When this is done he

[17] Nicollet apparently had difficulty finding a word to express this action. The italics are his.

moves over to the faculty, and as he goes by the pole he says to it again, *"Migwetch kâshâwenimiyun."* Before sitting down, he raises his hand as if he were blessing the assembly and proclaims, *"Nâ, nikanug, nikanug, kanagekana."* The assembly replies, *"Nâ."* The novice sits down, smokes, rests, and all has been accomplished as far as he is concerned.

Now a ceremony takes place that one could call the grand finale of the manifestation. It is as amusing to the participants as it is fascinating to the spectators. Inside the lodge, the whole assembly is in a turmoil. The faculty members have kept the instruments and go on singing. In the course of this commotion or frenzy, the medical body is splintered into groups, each group being characterized by a certain type of medicine bag. To accomplish this, some begin by going around the lodge depositing their bags in a certain place on the ground. They keep going around, and each member puts his bag on the pile made up of bags identical to his. After two or three rounds, there are different piles of bags on the ground, some made out of otter skins, others made out of owl skins, others again out of martens, eagles, etc. Then each member stands beside the pile containing his bag, and the sections are now formed. Then the bags are retrieved, and more rounds of the lodge are completed to the sound of chants and the instruments. The object of this dividing into sections in the course of the melee is to demonstrate that the various kinds of medicine all have the power. They now prove it by blowing each other out in a long-lasting and most entertaining squabble.

The conclusion of this celebration is supposed to take place at the setting of the sun. The grand finale is extended long enough to make it last until the exact time prescribed by the rites. Some time is kept aside for the banquet, which brings the ceremony to an end. Then one withdraws to one's dwelling where each doctor has yet to carry out the ceremony of closing his medicine bag. This cannot be done without another banquet even if it means consuming a mere handful of sugar. But these last rituals can actually be postponed until the next day, even for two or three days. This explains why private conferences taking place in various lodges last for several days after the *midéwiwin.*

As far as the novice is concerned, he still has to equip his medicine bag, his pharmacy, his *pinjigoosân.* The day following his initiation, he prepares a *madodiswôn* and invites the eight members of the faculty. They gather and deliberate among themselves on the kinds of plants they shall give their new colleague. Since there are eight members, the vapor ceremony must be carried out eight times, but the novice does not have to offer a banquet. However, he waits on them while they perspire and all the while renders homage to the sun by smoking. This ceremony lasts eight days, but it can be reduced to four if two steam baths are given daily, one in the morning, the other in the evening. The eighth time, the initiate is admitted with the faculty. They instruct him on the plants and their properties. This plant is that of such and such a snake, you must use it in such a way under the following circumstances; this one is that of the bear, that one of the *missabé*, etc.[18] These definitions mean that the spirit of the plant is the divine factor giving the plant its virtues and that it is this spirit which must be invoked in order to make such a plant effective. If the wrong manito is invoked or if a doctor does not reveal the real manito of a plant, all is lost. Finally, the novice offers a banquet that will mark the closing of his medicine bag.

The *midéwiwin* is a great manifestation among all the native nations of North America.[19] In the order of their religious ideas, it is their most solemn, their grandest ceremony, excepting the feasts following declarations of peace or war. One cannot imagine it without actually witnessing its performance among nations that have not yet dispersed or whose mores have not yet been adulterated by mingling with the whites.

The Chippewa of the sources of the Mississippi carry out these ceremonies with taste, in an orderly fashion, and with good co-ordination. They add wit and gaiety, and the crafty tricks they include are executed with finesse and skill, creating suspense and hilarity. All this seems to indicate that the puerility of their beliefs was inspired by the cleverest among them, and that they feel such happenings are only fit for entertaining the simple and deceiving the gullible.

[18] Elsewhere (below, p. 212) Nicollet defines this word as "the manito of hunters." Baraga (2:252) spells it *missâbe* and defines it as "giant."

[19] This statement is true only if interpreted to mean the general practice of medicine and of magical rites. The Midéwiwin Society itself, properly speaking, was limited to the Chippewa, although very similar rites were practiced by other tribes belonging to the widespread Algonquian linguistic family and also by neighboring tribes as indicated in Nicollet's description below of medicine ceremonies among the Sioux. See Hodge, *Handbook of American Indians*, 1:38–40, 836–838; Warren, *History of the Ojibways*, 77–79; Hoffman, in Bureau of Ethnology, *Seventh Annual Report*, 154, 160.

The Sioux, on the other hand, carry out these ceremonies with much gravity, little co-ordination, little intelligence, and no taste. But they seem to be aroused by such a strong faith, and they apply themselves with a candor, simplicity, and naïveté so thorough that one is necessarily interested (though from a different point of view) and inclined to overlook the awkwardness and irregularities with which the climactic parts of the rites are performed. By the same token, there remains something primitive, coarse, and barbaric among the Sioux, something the Chippewa, who are definitely more refined, no longer entertain. The Chippewa, who are also more intelligent, are better prepared for reform brought by civilization. For example, with the Sioux, the candidate is naked down to his waist, and below down to his toes. Their *midéwiwin* takes place in winter, and the candidate has to undergo temperatures ranging from 12° to 15° below freezing point for eight to ten torturous hours. It is a fact, however, that they are more humane toward women candidates, whose initiation is always postponed until spring. The Chippewa banished the nudity of the candidates, and if the initiation happens to take place during a cold spell, the festivities are celebrated in an enclosed and heated arena. Furthermore, the candidate, man or woman, will make his appearance dressed in the richest, the most beautiful and classical costume of his sex in line with the customs of his nation. A stranger cannot but admire the taste and artfulness revealed by the Chippewa in their way of reconciling elegance with the customs and requisites of modesty and decency.

The Sioux do not make much of an outlay for their costumes or for their general attire at the *midéwiwin* celebrations. They attend dirty and ragged, and their medicine bags do not conform to the rites. The women are infinitely better, and the most industrious among them appear in clothes trimmed with porcupine quills of great beauty. It is regrettable, under the circumstances, that some of the most handsome specimens of mankind, perhaps, in the whole world, should be indolent and indifferent to the point of neglecting to appear to the benefit of their inherent advantages. It is not so with the Chippewa. To them, these celebrations are a matter of national pride for which men and women prepare themselves long in advance. Thus they appear endowed with the advantages befitting their inclinations and traditions.

To get a good idea of the national costumes and traditions of these native nations, observations should be made during such celebrations rather than in times of war. In war their attire is motivated by one single objective, that of appearing hideous and terrifying. In such times, the predilections and customs of the nations are without meaning. Observe the Sioux or the Chippewa on the battleground, and you can hardly distinguish them. Observe them at a civil or religious ceremony, and there can be no confusion.

There is, nevertheless, a particular part of the *midéwiwin* that is more stately, more imposing, and more impressive among the Sioux than among the Chippewa or any of the other nations among whom I witnessed this manifestation.[20] It takes place at the beginning of the ceremonies when the medicine men enter the enclosure where the initiation will be held. The differences between the various ways of effecting this entrance do not lie in differences in the rites but are controlled by the geographical distribution of the nations on the territory they occupy.

The Chippewa are dispersed in bands too far apart for them to be able to invite one another and to gather together to give more pomp to their ceremonies. Each band relies on itself for a celebration on its own grounds, and it seems that Leech Lake is the only place where, thanks to a population of more than a thousand souls, one can observe such festivities at their best. With the Sioux, on the contrary, the seven tribes which compose this great nation are divided into small villages never too far apart to prevent them from visiting each other after a day's march.[21] When a *midéwiwin* is to be celebrated in a village, one can be sure all the other villages of the same tribe will send their delegations.

I attended several such celebrations held in winter and spring by the people of the lakes, *mendewakantous*.[22] The most spectacular took place on February 15, 1837. They were celebrating the initiation of the son of Big Soldier, a village chief on the Mississippi, nine miles

[20] Since Nicollet's journals of his travels elsewhere are missing, it is not known what tribes he observed other than the Chickasaw, whom he mentions by name (below, p. 222).

[21] The seven tribes of the Sioux referred to by Nicollet were: Mdewakanton, Wahpekute, Sisseton, Wahpeton, Yankton, Yanktonai, and Teton. See Hodge, *Handbook of American Indians*, 1: 378.

[22] Elsewhere, in an undated note among his papers, Nicollet spelled this *Mendè Ouakanton*. The accepted spelling is Mdewakanton. They were a division of the eastern, or Santee, Sioux.

below St. Peter.[23] The ceremony took place in an oak grove crowning a plateau halfway up the high hill of Pilot Knob, behind the facilities of the American [Fur] Company on the right bank of the St. Peter River. A great congregation of people, a camp with eighty lodges, more than three hundred *midé* men and women, eighteen inches of snow, a temperature of 6° to 10° Fahrenheit below freezing, and a northwest wind multiplying the effects of this temperature transformed this day into a spectacle such as civilized societies cannot imagine.

The natives had spent more than eight days coming together and making preparations. Each of the delegations of the various villages had its camp quarters with its tents and families, and the members of the medicine body formed as many separate faculties as there were villages. On the morning of the day of initiation, at about 9 o'clock, the *oshkabewis* of the faculty who were conducting the ceremony and initiating the son of Big Soldier traveled through the camp and surroundings proclaiming that the festivities were about to begin, adding from time to time that those arriving late would be noted and condemned to offering a banquet. At 11 o'clock, the great faculty announces it is ready to begin and to welcome the delegations.

MANITOKAZOWIN

This is the ceremony travelers mention most, yet I never saw a description of it. It is celebrated in times of distress, during hunting expeditions, when the land has been exhausted, and when families lie dying of hunger. The native who can no longer bear the spectacle of misery surrounding him, whose vain efforts on the hunting grounds result only in his own exhaustion, and who is at the end of his rope decides to implore the manitos to be charitable unto him. He is well aware that the manitos will not bring him anything to eat in his lodge, and, being a hunter, he implores the spirits to bring to him or guide him to the animals needed for food and clothing. Lastly he pleads with them to enable him to kill his prey. According to the natives, such a

[23] The identity of Big Soldier is not certain. The village nine miles below Fort Snelling was Kaposia, on the site of present-day South St. Paul. Its chief at this time was Big Thunder, and his head soldier (who may have been the man referred to by Nicollet) was named Big Iron. See Pond, *Two Volunteer Missionaries*, 32; Folwell, *Minnesota*, 1: 185, 202.

ceremony will be fruitful and the requests will be granted only if it is performed by a man with power—in other words, by a *midé*. The ceremony he will celebrate to call on the spirits is called *manitokazowin*. The celebrant is called *manitokazood*.[24]

The *manitokazood* must specify his requests and list them on a board. Should he visualize a family of bears, he must trace on the board a male bear, a female, and two cubs and do likewise for all other species. Furthermore, he must carve a wooden doll representing the *missabé*, the manito of hunters. He colors it. This statuette is called by the natives *mazinini* (plural: *mazininig*). The word means image or figure of a man. [The *manitokazood*] will ocupy a lodge for the night by himself. In it he plants the *mazinini* before him, and he surrounds it with four to eight little sticks, some painted red, others black, called *midewatigun*—sticks of the *midé*. The *oshkanzhiwôg* is planted into the ground next to the statuette, as well as the *jibïattig*—the pole of the dead. The drum (*mittigwâkik*), the *shishigwân* and the hammer are brought in, and when all is ready, he speaks unto the *missabé*, tells him his family is starving, asks for help, begs that he may be made as good a hunter as the *missabé* and implores that he be led to the family of bears, the object of his prayer. "I have power, but you have more than I," says he. "If you help me, my family shall survive."

The lodge is dark, there is no fire. He prays, eyes closed, and his imagination is exalted to such a degree that he actually believes he can see the bears, that they are wandering in the surroundings and have come to see him. Such a vision augurs well. The *missabé* is granting his wishes. He then fixes a definite time with him: "See to it I kill them tomorrow, in two days' time, or three," etc. When this oration is ended, he sings for a long time, eyes closed, increasing the suspense with the drum and *shishigwân*. He sees more bears. They have come to visit him. The direction whence they come in his imagination is the direction he must take to hunt them down. It is by this vision the *missabé* manifests his assistance to him. His chants concluded, his imagination full of visions, he withdraws from the lodge and invites his neighbors to a banquet. The things offered at this manifestation

[24] Baraga (2:219) gives *manitôkâsowin* as meaning "religious performance." The *ood* added by Nicollet to make the third person singular of the practitioner is obscure. For mention of the ceremony by earlier travelers, see Pierre François Xavier de Charlevoix, *Histoire et Description generale de la Nouvelle France*, 2:166 (Paris, 1744); Thwaites, ed., *Jesuit Relations*, 10:208 (Cleveland, Ohio, 1897); Henry, *Travels and Adventures*, 114, 115n.

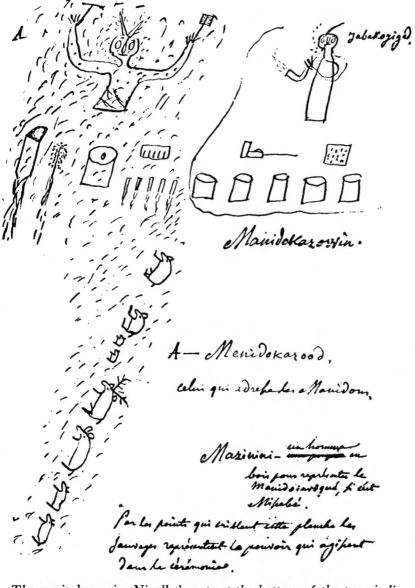

The manitokazowin. *Nicollet's note at the bottom of the page indicates that the dots on the drawing represent fields of spiritual force which according to the Indians invest the ceremony.*

are called *jibakojigon* — from *jibakwan* (the imperative), to make in a pot.

The banquet is intended for the *missabé* and for the animals called for. *Midé* as well as those who are not *midé* may attend. Even though passed out late at night, such invitations are never declined; the people come. The Amphitryon states the object of the banquet, conveys the *missabé's* intentions, tells of the bears that have appeared to him, and says, "Tomorrow, or the day after, go yonder, and you shall kill the bears." Under such circumstances, no one jealously covets the kill for himself, for he that slays such prophesied animals cannot retain them. Such prey belongs to the community present and the slain animal is completely sacrificed at another banquet where everybody is served. The animal is grilled even to the skin which is also eaten, and the remains can only be bones that are suspended from the trees or thrown into the water so that they may not be soiled. The share belonging to the *missabé* consists of the head, the four paws, the stomach and the entrails. The remainder of the animal is for the guests. During this banquet, the *manitokazood* makes an oration to the *missabé* and says unto him, "You had pity on me, but I also am charitable unto you." At the banquet held in honor of the *missabé* and the bears on the night he prayed, he [*the manitokazood*] was the one who issued the invitations, and therefore he is the one who should eat the share belonging to the *missabé* while the guests eat the share of the animals that were prayed for. For banquets are supposed to be offered to the spirits whose share is consumed by those responsible for the invitations.

The visions experienced by the *manitokazood* are an indication of the handicaps he shall encounter and the time it will take to track down the animals. He judges by the behavior of the animals in his vision. Should the bears enter the lodge and head straight for the pot prepared for the banquet, he concludes he shall kill them the next day without any difficulty. If, on the other hand, the bears stop at the door of the lodge, then it will take more time.

Those who are not *midé* and who must implore the spirits for animals to kill in order to feed their families must call on a *midé* to celebrate the ceremony for them. If the *midé* does not have trust in his own power, he must have recourse to another *midé* and himself supply the banquet and tobacco. In this case the former is a *jabakojiged* — he that "makes in a pot" or cooks for the *manitokazowin*.

The *manitokazowin* is carried out in a similar way for other kinds of requests made to the spirits. It suffices to change the *mazinini* into another object representing the manito to which the request is made. A person performing a ceremony requesting good health from his manito must, if the latter be a bear, use the head of a bear, or a bear medicine bag, or some representation of this animal cut out of fabric, the two layers of fabric being sewn together at the edges while the inside is stuffed with some kind of filling. A chained prisoner will perform an identical ceremony. He will ask his manito to give him the power to detach his bonds and be free. It is surprising how often such prisoners succeed in doing this—for example, Pashkwewozh, the murderer of Aitken's son.[25] Of course, in such cases there are no banquets, no instruments, and no statuettes. Under the circumstances, the prisoners say they perform the ceremony using their own power, and when they succeed they are recognized as great men.

War chiefs on the warpath celebrate a *manitokazowin* every evening. They implore the spirits of war and the birds of battle for assistance against their enemies. They ask for intelligence on the numbers and strength of the enemy and on where his forces are deployed. One might add that all *midé* at war feel entitled to perform their own unique ceremonies. Of course, in the morning when they divulge their findings, the conflicting results at which they all arrive more often than not contribute greatly to the defections involved. These turn out to be as numerous as their causes are frivolous, thus bringing to a halt many a native campaign. One can take advantage of such ceremonies to sway the natives in one's favor if one knows how to manipulate the mystical practices that have such an enormous influence on their lives.

Natives feel that the *manitokazowin* is a respectable ceremony. They do not make fun of it, nor are they amused by it as they are by the *jisakan*, which seems to have been contrived by quacks and impostors.

The *manitokazowin* for plants is an invocation to the manito of each plant that he may render it more powerful. State here and describe how Chagobay performed this ceremony at Leech Lake over

[25] For Aitken, see p. 135n, 141n. His son Alfred was killed at Cass Lake in 1836 by an Indian who became enraged because young Aitken had stolen his wife and refused to return her. The Indian was captured, escaped, and was recaptured and taken to Prairie du Chien for trial. The jury acquitted him. See Edward D. Neill, *History of the Upper Mississippi Valley*, 190 (Minneapolis, 1881).

the collection of plants he gathered on our trip. Describe the banquet, how the guests ended it by going around the lodge eight times and how they left through an exit vis-à-vis the entrance.[26]

THE *JISAKAN* – THE CEREMONIAL LODGE

The lodge is built with eight poles, sometimes only four. The poles are two or three inches thick and twelve, fifteen, or twenty feet high, depending on the exploits the conjurer thinks he can accomplish. The eighth pole is topped by its natural foliage, its head formed by several branches where he hangs or ties the objects he wishes to offer the spirits—tinklers, chimes, etc. Three singers with the drum, the *shishigwân* and the *oshkanzhiwôg* are there to help prepare the lodge. They take up their positions at the north end of the lodge. A congregation attends but cannot be placed on the side of the singers.

The singers tie the hands and feet of the conjurer, or *jasakid*, and push him into the lodge beneath the skins that cover it. Once inside he asks his servants for a pipe to smoke and says to the person handing it to him, "*Sâgâswê iwen*—Invite for the smoke." Thereupon, the servant calls the spirits of the four cardinal points. Looking north he shouts, "*Hohohoho, kokokoko kisâgâsweigo*—Owl, thou art invited to smoke." The people answer in the name of the spirit of the north, "*Ho!*—yes!" Looking east he shouts, "*Nenabozh, nenabozh, kisâgâsweigo.*"

The people again answer, "*Ho!*" To the south, "*Memengwâ,*" (butterfly), "*kisâgâsweigo,*" etc. To the setting sun, "*Animiki*" (thunder), "*kisâgâsweigo,*" etc. After these invitations, a silence prevails in the congregation; the people gaze toward the sky to watch the spirits descend. The conjurer begins to sing as does the choir. Then the lodge is seized by a commotion. There is an extraordinary display of noise and confusion. This is the descent of the spirits from the four corners of the horizon. There are eight of them, this number being sacred. The turtle arrives first, and she will be the last to leave.[27] She is the garrulous one, the spirit-interpreter, the secretary, the speaker for the faculty of the manitos. It is through her intercession that the spirits and the conjurer communicate with the people, and one must call

[26] For Chagobay see above, p. 19, 34, 64, 73.
[27] The calling of the turtle is described in Densmore, *Chippewa Customs,* 46, and Henry, *Travels and Adventures,* 158.

upon her to obtain information from the conjurer or the spirits. Each time a manito arrives, a tremendous thump hits the ground as if something heavy had fallen, and the lodge is violently shaken. The first time this happens the people shout, "Is it you, turtle, the great loquacious one—*kinnâ mishiken?*" (*Mikinak*—general term for turtle; *mishiken*—turtle that accompanies the spirits.)

Each time a spirit descends another thump is heard, and the lodge is shaken. When all the spirits are gathered, the faculty is actually in council, and conversation can be detected inside the lodge. This deliberation is held in an orderly fashion. Each spirit talks in his turn and each has a different voice. Soon the consultations will begin. A person in the congregation has a sick child and wants to know what she should do to cure it. She implores the turtle, but the latter turns a deaf ear.

"Talk, O, you old chatterer!"

The turtle still says nothing.

Then the *jasakid* is asked why the turtle refuses to answer. So the *jasakid* draws attention to the fact that all the things to be said were not said. The implorer adds, "Well, O talkative one, I shall give you tobacco and some blue fabric for making leggings. Talk!"

But the turtle still remains silent.

"But what is wrong with her?"

"She says you forgot the sugar."

"Well, O miser you, you shall have the sugar. Speak up!"

At this point the faculty deliberates. The members can be heard, each in turn, and the turtle announces the conclusion she has come to —the opinion of the faculty, that is. She says, "Your child has a piece of iron, a worm or some other animal in its stomach. It has to be withdrawn." Or she might say, "The sick one has a bear claw in its body, or porcupine quills," etc. Or maybe, "Your child is sick because he carries a bad name; it has to be changed." Or, "He that prescribed the child a medicine gave a bad medicine. He is a man of no power." Or else, "So-and-so is sick because he killed a bear, or a deer, and did not give any to the spirits. You must throw your dog into the water to feed the spirits. You must sacrifice it and offer a banquet."

In a serious case the father or mother consulting about a child or a relative will go as far as to include in their offering the following statement, "If you heal this person, I shall give you my daughter." The *jasakid* gives the serious matter all the consideration it calls for—or rather, the turtle does! The faculty, after having deliberated, delegates one of its members to the side of the sick one. The spirit is heard leaving, for the lodge is in a trance. While the spirit is away the deliberations of the council continue. The lodge quivers again. The spirit is returning to report to the faculty on the condition of the patient. The faculty deliberates further, and at last the turtle proclaims its decision: the soul of the patient is no longer in his body, it was ravished by an evil spirit. It is now confined far away. A stronger spirit must be dispatched to deliver it. And the family gives something more so that the soul shall be delivered and returned to the patient. (Indians are inclined to believe that when a sick man is at his worst his soul has already departed and he is dead, but also that he can be revived if his soul is returned.)

All these conjurations are performed with great skill and cunning. The natives are greatly amused by them but nevertheless believe in all the mystery that takes place. Anyone attempting to turn them away from these beliefs would be running a risk. In the course of these conjurations, gifts are repeatedly offered to the singers, who gather them, or to the *jasakid*, who receives them from under the folds of the lodge. After the ceremony, the *jasakid* and the singers have a feast. Their banquet, which follows no particular ritual, is held at the expense of the dupes of the day.

NANANDAWI IDIWIN – THE DOCTOR'S CALL

(From *nanandawi*, a verb. Third person of the imperative, *ônanandawiân*; infinitive, *nanandawiâ* – to take care of, to take under one's care, a doctor nursing a patient.) [28]

Take, for example, a sick child and consider the parent who wants to know the cause. First he cooks something and prepares some tobacco. He also gathers some cloth to offer as a gift, or something else that is not edible and hence called *sasagiwijigôn*. Those gifts that are edible are called *jibakoojigôn – jibakoojigônun*; the tobacco is called *pindakoojigôn* and *nun*, from *jibakwen* – to make in a pot, to cook, and *pindakwe* – to use, to make use of.

He then sends for a *midé* or for a practitioner who collects roots and knows their virtues, who nurses people, as some white men do,

---

[28] Densmore defines *nenandawiwed* as one who treats the sick by administering remedies. *Chippewa Customs*, 13.

although they are not *midé* or regular doctors. There are many such practitioners among the natives, conjurers at the same time, but they cannot accomplish anything, and they are not admitted to the *midé-wiwin*. A person in need of a medicine man goes to him and says, "*Kisâgâsweigo*—come and smoke." If there are several of them invited he says, "*Kisâgâsweigom*." The man comes, he is presented with a pipe, and if the patient he examines is ill, he accepts with thanks saying, "*Nâ, nikan, nagenâ*," or else, "*Kanagekana*." If he is not a *midé* he says, "*Nâ, nisagimâm*." It appears that *kanagekana* is an abbreviation for *nâ, nikan, nagenâ*.

While he smokes, the family tells him about the patient, and they mention that they would like him to take the case. The dish containing food is pushed toward him. His reply to all this is, "*Ho!*" After some meditation, he makes an oration to his manito asking for a revelation on the condition of the patient and for an inspiration on the selection of the plant that should be applied as a remedy.

He makes a point of explaining to those present that his manito is a *kitshimanito*,[29] and he says unto the latter, "Help me, assist me, thou art a great manito, thou must exorcise the *maji-ayâ-awish*." The latter is an evil animated thing such as a worm, a porcupine, any kind of insect or animal that has not been consecrated a manito of medicine. The bear and the snake are therefore excluded, for they are great manitos that one cannot abuse without exposing oneself to their wrath. And he will say, "You must drive away the *maji-ayi-iwish*," referring to inanimate but malignant substances and matter such as a piece of wood or iron, or a green-yellow liquid such as pus, etc., that he feels reside in the body of the patient. Boils and buboes, and so on, are caused by animals and insects. Bile is animated, so he calls it *maji-ayâ-awish*. Stones, bones, fishbones, etc., are *maji-ayi-iwish*. When referring to an endemic disease prevailing in an unhealthy place or country they say *maji-akki*.

When he has decided which healing plant applies, he utters another supplication begging the manito of the plant to instill in it power. If he leaves the plant behind, to be administered in his absence, it will be masked and he will not tell what it is. Instead he will declare that the plant is his manito and will recommend the manito be invoked before the remedy is administered.

[29] Baraga (2:193) defines *kitchi* as a prefix meaning great, large, or pre-eminent.

When the consultation has reached this point, including a slight repast, the doctor will pursue his art no further without making it beneficial to his profession, unless he be the only doctor in the country. Therefore he will send out invitations to a certain number of persons, men and women, *midé* or not, to whomever he wishes. The guests arrive with their dishes under their arms, pipes in their hands. The doctor stuffs their pipes and declares, "Light your pipes, smoke to the spirits of the above and below."

The guests reply as if expressing their gratitude, "*Nâ, nikanug, kanagekana*," if the doctor and patient are *midé*, or "*Nâ, nisagima-mug, kanageka*," if they are practitioners, or "*Nâ, nikan nisagimam, kanageka*," if one is *midé* but not the other.

When these things have been said, the doctor makes a speech, *ayâ nimitagooziwin*, stating why he was called. He divides up the food, more gratitude is expressed, and everyone eats. Then the doctor speaks with an inspired tone of voice, takes the *shishigwân* in his right hand, the *oshkanzhiwôg* in his left, and declares, "*Nâ, kanagekana.*"

Whether they have finished or not, everybody stops eating at this signal, and the doctor makes a fiery oration to his manito and to the spirit of the plant. He implores, begs, beseeches, commands, and directs the spirits to deliver the patient from the *maji-ayâ-awish* or from the *maji-ayi-iwish* in his body. He sings a song, frets, and grows excited. He then reverts to his oration, but this time the guests listen standing up. Then comes another song during which the guests dance showing their empty dishes to the spirits of the above and below. The dancers dance around the lodge, and as each one reaches the door he stops and utters a "*We − ho! hohohoho − ho!*" says "*Kanagekana*," exits, and leaves. The song they sing as they dance is composed of a single word: *ninanandoma â* (repeated, meaning I call him, I call him − the manito of the plant).

In these medicine and banquet ceremonies, the number of times the guests rotate around the lodge before they leave depends on the number of persons making up the faculty of the ceremony. Since there is only one doctor in our case, they dance around the lodge but once.

The manitos are now appeased, and the doctor who is the only one to have stayed behind calls for his *pinjigoosân* or medicine bag, and searches within it for what he needs. All the while he sings: "*Anin-diwendabiôu − â* (repeated − *â* is a fill-in) − Where art thou? Where art thou? Where art thou to be found?" And when he finds what he wants, he adds, "*Yâaa! yâaa — hoho! hoho!*" taking it in his hands. He prepares the remedy in a shell or dish, saying, "*Mayi ode, mayi ode, wi-i-wi* — He crawls, he crawls, he crawls." He talks to the manito and sings: "*Wajiwônne, tâmâdwejiwône* — The mountains, the mountains that roar."

He walks around the lodge holding out the potion he is about to administer while the patient gets ready to receive it. The doctor comes saying, "*Hwa! hwa!*" The patient swallows and absorbs the potion to the sound of, "*We—hohohoho—ho—ho!*" He speaks to the medicine man and to the manito, "Do not stop, purify the body, drive away the *maji-ayâ-awish* or *maji-ayi-iwish!*"

[The doctor] closes his *pinjigoosân*, has it carried to his abode, and stays behind awhile. He then takes the gifts presented to him, urges the spirits to stay in the lodge, to watch over the patient, and to cure him. He makes his way around the lodge singing, "*Wabamishin*," showing the gifts to the spirits of the above and below. Arriving at the door [he pronounces] "*We—hohoho—ho—ho! kanagekana*," and leaves.

The doctor continues to treat his patient, visits him every day, but does not repeat the ceremony. However, it is necessary to present him with gifts, or at least to give him something to eat, otherwise he will not ever return to the lodge, for his manito would withdraw his power and the patient would die.

In a case like the present one, or in other cases where medicine men are sought for their remedies, for some kind of a revelation, or a secret, the most precious gift one can offer them in the way of edible matter is a dog. Such is their favorite food—any kind of a dog, whether he be fat or reduced to skin and bones. Such is also the offering to which the spirits are most partial. Since the *midé* eat in lieu of the spirits, dogs are what one should offer to them, and dogs on the menu make for the most solemn banquets. The next in line after the dog in the way of an offering is the *madodiswōn*, or vapor bath.

The *nânandawi idiwin*, the main characteristics of which I have described, reveals the practicality of Indian methods in matters of medicine. The ceremony is a common one among Indians. It is that which strangers are most likely to see because it can take place any time while the others are merely occasional and performed only at certain seasons of the year. The *nânandawi idiwin* is the ceremony travelers have so frequently mentioned in their records under various names and which, because they were unaware of either its end or connection with the doctrine in general, they have interpreted so differently.

We shall understand why the ceremony manifests itself in so many different forms, although the essence of it—its rites and motives—always remain the same. The diversity of form with which it is performed is due to the diversity of diseases.

Point out here:

1. The case described when among the Chikasas [*sic*].[30]
2. Some cases taken from travelers, particularly Henry.[31]
3. The case of the Leech Lake woman whose very sick only son of ten years of age asked that medicine be sung to him for his entertainment. Ten doctors were brought along and they decided to sing four songs each, during which, in accordance with their rules, the patient cannot sleep, etc.
4. The case of the child delivery wherein the power of the crayfish was invoked.

[30] This reference indicates that Nicollet had been observing the Indians throughout his travels in the United States. His account of this ceremony among the Chickasaw has been lost.

[31] See Henry, *Travels and Adventures*, 115–118.

APPENDIXES

Appendixes

1. Names of Lakes and Streams

Nicollet recorded names of geographic features in a number of different places: his journals, his astronomical notebook, two manuscript maps dating from 1836 and 1837, and the 1843 published map. In addition, many appear in a manuscript table of distances preserved among his papers. In most cases the names recorded differ somewhat in spelling, language, or meaning. Although Nicollet generally followed prevailing usage, in a few cases he actually named a lake or river, then, as often as not, he changed his mind. Some variations appearing on the 1843 map appear to have been errors of the engraver, but there is no way to be sure.

The table below includes lakes and streams mentioned in the diaries here published. They are listed alphabetically by the modern name, and the various names given by Nicollet are indicated in the four columns to the right. The notation "not named" indicates that the feature is described in a journal or shown on a map but not named. The two manuscript maps overlap somewhat, and where different names appear for the same feature, both are given, divided by a slash mark (/). The one on the 1837 map is identified by an asterisk. On the 1843 map Nicollet often gave both the Indian name and the English meaning. Not all the places are listed in the Astronomical Notebook and the Table of Distances, and names from these are given only when they differ from the other sources or provide additional information. These two sources are abbreviated as T.D.—Table of Distances—and A.N.—Astronomical Notebook.

MODERN NAME	JOURNAL	1836 and 1837 MAPS	1843 MAP	OTHER NICOLLET NOTES
Abe Lake (Cass Co.)	Not named			
Alcohol Creek (Hubbard Co.)	Not named			
Alice Lake (Hubbard Co.)	Ossawa Lake	(Illegible)	Assawe Lake	Ossawa Lake or Yellow Perch Lake (A.N.)
Lake Andrusia (Beltrami Co.)	Not named	Lake Livingston (for Edward Livingston, U.S. secretary of state)	Not named	
Angel Creek (Wis.)	Not named			
Apple River (Wis.)	Wabizipinikan Sibi	Green Stone River	Wabezipinikan River	
Arrow Lake (Hubbard Co.)	Not named	Not named	Lake Irving [1]	
Ball Club River (Itasca Co.)	La Crosse River	Lacrosse River	Pagadowan River	La Cross River or Pāgâ Adowân Sibi (T.D.)
Ball Club Lake Lake (Itasca Co.)	La Crosse Lake	Lake La Crosse	Not named	
Bass Brook (Itasca Co.)	Crapet River	Not named	Not named	
Bass Lake (Cass Co.)	Turtle Lake [2]	Philadelphia Canal	Lake Eccleston (for Bishop Samuel Eccleston of Baltimore)	

[1] On the 1843 map a lake which might be either Arrow or Fern Lake is incorrectly labeled Lake Irving. Lake Irving, named by Schoolcraft for Washington Irving, is correctly identified in Nicollet's diary and on his manuscript maps.

[2] As noted in the text (p. 73n.) Nicollet apparently treated present-day Bass, Coffin, and Thunder lakes as a single body of water, which he lumped under the name Turtle Lake in his diary and labeled Philadelphia Canal on the 1836 map and Lake Eccleston on the 1843 map.

MODERN NAME	JOURNAL	1836 and 1837 MAPS	1843 MAP	OTHER NICOLLET NOTES
Bassett Creek (Crow Wing Co.)	Not named	Not named	Fall Creek	
Bear Creek (Clearwater Co.)	Not named	Not named	Not named	
Lake Bemidji (Beltrami Co.)	Lake Travers	Chippewa Lake Travers	Lake Pemidji	Pemiji Gomâg (T.D.)
Benedict Lake (Hubbard Co.)	Not named	Not named	Not named	
Big Rice Lake (Cass Co.)	Duck Lake	Lake Rosati (for Bishop Joseph Rosati of St. Louis)	Lake Rosati	
Big Sandy Lake (Aitkin Co.)	Sandy Lake	Sandy Lake	Sandy Lake	
Big Swan Lake (Todd Co.)	Swan Lake	Not named	Not named	
Birch Creek (Hubbard Co.)	Ossawa River	Not named	Not named	
Blackberry Brook (Itasca Co.)	Little Island River [3]	Blueberry River	Blueberry Creek	Minikan Sibiwisen (T.D.)
Boy Lake (Cass Co.)	Boston Canal	Boston Canal	Lake Hassler (for Ferdinand R. Hassler)	
Boy River (Cass Co.)	Petit Enfant River and Indian Gardens River	Indian Garden River	Little Boy or Kwiwissens River	
Brule River (Wis.)	Bois Brulés River	Burntwood or Wissakuda Sibi *	Wissakude or Burnt Wood River	

[3] Here Nicollet appears to have been confused. The present Blackberry Brook corresponds to the stream described by the explorer as Trout River. However, the nearby stream which he names in his diary Little Island River appears on his maps under the name Blueberry Creek. On modern maps it is unnamed.

MODERN NAME	JOURNAL	1836 and 1837 MAPS	1843 MAP	OTHER NICOLLET NOTES
Lake Calhoun (Hennepin Co.)	Lake Calhoun	Not named	Lake Calhoun	
Cass Lake (Cass & Beltrami)	Cass Lake	Cass Lake	Cass Lake	Cass Lake or Kamiskwâkokâg (T.D.)
Cedar Creek (Crow Wing Co.)	Red Cedar Lake River	Not named	Not named	
Chambers Creek (Clearwater Co.)	Not named	Not named	Not named	
Chase Creek (Wis.)	River Where Canoes Are Made or Attonowining	Attonowining River	Attonowining River	
Chill Creek (Clearwater Co.)	Not named	Not named	Not named	
Clam River (Wis.)	Clam River	Clam River	Kayesikang or Shell River	
Clearwater River (Wright & Stearns)	Clear Water River or Ka Ouâ Kummik Tigoue Yag	Clearwater River	Kawakomik or Clear Water River	
Coffin Lake (Cass Co.)	Turtle Lake [2]	Philadelphia Canal	Lake Eccleston (see Bass Lake)	
Coon Creek (Anoka Co.)	Kitta-jouan or Little-Big River	Not named	Peterah River	
Cranberry River (Wis.)	Mashkigi Minikani Sibi or Cranberry River		Cranberry River	
Crooked Creek (Pine Co.)	Everflowing River	Everflowing River	Everflowing River	

MODERN NAME	JOURNAL	1836 and 1837 MAPS	1843 MAP	OTHER NICOLLET NOTES
(Cross Lake) (Crow Wing Co.)	Lake Travers or Lake Davenport (for William Davenport, commander at Fort Snelling)	Lake Davenport	Lake Davenport	
Lac Court Oreilles (Wis.)	Lac Court Oreilles	Lac Court Oreilles *	Ottawa Lake or Court Oreilles Lake	
Crow River (Wright & Hennepin)	(Entry missing)	Crow River	Karishon or Crow River	
Crow Wing River (Cass & Morrison)	Crow River or Chippewa Crow River	Raven River	Crow Wing or Kagiwigwan River	Kakâghi Ouigouân Sibi, Rivière aux Plumes de Corbeau or Crow Quill River of the Chippewa (A.N.)
Daggett Brook (Crow Wing Co.)	Not named	Pine Branch and West Fork of Pine Branch	Not named	
Daggett Lake (Crow Wing Co.)	Not named	Not named	Not named	
Deer Lake (Crow Wing Co.)	Hay Lake or Kâmuskusi Wâ Gamag	Hay Lake	Mashkosiwah Lake	
Deer River (Itasca Co.)	Deer River	Deer River	Deer River	Deer River or Wâwâshkesh Sibi (T.D.)
Dry Creek (Chisago Co.)	Mokiginowish River	Mokiginowide River	Mokiginewish River	
Eagle Lake (Crow Wing Co.)	Not named	Not named	Not named	

MODERN NAME	JOURNAL	1836 and 1837 MAPS	1843 MAP	OTHER NICOLLET NOTES
Eau Claire River (Wis.)	Clear Water River	Clear Water River *	Wayakomig River	
Elk Lake (Clearwater Co.)	Not named	Not named	Not named	
Elk River (Sherburne Co.)	(Entry missing)	St. Francis River	Kabitawi River	St. Francis River, Parallel River, River Beside Another, Kâbita Oui Tigoué Yâg (A.N.)
Elm Creek (Hennepin Co.)	Not named	Rush River	Wanyecha River	
Fish Creek (Wright Co.)	Kibiskabiti- goué-yâg, Meander River, or Big Point River		Bend Creek	
Fish Creek (Wis.)	Shishkaweka Sibi, Shish- kawekanig Sibi, or Fish River *		Not named	
Garfield Lake (Hubbard Co.)	Not named	Not named	Not named	
Lake George (Cass Co.)	Otter Lake	Lake Bruté (for Simon Bruté de Remur of Baltimore)	Lake Enkes (for Johan Franz Encke, German astronomer)	
Goose Creek (Chisago Co.)	Red Cedar River	Red Cedar River	Red Cedar Creek	

⁴ Nicollet translates Shishkaweka or Shiskawekanig Sibi as Fish River but also notes that it is "some kind of fish." This may mean that he was referring to the Siskiwit River, the name of which derives from the fact that siscowet — more commonly called cisco — were caught there. See above, p. 152; Appendix 6, p. 265; Ross, *La Pointe*, 182, 184.

MODERN NAME	JOURNAL	1836 and 1837 MAPS	1843 MAP	OTHER NICOLLET NOTES
Gulch Creek (Hubbard Co.)	Not named	Not named	Not named	
Gull Lake (Cass Co.)	Gull Lake	Gull Lake	Gayashk Lake	
Gull River (Cass Co.)	Gull River	Gull River	Gayashk River	Kakäyash Konsikâg Sibi (A.N.)
Halfway Brook (Benton Co.)	Not named	Not named	Not named	
Hart Lake (Hubbard Co.)	Not named	Not named	Not named	
Hay River (Crow Wing Co.)	Manito Sibi Ouissen	Manito River	Manito River	
Hennepin River (Hubbard & Beltrami)	Not named	Not named	Not named	
Home Brook (Cass Co.)	Not named	Not named	Not named	
Horseshoe Lake (Itasca Co.)	Not named	Not named	Not named	
Hubbard Lake (Hubbard Co.)	Not named	Not named	Not named	
Inguadona Lake (Cass Co.)	New York Canal	New York Canal	Lake Gauss (for Karl Friedrich Gauss, German mathematician)	
Iron River (Wis.)	Piwâbikû Sibi or Iron River	Piwapiki Sibi/Iron River *	Piwabik or Iron River	
Lake Irving (Beltrami Co.)	Lake Irving	Lake Irving	Not named [1]	

MODERN NAME	JOURNAL	1836 and 1837 MAPS	1843 MAP	OTHER NICOLLET NOTES
Lake Itasca (Clearwater Co.)	La Biche Lake	Itasca Lake (named by Schoolcraft)	Itasca Lake	Itasca Lake, Elk or La Biche Lake or Omosbkas Lagäigōn (A.N.)
Jerseth Creek (Wis.)	Not named			
Joe Gould Lake (Itasca Co.)	Pakégumâg Lake	Pakegomag Lake	Pakegomag Lake	Pakégamâ (in miscellaneous geographical notes)
Kabekona Bay (Leech Lake)	Not named	Lake Gratiot (for General Charles Gratiot)	Not named	
Kabekona Lake (Hubbard Co.)	Kâbékanâ Lake	Kabekona Lake	Kabekona Lake	
Kabekona River (Hubbard Co.)	Kâbékanâ Sibi	Kabekana River	Kabekona River	
Kettle River (Pine Co.)	Rivière Chaudière or Kettle River	Kettle River/ Akiko Sibi or Rivière Chaudière *	Akkik or Kettle River	
Lake of the Woods (Wis.)	Not named	Not named	Not named	
La Salle River (Hubbard Co.)	Not named	Not named	Not named	
Laura Creek (Cass Co.)	Indian Gardens or Little Boy River	Not named	Kwiwissens River	
Laura Lake (Cass Co.)	Tamarack Lake or Hawthorn Lake	Lake Michael (for Bishop Michael Portier of Mobile, Ala.)	Lake Portier (for Bishop Portier)	

MODERN NAME	JOURNAL	1836 and 1837 MAPS	1843 MAP	OTHER NICOLLET NOTES
Leech Lake (Cass Co.)	Leech Lake	Leech Lake	Leech Lake	Kah-suguswâ-yema-kâg, or Where Leeches Are Found (in miscellaneous geographical notes)
Leech Lake River (Cass Co.)	Leech Lake River	Leech Lake River	Leech Lake River	Kasagāskwây-imekâg Sibi (T.D.)
Little Elk River (Morrison Co.)	La Biche River or Omoschkôs Sibi	Elk River	Elk or Omoskos River	Omokoso Sibi (in miscellaneous notes)
Little Gulch Lakes (Hubbard Co.)	Not named	Not named	Not named	
Little Mis-sissippi River (Beltrami Co.)	Not named	Not named	Not named	
Little Pine Lake (Crow Wing Co.)	Not named	Not named	Not named	
Little Rice Lake (Itasca Co.)	Not named	Not named	Not named	
Little Rock Creek (Benton Co.)	Rock River or Kouâbika Sibi	Little Rock River	Pikwabic or Little Rock River	
Little Willow River (Aitkin Co.)	Little Willow River	Little Willow River	Little Willow River	
Lower Hay Lake (Crow Wing Co.)	Manito Lake	Not named	Not named	

MODERN NAME	JOURNAL	1836 and 1837 MAPS	1843 MAP	OTHER NICOLLET NOTES
Lower Tamarack River (Pine Co.)	Eninandigo Sibi, Rivière aux Epinettes, or Fir Spruce River	Eninandigo River	Eninandigo River	
Lower Trelipe Lake (Cass Co.)	Little Whitefish Lake	Lake Eccleston (see Bass Lake)	Lake Deluol (for Rev. Louis Regis Deluol of Baltimore)	
Mayo Creek (Cass Co.)	Gull River	Gull River	Gayashk River	
Mayo Lake (Crow Wing Co.)	Long Lake	Not named	Not named	
Mille Lacs Lake (Mille Lacs & Aitkin)	Mille Lacs	Missi Sagai- goning or Mille Lacs	Minsi Sagai- goning or Mille Lacs	
Mississippi River	Mississippi River	Mississippi River	Mississippi River	
Mitchell Lake (Crow Wing Co.)	Not named	Not named	Not named	
Monimin Lake (Beltrami Co.)	Not named	Not named	Not named	
Moss Lake (Cass Co.)	Moss Lake (named by Schoolcraft)	Moss Lake	Moss Lake	
Mud Lake (Cass Co.)	Muddy Lake	Muddy Lake	Lake Bessel (for Friedrich Wilhelm Bessel, German astronomer)	
Namekagon River (Wis.)	Namekagon River	Namakagon River/ Makagon Sibi *	Namekagon River	

MODERN NAME	JOURNAL	1836 and 1837 MAPS	1843 MAP	OTHER NICOLLET NOTES
Nebegamon Creek (Wis.)	Sleeping Bear River or Nibegomowin		Nibegomowin or Sleeping Bear River	
Nicollet Creek (Clearwater Co.)	Not named	Not named	Not named	
Nicollet Lake (Clearwater Co.)	Not named	Not named	Not named	
Otter Creek (Wright Co.)	Migady-ouin Sibi Ouissen or Little Battle River	Migadiwin Creek	Migadiwin Creek	
Ottertail Lake (Otter Tail Co.)	Big Otter Tail Lake	Otter Tail Lake	Otter Tail Lake	
Ox Creek (Wis.)	Buffalo River	Not named	Pijiki River	
Pembina River (No. Dak.)	Pembina River or Anibi-minanisibi			
Pike Creek (Morrison Co.)	Little Falls Creek	Little Falls Creek	Little Fall Creek	Little Rapids Creek (A.N.)
Pine River (Crow Wing Co.)	Pine River	Pine River	Pine River	Jingouâ Kouâ Sibi (A.N.)
Platte River (Benton Co.)	Broken River	Broken River	Pekushino River	
Pokegama Lake (Itasca Co.)	Not named	Not named	Not named	
Pokegama Lake (Pine Co.)	Pakagâma Lake	Pâkegomag Lake/Pakag-amag Lake *	Pekegomag Lake	
Portage Creek (Cass Co.)	Not named	Not named	Not named	
Portage Lake (Cass Co.)	Not named	Not named	Not named	

MODERN NAME	JOURNAL	1836 and 1837 MAPS	1843 MAP	OTHER NICOLLET NOTES
Prairie River (Itasca Co.)	Prairie River	Prairie River	Mashkudens River	Rivière aux Petites Prairies or Mash-koodensirvi Sibi (T.D.)
Pug Hole Lake (Crow Wing Co.)	Not named	Not named	Not named	
Rainy Lake	Rainy Lake		Rainy Lake	
Raspberry River (Wis.)	Miskwi Minikan or Raspberry River		Miskwimin or Raspberry River	
Red River	Red River	Red River	Red River of the North	
Rice Creek (Anoka Co.)	Wild Rice River or Manomin-ikan Sibi	Village River	Ottonway River	
Rice Creek (Itasca Co.)	Not named	Not named	Not named	
Rice Lake (Itasca Co.)	Not named	Not named	Not named	
Rice River (Aitkin Co.)	Wild Rice River	Folle Avoine River	Manomin River	Folle-avoine River or Manominikan Sibi (T.D.)
Ripple River (Aitkin Co.)	Muddy River	Muddy River	Muddy River	Sipashkooyish Kirvakag Sibiwisen (T.D.)
Rock Creek (Chisago Co.)	Little Rock River	Little Rock River	Little Rock Creek	
Rocky Run (Wis.)	Not named			
Lake Roosevelt (Crow Wing & Cass)	Crooked Lake or Balti-more Canal	Baltimore Canal	Lake Chanche (for Bishop John Chanche of Baltimore)	Lac Croche des Sauvages (A.N.)
Rum River (Anoka Co.)	Rum River or Chkodéou-âbo Sibi	Rhum River	Iskode Wabo or Rum River	

MODERN NAME	JOURNAL	1836 and 1837 MAPS	1843 MAP	OTHER NICOLLET NOTES
Rush Creek (Chisago Co.)	Reed River	Reed River	Reed Creek	
Rush Lake (Crow Wing Co.)	Not named	Not named	Lake Plympton (for Joseph Plympton, commander of Fort Snelling)	
Rush River (Wis.)	Rush River, Pakwaika Sibi, or Apakwaika Sibi		Apakwa River	
St. Croix River	St. Croix River	St. Croix River	St. Croix River	
St. Croix Flowage (Wis.)	Wild Rice	Not named	Not named	
Lake St. Croix (Washington Co.)	Not named	Lake St. Croix	St. Croix Lake	
St. Francis River (Sherburne Co.)	(Entry missing)	East Branch St. Francis River	St. Francis or Wicha- niwa River	Leaf River, Kâbita Oui Tigoué Yâg, or Parallel River (A.N.)
St. Louis River (St. Louis Co.)	Wekwâ Kichi Gummi Sibi, St. Louis River, or Fond du Lac River	St. Louis River	St. Louis River	
Sand River (Pine Co.)	Sandy River	Sand River	Sand River	
Sandy River (Aitkin Co.)	Not named	Not named	Not named	Sandy Lake River or Kamitawanga Gomâg (T.D.)
Sauk River (Stearns Co.)	Osâgis or Sâgis Sibi	Sâkis River	Osakis River	

MODERN NAME	JOURNAL	1836 and 1837 MAPS	1843 MAP	OTHER NICOLLET NOTES
Schoolcraft River (Hubbard Co.)	Laplace or Ossawa River	Laplace River (for Pierre Simon Laplace, French mathematician)	Laplace River	
Sibley Lake (Crow Wing Co.)	Long Lake or Kâghinô Gamac	Lake Sibley (for Henry H. Sibley)	Lake Sibley	
Silver Creek (Wright Co.)	Sibi-ouissen or Little River	Little River	Not named	
Siskiwit River (Wis.)	Shiskaweka Sibi or Shiskawe-kanig Sibi [4]	Not named	Not named	
Six Mile Brook (Cass Co.)	Not named	Not named	Not named	
Snake River (Pine Co.)	Snake River	Snake River/ Kinebigo Sibi [*]	Kinebik or Snake River	
Splithand Creek (Itasca Co.)	Main Coupée or Cut Hand River	Cut Hand	Cut Hand Creek	Kishkiningi Sibiwisen (T.D.)
Spring Brook (Cass Co.)	Not named	East Fork of Pine Branch	Not named	
Spring Lake (Hubbard Co.)	Not named	Not named	Not named	
Spunk Brook (Stearns Co.)	Sagatagan Sibi or Spunk River	Spunk River	Sagatagon or Spunk River	
Spunk Lake (Stearns Co.)	Sagatagan Sagahagan or Spunk Lake	Not named	Not named	
Steamboat Bay Lake (Cass Co.)	Not named	Not named	Not named	
Steamboat Lake (Hubbard & Cass)	Kâbak Saghidawâg or Lake Kabuka	Not named	Not named	

MODERN NAME	JOURNAL	1836 and 1837 MAPS	1843 MAP	OTHER NICOLLET NOTES
Steamboat River (Hubbard & Cass)	Kabukasâ or Kabuka River	Kabuki Sagidawâ	Pake Sagidowag River	
Stony Brook (Cass Co.)	Not named	Not named	Not named	
Sucker Brook (Hubbard Co.)	Not named	Not named	Not named	
Sucker Creek (Clearwater Co.)	Not named	Not named	Not named	
Sunrise River (Chisago Co.)	Sunrise River or Memokage Sibi	Sunrise River/ Memokage Sibi *	Memokage River	
Lake Superior	Lake Superior	Lake Superior	Kichi Gummi or Lake Superior	
Swamp Lake (Cass Co.)	Not named	Not named	Not named	
Swan Lake (Itasca Co.)	Not named	Great Swan Lake	Swan Lake	
Swan River (Itasca Co.)	Swan River	West Swan River	West Swan River	West Swan River or Wabiziwi Sibi (T.D.)
Swan River (Morrison Co.)	Swan River or Ouâbisi-oui-sibi	Swan River	Wabezi or Swan River	West Swan River (A.N.)
Thunder Lake (Cass Co.)	Turtle Lake or Philadelphia Canal	Philadelphia Canal	Lake Eccleston (see Bass Lake)	Lac aux Tortues des Chippewa (A.N.)
Trade River (Wis.)	Attanwa Sibi	Attanwan River	Attanwa River	
Trout Lake (Itasca Co.)	Trout Lake [6]	Trout Lake	Trout Lakes	

[6] See above, p. 130n. Trout Lake is identified in the diary as the source of a river entering the Mississippi at about the same place as present-day Blackberry Brook. Yet on his maps Nicollet shows a series of small lakes feeding this stream, which is still labeled Trout River. Another large lake is shown with an outlet flowing into Swan River. On the 1836 map this large lake is correctly labeled Trout Lake, but on the 1843 map it is not named.

MODERN NAME	JOURNAL	1836 and 1837 MAPS	1843 MAP	OTHER NICOLLET NOTES
Trout River (Itasca Co.)	Trout River [6]	Not named	Trout Creek	Kanamegosikag Sibiwisen (T.D.)
Two Rivers (Morrison Co.)	Two Rivers or Kanijô-tigoué-hâ	Two Rivers	Two Rivers	
Upper Gull Lake (Cass Co.)	Not named	Not named	Not named	
Upper Hay Lake (Crow Wing Co.)	Kawâ-we-é Gumag or Round Lake	Circular Lake	Lake Gratiot (see Kabe-kona Bay)	
Upper Rice Lake (Clearwater Co.)	Lake Hauteur de Terre or Ayawaiway Satagan Sagahegain	Rice Lake	Rice Lake	
Upper St. Croix Lake (Wis.)	Upper St. Croix Lake	Not named	Upper St. Croix Lake	
Upper Tamarack River (Pine Co.)	Upper Fir Spruce River	Little Eninandigo River	Little Eninandigo River	
Vermilion Lake (St. Louis Co.)	Vermilion Lake		Vermilion Lake	
Vermillion Lake (Cass Co.)	Not named	Not named	Not named	
Vermillion River (Cass Co.)	Vermillion River or Unâmunâsibi	Vermillion River	Wanomon River	Wanomon Sibi (T.D.)
Watab River (Stearns Co.)	Ouâtab, Wâhtab, or Little Sâkis River	Watabi River	Watab River	
Whipple Lake (Clearwater Co.)	Not named	Not named	Not named	
White Oak Lake (Itasca Co.)	Not named	Not named	Not named	

[6] This river was incorrectly identified by Nicollet. See footnote 5 above.

MODERN NAME	JOURNAL	1836 and 1837 MAPS	1843 MAP	OTHER NICOLLET NOTES
Whitefish Lake (Crow Wing Co.)	Whitefish Lake	White Fish Lake	Kadikomeg Lake	Kadikumagokâg or Lake Where There Are Many Whitefish (A.N.)
Willow River (Aitkin Co.)	Willow River	Willow River	Willow River	
Wilson Creek (Wis.)	Not named	Not named	Not named	
Lake Winnibigoshish (Cass & Itasca)	Lake Winnipec or Winnipac	Lake Winipik	Lake Winibogoshish	Lake Winipik Winibigoshish Sagäigōn (T.D.)
Wolf Lake (Beltrami & Hubbard)	Not named	Lake Woodbury (for Levi Woodbury, secretary of the navy)	Lake Vandermaelen (for Philippe Vandermaelen, Belgian cartographer)	
Wood River (Wis.)	Whitewood or Basswood River	Whitewood River	Wigobimis River	
Yellow River (Wis.)	Yellow River	Yellow River/ Wassawa Gomig *	Wassewa or Yellow River	

2. Table of River Mileages from Fort Snelling

In the table below Nicollet's calculation of distances on the upper Mississippi is compared with the corresponding figures arrived at by the United States Army Corps of Engineers in 1939. Some of Nicollet's figures are drawn from a table of river distances included in his *Report* (p. 124). The rest are from a manuscript table among his papers in the Library of Congress. The modern mileages are from United States Army, Corps of Engineers, *The Middle and Upper Mississippi River*, 159, 163, 285–288 (Washington, D.C., 1940).

MILES FROM FORT SNELLING

Place (Modern name)	Nicollet	Corps of Engineers
St. Croix River	42	34.2
Falls of St. Anthony	8	8
Rum River	27	25.9
Crow River	37	34.1
Elk River	46	39.3
Clearwater River	88	69
Sauk River	110	84.5
Watab River	113	86.9
Swan River (Morrison Co.)	149	115.5
Little Elk River	159	122.3
Nokassippi River	177	136.5
Crow Wing River	189	144.9
Rabbit River	207	167.3
Pine River	237	178.3
Little Willow River	267	204.3
Ripple River	277	211.2
Rice River	289	220
Willow River	302	232
Sandy River	334	260.1
Swan River (Aitkin Co.)	372	292.5
Prairie River	427	332
Grand Rapids	435	335
Pokegama Lake	439	338.4
Vermillion River	456	354.8
Deer River	468	369.9
Ball Club River	480	376
Leech Lake River	483	378.3
Lake Winnibigoshish (inlet)	533	418.3
Cass Lake (inlet)	563	438.3
Lake Bemidji (inlet)	607 *	458.5
Schoolcraft River	610	460.6
Lake Itasca	707 *	520.7

* Figures given here are from Nicollet's manuscript table. In his *Report* they are 608 and 698.

3. Nicollet's Bibliography on the North American Indian

At the time of Nicollet's death in 1843 his library, extensive for a man of his means in that day, was inventoried, and a record of the books he owned is preserved among his papers. The assessor's entries— sometimes vague and fragmentary—are reproduced in small capitals in the list below. They are followed by the full title of the work, so far as this could be determined by the editor. The first group includes Nicollet's books relating to the Indians published before 1836 and with which he was presumably familiar at the time he made his trip to the sources of the Mississippi.

HISTOIRE DE NOUVELLE FRANCE. This could refer to Pierre François Xavier de Charlevoix, *Histoire et description generale de la Nouvelle France* (Paris, 1744). Nicollet was familiar with this book as he mentioned it in an earlier journal as well as in his report. It was widely accepted as a basic authority.

BOSSU'S TRAVELS. Jean-Bernard Bossu, *Nouveaux voyages aux Indes Occidentales; contenant une relation des differens peuples qui habitent les environs du grand fleuve Saint-Louis, appellé vulgairement le Mississippi* (Paris, 1768). An English translation, *Travels through the Part of North America Formerly Called Louisiana*, appeared in London in 1771 and a sequel was published in Amsterdam in 1778 under the title: *Nouveaux voyages dans l'Amérique Septentrionale*. It is impossible to know which one Nicollet possessed, but it was probably the English translation as the assessor lists it in English.

HARMON'S JOURNAL. Daniel William Harmon, *A Journal of Voyages and Travels in the Interior of North America* (Andover, Mass., 1820).

HENRY'S TRAVELS. Alexander Henry, *Travels and Adventures in Canada and the Indian Territories between 1750–1776* (New York, 1809).

MAJOR LONG'S 2D EXPEDITION. Probably William H. Keating, *Narrative of an Expedition to the Source of the St. Peter's River* (Philadelphia, 1824).

VOYAGE DANS LES DEUX LOUISIANES. François-Marie Perrin du Lac, *Voyage dans les Deux Louisianes, et chez les nations sauvages du Missouri, par les États Unis . . . 1801, 1802, 1803* (Paris and Lyon, 1805).

PAMPHL. REMARKS ON N. AMER. INDIANS. This may have been Philadelphus, [pseud. for Saxe Bannister], *Remarks on the Indians of North America in a Letter to an Edinburgh Reviewer* (London, 1822). It earnestly defends the character of the Indian.

PAMPHL. CONG. DOC. ALLEN'S REPORT OF EXPED[n] TO THE N.W. INDIANS. James Allen, *Journal of an "Expedition into the Indian country," to the source of the Mississippi, made under the authority of the War Department, in 1832* (23 Congress, 1 session, *House Documents*, no. 323 – serial 257).

PAMPHL. EXAMIN. RESPECTING THE HISTORY, TRADITIONS ETC. OF THE N. AM. INDIANS. Unidentified.

In addition to the above list, Nicollet undoubtedly read the following books, which are specifically mentioned in his report and diary:

Jonathan Carver, *Travels through the Interior Parts of North America in 1766, 1767, and 1768* (London, 1778).

Baron de Lahontan, *New Voyages to North-America* (The Hague and London, 1703).

John Tanner, *Narrative of the Captivity and Adventures of John Tanner* (New York, 1830).

Comte de Volney, *Tableau du climat et du Sol des Etats Unis* (Paris, 1803).

Various volumes of the *Jesuit Relations*.

Books on the Indian published after 1836 which Nicollet owned at the time of his death were:

CATLIN'S INDIANS. George Catlin, *Letters and Notes on the Manners, Customs and Condition of the North American Indians* (London, 1841).

MEMOIR SUR LES LANGUES DU L'AM. DU NORD. Possibly Pierre Etienne DuPonceau, *Mémoire sur le systeme grammatical des langues de quelques nations Indiennes de l'Amérique du Nord* (Paris, 1838).

4. Geographical Notes

THE PRAIRIE

[*The following descriptive passages appear in Nicollet's diary after an entry dated October 12, 1836, in which he tells briefly of a visit to Fountain Cave, below Fort Snelling. They obviously belong to a later date and another expedition, but there is no hint as to the time or place at which he made the observations.*]

Today we found the edge of the prairie spreading as far as the river at a height of twenty-five feet above water level. Our bearing was NW. The weather was very warm. The country presented a plain, spreading as far as the eye could see, without any substantial change of level and for the most part without woods or even the slightest cluster of shrubs. It is an endless expanse without a single rise, a sea of greenness without islands of woods. The country we had left behind us had dissolved into the horizon, and all the eye could see was sky and prairie.

At 4 o'clock we noticed an island of woods to the left. At 5:00, we saw another. At first this immense, uninterrupted horizon seemed both astonishing and admirable. But when the eye has probed the depths in every direction and discovers that this immensity does not stretch as does the sky above beyond the eye's reach, when the admirer sees the biggest of animals fleeing with all their might only as black specks that seem to move no more than flowers or grass swayed by the wind, when he realizes that with each season this stirring greatness brings disastrous perils — that in spring he may well perish there in the spongy mires of the sunken hollows, that in summer he may well die of thirst or of a fever carried by swarms of insects, that in the fall, fires backed by winds may in a matter of hours transform this magnificent green, flowered and living, into a shroud of mourning strewn with the skeletons of all the creatures that breathed there, that winter may yet cast another shroud, a white mantle two to four feet thick capable of blinding him should the sun shine bright or of burying him under a mountain of snow should the wind blow strong — then, gloom dissolves the magnificence of this scene and proves once more that in a desert man's glimpse of delight comes shadowed with the forebodings of fear and sorrow.

We had not been going long when the land betrayed the first signs of an increasing barrenness, so typical of plains. The woods dwindled in number and size, and we were forced to camp a little earlier than usual so as to be able to find enough wood to cook supper and keep us warm for the night. We reached another narrowing of the river. There the current, forced between high banks, acquired such speed that counter currents were formed. Some islands rose in this portion of the river, dividing it into sections through which the water sped as quickly as through the straits.

When one is able to reach the top of some elevation or other in this vast region, he always gets the impression of being in the center of immense, perfectly level plains, and the horizon invariably seems to be limited in all directions by chains of hills which, taking into account the distance at which one supposed them to be, appear like mountain ranges. If some forests or clusters of trees happen to be there also, the illusion is greater and more misleading yet. However, it is only by comparison that this country deserves to be called a plain, for its surface is greatly diversified by long bands of primitive deposits, by depressions, gullies, small mounds, accumulations of sand and gravel, spaces crisscrossed by lakes, ponds, and swamps. The latter are invariably bordered by trees that fires cannot approach. Although the general outlook and the apparent surface are not spoiled by these irregularities, they do make the country broken and varied for the traveler.

The first flower we pick [*in the spring*] is coltsfoot. A few days later other species are in full bloom, especially white anemones [*probably pasqueflowers*], which are the most abundant.

Vegetation consists mainly of a few herbaceous plants, moss, and some flowering dwarf-sized shrubs. The fox was the only animal we saw. Hawks, gulls, plover, and phalaropes make up the list of birds encountered in these cold and barren plains. But as we passed along the edge of the island, we disturbed some deer, elk, geese, cranes, gulls, and some swans which were all eating peacefully near the shore.

LAKES AND SWAMPS OF THE
MISSISSIPPI HEADWATERS

Kâbékanâ [*Kabekona*], Muddy [*Mud*] Lake, etc. These stagnant waters are occupied by a large quantity of vegetal matter of a pulpy, tender, and spongy consistency decomposing very easily. Each winter a portion of this vegetation dies. Gravity attracts it to the bottom where it forms a thin layer. The following year another layer settles upon the first and so on.

The substances undergoing the laws of chemical decomposition turn into a compost, the density and homogeneity of which varies in quality and perfection with the age of the deposits. It is therefore clear that the peat is the function of the nature of the sedimented vegetation and that the older the layers, the more difficult it is to recognize the plants having given off the compost.

Wild waters penetrating a river bed increase the volume of the latter, causing the water to overflow into the adjacent flat lands on either side. The greater the surface of the land flooded, the less the depth of the water and the greater the number of obstacles it encounters. The current is then slowed down and the waters deposit the substances suspended in them, building up a thin coat of sediment. But in the river bed where speed is maintained the sedimentation cannot take place in the same way. These phenomena occur each time the river floods its surroundings, causing borders to rise. The more floods there are, the greater the height of these borders.

The application of these principles explains the different stages in the secular developments of nature that are to be seen in the regions around the sources of the Mississippi. The effects can be traced back to the first time these forces were applied to the rivers and lakes that flooded the shallows, steppes, or marshes that compose the region from Lake La Biche [*Itasca*] on down through Lake Travers [*Bemidji*], Cass, Winnipak [*Winnibigoshish*], Eagle Nest Swamp, Oak Point and so on, to Pakégamâg [*Pokegama*]. However, such an analysis should not be limited to a single zone; to carry it out one should apply a philosophical approach which, lacking observations made during centuries, employs extrapolation, which is what the astronomers apply in their research into the physical constitution of the universe, as do agricultural engineers when they want to determine the progress of a forest. It imports little to know the absolute age of the individual item; determining the laws of their relative ages and of the development of their growth is enough.

With regard to the low-lying places I have just mentioned, they are still undisturbed and they present in full development the forces which unite to form a postdiluvian land before our very eyes.[1] Gravity, water, and wind carry off the debris originating from destructions caused by the same forces upon previous formations, and transform liquid basins first into marshy prairies, then into valleys irrigated by creeks, finally into hills covered with forests.

A large lake covers a region with pure deep water. At the limits of its empire begins the kingdom of vegetation. It has its tributaries

[1] This and other references to a postdiluvian epoch reveal that at the time of writing Nicollet still accepted the neptunian geological theory propounded by Abraham Gottlob Werner — a theory he was later to abandon in favor of the more modern stratigraphic approach. See Bray, in American Philosophical Society, *Proceedings*, 114:37–59.

and it also pays its tribute. A rock rolls into it, a tree topples over, an animal dies here, a butterfly, an insect, a speck of dust drop upon it there. The deed is done; an invasion has been launched; the empire of these waters is forever upset; the equilibrium of the waves is broken; a new order shall prevail and dwell on forever.

This incident has caused a certain place in the bed of the lake to rise. But this rise also happens to shelter a mysterious seed. The seed finds this environment favorable to its development. A living stem appears, grows, conceives, and dies. A family succeeds it; it also grows, multiplies, and dies. Generations follow and they too multiply. So the first stem becomes a plant with several stems, and the plant then becomes a cluster composed of several plants. More clusters appear near the first one; each one increases its domain; the domains link up, unite, and before long form a submarine kingdom thriving at the expense of the waters.

However, this kingdom is still concealed from the world. Its existence is due to an incident. Another incident can now destroy it, so it must be reinforced. Neighboring territories will supply the reinforcements, and among the new families sailing in on the wind there soon appear and thrive those that are dominated by rushes and reeds. The latter, subject to the same laws, soon call for willows and all kinds of shrubs with berries. Then comes the turn of the ruling trees, and they too settle and become natives of the new empire. Among them are those that draw life from humid soil, those that only like the freshness of water, and so on, and the time comes when there is no more lake. Its dazzling waters have shrunk to the size of a silvery ribbon flowing through green fields carrying life and fertility among the families that overran its domain.

Then all is in readiness for the arrival of the king of the earth. He shall appear with a hatchet, a plow, and his domesticated animals. The hatchet will thin out the forest, the plow will cut through the soil, and the animals will trample and crush the ground, causing it to lose its saturated, spongy quality. Stray dirty waters will drain away down the steepest slopes. Ferocious wild animals will flee, dangerous reptiles will perish, bloodthirsty insects will scatter, the air will be invigorated, and sanitary water shall be drawn from wells. Finally, nature's own strength will be multiplied and with man's triumph, civilization shall rule.

Such is the admirable rotation of phenomena we are witnessing today as it takes place on both shores of the Mississippi, rapidly and magically. In a few years many lakes, marshes, and ponds will have disappeared following man's first intervention with nature. Such is also the impending destiny of the region I am describing. The generations of the coming century, if my map ever reaches them, will no doubt disbelieve the things it shows as being the facts of today. It is necessary to make haste in order to take nature by surprise while it is still in a quasi-virgin state and while the consequences of its laws are still open before us. In this respect, the Mississippi, as it flows from its sources to the Gulf of Mexico, generously displays the various stages of its postdiluvian formation — so generously that one could not have made better observations had one been there in the course of the ages that followed the last general upheaval sustained by our planet. It was this great catastrophe that initiated the new equilibrium regulating today's natural forces. Because of the vast spaces abandoned to the action of the forces unleashed by vegetal soil and landslides, soft and salt water erosion, dune formation, etc., the geologist can properly observe with more chance of success the various postdiluvian terrain formation along the shores of this river. [This is particularly true of] Leech Lake, which some day will be divided into two sections by a growing stretch of land forming a strait that links the main body of the lake to the northwest with the southwestern bay, and also of Muddy Lake, two thirds of which has already been taken over by vegetation, and Eagle Nest's great savanna, and all the land stretching from Pakégâma to Sandy Lake ready as of now to be exploited by the farmer.

LEECH LAKE

The perimeter of the lake is at least 160 miles. Twenty-seven rivers empty into it coming from every direction on the horizon. Only one river flows from it to join the Mississippi; its name is Leech Lake River. There are nine large bays and very many small ones. There are six large capes and many small ones. The population exceeds 1,000 inhabitants, more than 200 of which are warriors.

The soil on the shores and around the lake is fit for the best of farming. It can be tilled to produce food in small or large quantities. There are several types of clay, some of which are very fine, either mixed with talcous rock sand or superimposed on it, but always covered with a layer of vegetation that is occasionally very rich. The forest trees are of healthy growth and some are very old. They do not seem to be as susceptible to the disease which afflicts the trees of forests farther south and west. Elm; hard and soft maple; red, white, [*one word illegible*], and other oak; red and yellow pine; spruce, larch, balsam, cedar, basswood, birch, poplar, ash trees, and above all, the sugar maple. Small trees are also plentiful: wild plum, wild pear,[2] and cherry trees; blueberry, blackberry, raspberry, and hawthorn bushes.

The lake has an overabundance of leeches, hence its name, *Kahsuguswâyema-kâg*, meaning where leeches are to be found.

The lake contains whitefish, tullibee, the *mushkonoshâ*,[3] jack fish, pike, sucker, pickerel or golden carp, and other species. Game — several kinds of ducks, bustard geese, pelicans, loons, gulls, fish hawks, bald eagles, wolves, bears, fishers, muskrats, minks, raccoons, foxes, martens, porcupines, ground hogs or woodchucks, weasels, red, striped, and flying squirrels, and three species of turtles, one of which is ten to fourteen inches large.

The climate is conducive to good health, winters being less subject to sudden and frequent changes than in the northeastern states. The seasons are regular. There are one or two hail storms in July every year. There are occasionally some tornadoes, but seldom.

The bays of the lake and the shores of rivers supply great quantities of wild rice. At harvest time the Indians venture with their canoes into the rice paddies. One harvester scoops the head of rice over the boat while another shakes it, causing the grain to fall into the canoe.

5. *Notes on the Beliefs and Customs of the Indians*

[*These fragmentary memoranda, questions, and observations were found among Nicollet's papers in the Library of Congress. They are unconnected, undated, and often unfinished, yet they supplement in many ways his more structured essays and strikingly reveal the direction of his thought.*]

Notes to be used when examining the following points:

[2] Nicollet wrote this name in English. Exactly what kind of shrub he meant is not clear.

[3] Baraga (2:224) spells this *mashkinoje* and defines it as "a kind of pike."

1. Before meeting the whites, did the Indians of North America ever know or practice a doctrine, idolatrous or superstitious deserving of the name Religion?

2. Did they ever acquire an exact notion of property, of what is yours or mine, of bartering, contracts and treaties?

3. Is their cruelty bred by vengeance? Have they ever known this passion? Their cruelty, is it not rather the inevitable result of mores stemming from the necessities of man reduced to the state of nature?

* * *

Since the natives have no notion of government, of political organizations, or of law we cannot apply our concepts to them and say that they are republicans, democrats, demagogues, radicals, or agrarians. They simply abide by the law of nature. Thanks to nature, all that exists breathes and lives. Man must also dress and seek shelter. Earth belongs to man. Thus the child in a crib, the old man approaching death, a woman in pain, the idiot or the cripple, all can say, "It is mine" and "I want some," just as the young man, the warrior or the strong hunter can. But no one may say, "I want it," "I want all of it," or "I want such a portion for myself, exclusively for me."

Nature has attached another law to this common right of universal property entitling one to pleasures. It is the law of conservation and all its corollary woes. Thus he that rejoices today is well aware he may suffer tomorrow. Therefore his soul tells him, "Do unto him today as you would have him do unto you tomorrow." He goes forth and collects the fruits of the earth, keeps some for himself, able to enjoy them, and brings some to his fellow man who is in distress. Thus the native says, "I bring you to eat," not "I give you to eat." To bring, to present, to offer, to let someone take are so many entries in the primitive Indian vocabulary. To give, to sell, to refuse, to prevent from taking, to make someone pay are words unknown to them.

There is a law, a law inspired into men but of which all traces have disappeared in civilized languages. One still finds it aglow in the hearts of natives who under the influence of our ideas we treat as destitutes, beggars, wretches, and undignified beings. Woe unto the first man that brought from the depths of hell the words "to possess" and "to sell," substituting them among men for the words "I have all but nothing is mine" — words originating in heaven.

Let us reflect and meditate upon this. Never was a heart better prepared to receive the word of Christ than that of the native who is all *charity* in the Gospel's sense of the word. To the native this notion of charity is inborn, or rather, inspired. There stands another road open unto the ardors of modern apostles. May God inspire them while there is still time.

* * *

. . . . "You talk to me of your *Gizhik* above. You make me laugh. How can we go there? Where is the little path leading to heaven — *Anindi iyû mikans gizhigong enamoog?*"

There we find the worst stumbling block that the missionaries have to face. These people cannot go beyond the perceptible. This is therefore where one must begin. One must make men out of them before attempting to make Christians out of them.

* * *

The restlessness of the natives cannot be stilled. They cannot be, like civilized people, compelled to stay in a permanent residence. Neither does one dare interfere with their trade or commerce without inciting them to riot and hate. All this is based on the love of liberty which is spontaneous among the natives. We cannot without being unjust deprive them of their original right of property over the lands upon which Providence placed them by birth. It is ridiculous to suppose contracts entered into with people whose simplicity and ignorance render them incapable of contracting will ever take place, or if they do, will be honored. If some day an individual among these people is shrewd enough to claim the land upon which he was born by virtue of nature, his very claim will be founded on the fact that his forefathers had no right to dispose of it.

* * *

The greatest obstacle civilized men must overcome is the [Indians'] deeply rooted presumption that the Master of Life has dispensed among the various races of humanity all that which their nature demands — that the blessings civilized man enjoys do not apply to the Indians, who have no need for them. Although the Indians admire our advantages and recognize that they also could attain them, they say, "These things are befitting to the whites, not to us."

This very presumption supports the perpetual state of belligerency that exists between their nations. The Sioux and Chippewa cannot explain the origin of the wars they have been waging against each other for centuries except by saying that the two nations, having met as they were hunting on the same grounds, could not communicate because of their difference in language; therefore they concluded the Master of Life must have been opposed to their friendship. Hence their conviction of the necessity of mutual extermination, but also their belief in durable peace and friendship between nations having no language barrier.

The difficulty of studying the Indians in their proper environment is in direct proportion with the importance of doing it. They are jealous and suspicious individuals and they find it hard to associate with strangers or to trust them. Those who are not familiar with Indians or their language cannot live with them or go with them from camp to camp, following the vicissitudes of the seasons and exposing themselves to the deprivations and exhaustion that only Indians can overcome. The courage, physical strength, and unique perseverance that are necessary are seldom found among [civilized] men. Our literature would profit greatly by knowing more about it.

* * *

The custom or usage of each family having grounds that are recognized as theirs for hunting purposes, or for fishing and tilling, is an exclusive right.

The usage of placing corpses upon scaffoldings seems to have no purpose other than to protect the body from the voracity of the wolves. It does not appear that any religious or sentimental idea or opinion is attached to this tradition. The custom is more likely to be practiced by the Indians of the plains and prairies. Furthermore, such scaffoldings are often temporary. In this case they are used when someone dies on a hunting expedition until the family returns to the place that is considered the homeland of the deceased where his graveyard is to be found. In some cases, instead of placing the body on a scaffolding they bury it, again with precaution, so that wild beasts are kept away from it. Usually the way a dead person is to be disposed of is prescribed by the deceased before his death. If this has not been done, then the family or circumstances decide.

In general the Chippewa are prolific. There is a high rate of sterility among the Sioux. Abortions and infanticide are very frequent acts among women of both nations. Their only punishment for it consists in their being called wicked women or bad mothers. Incest of all degrees is not unknown.

* * *

THE PILLAGERS, OR LEECH LAKE CHIPPEWA

1. Their homeland is the lake. They have been there as far back as man can remember. If they go away hunting for weeks or months, they always come back. In this respect, they are neither nomads nor cosmopolites, any more than the whites who travel for months, even years on end, about their affairs. The Chippewa and all the other natives leave, taking with them their abode, their household furnishings, and their families, but always for a limited time. They return as soon as possible. The whites do not take their houses with them because they build others wherever they need to spend a part of the year. I do not know why nations are distinguished as being permanently settled people or wandering nomads. All the nations as the whites found them still have their descendants on the same soil. The only changes brought about were those imposed by war, by treaties, or the exhaustion of the land. Do we not find similar examples all over the globe resulting from the same causes, even among the most highly civilized nations in modern or ancient times?

2. Construction of their winter and summer lodges. Their utensils. Their skill at working with birch bark, with rushes and reeds from lakes and rivers. The contrast between their lodges and those of the Sioux who are their neighbors and enemies. Why?

3. Their food. Game, fish, turtles, and wild rice, an abundant natural product that grows in the bays of lakes and on the rivers that flow into them. Some Indians have begun to grow corn, potatoes, pumpkins. But the Pillagers are ready to steal whatever is not given to them. Also, during the spring season they harvest maple syrup. They live off this manna for weeks on end. Few families have enough foresight to hoard supplies for the remainder of the year.

Fishing is good all the year round, but in spring and fall it is most plentiful. Nets set up before nightfall sometimes bring in 500 to 1,000 fish the next morning. They then dry the fish and preserve it for as long as they can refrain from eating it. They also dry the flesh from the hindquarters and sides of several kinds of animals, particularly deer, and preserve this meat for a long time.

Next to food — even prior to food in the order of importance of their needs — one must place smoking tobacco. It is impossible to realize what an addiction this is with them. When I arrived among these people, they had been without any tobacco for two or three weeks, and they found themselves reduced to cutting up the stems of their pipes and their pouches impregnated with the taste of tobacco and smoking that.

4. Customs. How families give names. These names are seldom official. They only talk of their totem names which are the names of the clans to which they belong. The totem institution is one of their customs, as are the prerogatives thereof, such as: rank, inheritance, alliances, and misalliances. The outstanding clan names are: bear, swan, stork, osprey, etc.[1] An example for a boy is *Missabay*, Giant or *Niganebitank*. For a girl, Red Sky, Sky Woman, etc.

5. Marriage. Polygamy. It is limited by their means of existence. Children. Care of the newborn. Description of the crib so tastefully made and so convenient for the mother who can attend to her domestic work without losing sight of her little one. Diapering. The use that mothers make of down drawn from cattails mixed with rotten wood, dry and finely ground, to keep the child as dry and comfortable as possible. Death. Their burial rites, in the ground or above it on a scaffolding, depending on the will of the deceased or of his family, should he not have expressed his desires. The skin of a swan which is not considered sacred is also used to envelop a child.

6. Men's dress. Women's attire. Customs of war.

7. Division of work. Men make canoes, weapons for hunting and for war. Women do housework and build lodges, they fish and make fishing tackle, etc.

8. Religion. Like other native nations they have no notion of a creator, no religion, no notion of immortality. Death is a voyage to the west made by the spirit of the body. The Milky Way is the path followed by the spirit.

9. Their concept of property. Very primitive. They either give, or things are given to them.

[10.] Jealousy, revenge. An insult, an offense, or jealousy may be avenged on any person or object provided it is remotely or closely connected with the individual who committed the offense. The brothers or parents of the offended person will carry out an act of vengeance should he be unable to do it himself. Revenge can be taken even

[1] See below, Appendix 6, p. 266. For a discussion of the totem system and a list of clans, see Warren, *History of the Ojibways*, 41–53.

on a child in a crib, or on animals, by poison or homicide. I know of a prominent trader who is hated by the natives. He has children of Indian mothers on all sides. He abandoned his first native woman and their several children to go off and live with another younger one. The abandoned mother is held in very much esteem and it was all she could do to prevent her brothers from killing the trader. This poor woman never leaves her lodge without her last child and an escort lest the natives kill or poison the baby to satisfy their hatred of its father.

*   *   *

LOVE SONGS

1. When in love the young man leaving for war calls his loved one "sister." She refers to her lover as "brother."

> *Misunka dan*
> My dear brother
> *Eyache: kakishmanyanche*
> Tell me: although they make me suffer
> *Sakim outekta*
> Together we shall die
> *Eya*
> Tell me
> *manko maninan*
> on the earth marching
> *tanke*
> my sister
> *niyedo*
> this now

The warrior sings these words as he marches off to war. They express those words his mistress told him before he departed. His mistress has a mother who is opposed to their marriage and this is what she is referring to when she says, "although they make me suffer."

2. A warrior off to the battlegrounds sings that his glory shall either surpass that of all warriors or he shall die.

> *Akichita tatanka kuwamanipicha, akichita iy otan*
> *Michidākon, akichita waniche ey a mikzuyayukanpo*
> Of me a memory shall remain
> *Wicharincha kiapecha tiyata*

The elders, chiefs of the spirit among us
As the warriors march off to hunt the oxen,
I have of myself a soldier made,
Oh, you old chiefs from our land, say in remembrance of me
that there are no more soldiers.

(In their allegorical style, to kill an ox, or to hunt down the oxen
means to kill a man, to go to war, etc.)

A warrior bidding farewell to his family, wife, children, says as
he marches off to war:

A-nan-mankiroptan-yukanpo, zuy ahendi-nanji
Listen well unto me, when the party shall arrive
Kihan, onman-turte-kashtaon nanman yakironpik tache
From this one or that one you shall hear of me.

When the soldiers are posted in a dangerous area where death may
well be the outcome of their mission, they proclaim: *"Mitanchan
erpewakige,* I cast off my body." When a chief details a soldier at the
door of a white man's house or sends him with the whites to protect
them from harm, he will give him a medal or some other token of his
authority, saying unto him, "You shall sacrifice your body; you shall
cast off your body to save the whites and the welfare of the nation."
And when he sees a white man in danger he says to the soldier, "Give
him your body. *Nikanchanki wichakuwo,* give your body for them."
Such expressions are orders commonly given by chiefs to their men.

As a rule in wartime, all participants must tell the truth or expose
themselves to defeat. If a warrior sings a war song or a love song containing allusions against the wife or daughter of another, such a warrior must proclaim openly that he sings the truth. If he happens to be
slandering, the husband or the parents seek revenge at war. If on the
contrary he speaks the truth, nothing can be done to him, neither to
the wife, nor to the daughter. It is up to the husband or to the wife
to bear the affront.

3. A young girl says to her sister, "There is a young man I have
heard about and when I am out I am on the verge of tears."

Hokshidan wan iananwaron onkan chouwe danka
And my dear sister
Tankān nanwaji wache — yanonsechache
Outside I place myself — I am about to weep.

4. A warrior married to a woman who loved another warrior

without the latter being aware of it questions her about it. He wants to make sure it is the truth, if they met, spoke, and made love. She sings:

> *Kuwadan wichiwan rektache mikiyedan yahidadechin*
> Come here that I may call you near me when you have passed.
> *He takeha keyecha iwanrkakish-manyanche ehaesh*
> He says you spoke to me — he questioned me causing me distress
> *Tokhe tannriye checheyash anan unkirmbektache*
> But even if he were to say much, we shall keep it a secret.
> *Tanke heyedo*
> My sister says so.

These last words are supposed to be said by the preferred lover as he goes off to war, his thoughts being turned toward the words she must be singing in his absence.

When lovers talk to one another, or when they talk about the subject of their love, they pronounce the following words: "*Mita-wichin*, my love, my life," etc.

* * *

DANCES

1. *Ogitshida nimmiwin*. This is the dance of the braves, of the warriors, or Strike-the-Pole Dance. Women do not attend unless they were also at war and even then they do not dance, only sing. Children are not allowed. It is a public tribune for the Indians where they relate, as they single out particular events of their lives, anything passing through their minds. This is the dance they perform before strangers that have come to their country, when they wish to draw attention to themselves. They use the dance to express themselves in harsh statements.

It is danced by one or several persons at the same time.

2. *Opwâgoni nimmiwin*. Neither women nor children may participate, and here there are no exceptions. Only two persons perform, each one holding a calumet or pipestem in one hand, the *shishigwân* in the other. They use these instruments for making gestures that are sometimes quite far-fetched. It is a dance celebrating peace, or manifestations related to peace.

3. *Kamaziwin*. This is the hair or scalp dance. It is performed when the warriors return from war with scalps. All are permitted at this dance, which lasts several days. The Chippewa dance it only in day-

time, on the village square. It is a manifestation of joy which they also practice when they have prisoners. The latter are forced to attend but they are nevertheless treated well.

4. *Ôzhawânogawin*. It is a peace dance performed with the calumet. Women are allowed. It is quite a potpourri of the nation, where women make up for not being permitted to participate in the other dances in which men only can take part. It is also the dance of the lovers. Men and women at the climax take to blankets and cling together by pairs, hide two by two as they dance around the lodge, advancing in turn toward each other as they yield to voluptuous gestures that go unnoticed by the audience. At night, libertines quench the fires and the games they play become more and more mysterious. Meanwhile, other libertines, not so fortunate, revive the fires as the mysteries develop, thus throwing cheerful confusion into the melee.

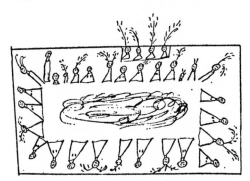

The ōzhawânogawin *or peace dance*

The liberties tolerated by this dance not only take place between the youth of the same nation, but also between members of the two sexes of two peacemaking nations, even though they are not acquainted. For the sake of the honor of the Indians, I must add that this dance has an abominable reputation among a great number of respectable Indians who do not allow their children to attend.

5. *Animooka Nimmiwin*. The Dog Dance. A family, or men, women and children who are hungry or are in need of something, gather and then go begging from lodge to lodge as dogs go wandering from door to door to find sustenance. They dress up in wolf or dog skins, imitate dogs following a scent, singing along or jumping, or walking on all

fours, yelping, barking, howling, etc. A piece of wood covered with animal fur attached between their legs completes the resemblance. When they come to the door of a lodge they sing one or two songs, enter and keep on singing. If anything is handed to them, they begin to dance by way of thankfulness, women on one side, men on the other, without mixing as they do in the *Ôzhwânogawin*. If no one gives them anything they wander through the lodge, sniffing away wherever they think there might be something they want. However, they will not help themselves to anything, even if perchance they stumble on something that had not been offered to them. After this, they withdraw and start anew elsewhere. Some members of the band carry a bag to hold gifts. They seldom fail to gather a good collection of things. A lodge really has to be stripped of everything for these beggars to come out of it empty handed. This dance is the dance of the beggars. It is more likely to be practiced by those who are not of the medicine faculty, for the members of this institution have means that are more skillful, subtle, and more dignified by which to procure their needs. These begging dogs also dance *with the dead ones*, at the graveyard, in order to obtain something from them also.[2] The parents come to answer for or give instead of their dead. Sometimes the dancers also visit the houses of the white man, if perchance there are any in the region.

The Buffalo Dance is no longer performed by the Chippewa. To witness it one must visit the nations of Missouri where this animal still exists. The Sioux from the west still practice it.

When at some of these dances the drum is allowed, the kind used is none other than the tambourine with jingles.

* * *

OHITIKA, THE TERRIBLE

Once upon a time, among the tribe of the Yanktonwannan [*Yanktonai*] there was a man born of a poor family who as long as his youth lasted remained without any parents. Orphaned, he would collect his food going begging from lodge to lodge, and when a piece of meat was handed out to him he would leave and the youth of wealthier families would tease and abuse him. One day he said to these rascals, "You ill-treat me, as I am poor, without support, and a mere child. But let me grow, and the day will come when I shall strike all of you

[2] The italics are Nicollet's.

down." And when he spoke this way, the young ones would mock him further, tear the meat away from him and give it to the dogs.

He did grow in body, but also in bravery. His first act of war was a strange one. He happened to be on the warpath with a party of fifty warriors. Having made contact with a large group of enemy braves that surrounded them on a prairie, they were forced to employ defensive tactics and dug trenches and ditches. The young warrior had already spent all his arrows as the battle raged on undecided. The other warriors of his party noticed his precision and courage and brought to him in turn their own arrows as he ran out of them. Finally nightfall brought an end to the battle and saved them. The young man, after having killed many an adversary, was the only one able to withdraw with three scalps, all three taken from warriors who had fallen on the edge of the trench into which they had penetrated in order to slay with their lances the braves within.

Back at the village, on the strength of his newly acquired reputation, he proclaimed that the time had come for him to avenge the affronts sustained during his youth. He terrified one and all with acts of violence indiscriminately committed. He struck people, killed those who had insulted him, seized wives before their very husbands, carried off daughters from their fathers' tents, kept them several days and then sent them back. He was victorious in all his undertakings, spread terror and became known as the infamous Ohitika, the Terrible. His elimination was proposed and debated. Plots were organized. One night the conspirators found him in a lodge among other people. The latter were told to run for their lives, and from outside the lodge arrows were shot into him, three of which struck home. In spite of this he came out of the lodge, stormed the assassins, killed one and chased the other away. On another occasion he happened to go to the spring where the young girls drew water. There he seized the wife of another man, dragged her by force some distance away from the camp, molested her several times and brought her back to her husband. This man sought revenge by shooting him in the head with a gun just as he was playing the circle game with some other natives. But The Terrible noticed what was happening, turned his head in the nick of time, and instead of blowing his brains out the bullet simply grazed his skull above the ear.

He recovered from this also and these miracles convinced him of his predestination and that supernatural powers protected him. He then proclaimed to the nation that he was invincible, that he could not be killed by any one of them nor by all, that thunder alone or the bear were the only spirits capable of conquering him. The tribe felt that it was useless to try to destroy him; they resolved to tame The Terrible by treating him well.

A council was held, and the motion carried that a magnificent lodge would be built in his honor. It was to be the largest and the tallest one of all. It was to be well painted, richly furnished, and carpeted with dyed buffalo skins. The two best horses available were tied to his door, and the prettiest girl in the nation was brought to him as his wife. He was elected chief of the tribe. Bygones were to be bygones they promised him, and they also swore an unconditional submission to him. To avoid all sources of irritation a spokesman was attached to his person; their best speaker was selected to whom The Terrible need only communicate his orders or desires to have them transmitted at once to the people, who would comply. Under such conditions The Terrible remained happy and peaceful for three or four months. But then it happened that a young man took the liberty of saying a few words to his wife. He seized the man, tore off his hair and clothes, and abandoned him naked. His fury had been awakened, and in spite of all the consideration granted him, he became more fearful than ever.

There was a man in the tribe, a widower who had two children, twins. Although he had already been a widower for four or five years, his sorrow was such that he vowed he would mourn his wife during the rest of his life. He had no lodge of his own, for this would have entertained too many memories of his happy days. He wore his hair long and disorderly, and his face was painted black. His body and clothes were neglected and stained with dark-colored smudges. His arms and legs were streaked with self-inflicted scars dating back to the death of his wife. His only consolation was to be with his twins. He loved them dearly and never left them, and they never left him, even at night when they slept in his arms.

Wichawi waricha — the widower

Chepka — twins

A great buffalo round-up took place. It had been ordered and commanded by The Terrible.

Death Song chanted by the daughter of The Terrible as she walked through the camp after her father's death:

Oyate piyada pinondo, ohitika tedo eyapido
My nation, you shall be satisfied, for it is said The Terrible is
dead.
They raised a high mound to cover his body
And the sun shall climb over it without warming his body.
Am petu wikin tanchan aomanshte hiyayekteshni

6. Ojibway Vocabulary and Picture Writing

*[Some of the following definitions and vocabulary notes are scattered
through the text and margins of the diary and Indian chapters. Others
are separate memoranda found among Nicollet's papers.]*

Weapons and signs represented on bark.

1. *mittigwânwi* — an arrow
2. *nabagikoman* — flat knife with two sharp edges
3. *tshimokoman* — the big knife
4. *pashkizigôn* — the rifle
5. *pindakadewân* — the powder horn
   pindâssinajigôn — shot pouch
6. *wâgakwâdons-ôpwâgôn* — the small pipe-hatchet
7. *wâbozobwân-pagâmagôn* — war club, a weapon looking like the
   thigh of a rabbit
8. Another variety of the *pagâmagôn* bearing the same name
9. *pikwâkwâd-pagâmagôn* — another variety of war club. Its tip is
   a ball with the extremity of a lance planted in it.
10. *kigidookig gïedôsh ôpwâgôn* — the calumet or stem and the pipe;
    kigidookig — the stem used at the council — the calumet, from the
    verb *kigidon*, to speak in council.
11. *wâgânakibijigôn* — a branch, symbolizing war. It is a long branch
    of a tree, or a bush, two or three inches thick, curved at the top.
    Its leaves are left on it, and a lance is attached at the top. This
    symbol is posted in the canoe of the *oshkabewis* marching forth
    with a party, indicating thereby that the party is on the warpath.
    Wherever it is planted it means war. Flags are never raised beside
    this symbol because they are the emblem of peace.
12. *wâgakwôd* — ordinary hatchet, the metallic part of it
    wagakwôd-wâttig — the handle of the hatchet. In order to name

the instrument as a whole one must say, *wâgakwôd gïedosh
wâgakwôd-wâttig.*

13. Another kind of *wâgânakibijigôn* — branch of war, without a
lance.
14. The lance is replaced by the tomahawk (No. 9).
15. The birds of No. 14 are those of war. This group is used in the
councils and ceremonies pertaining to war. The branch is always
the basic sign of war. It is placed with other instruments of war
to express feelings of belligerency more strongly. However, the
flag and calumet are never placed with it.
16. *wabimoojitshagwân* — mirror
17. *shimagôn* — war lance
18. *mittigwab gïedosh pindamoo ân* — the bow and quiver
19. *migwânnikikiweoon* — the flag made out of feathers. It is the flag
of the natives, their emblem of peace always displayed at peace
rallies, but they carry it only when they do not have those given
to them by the whites, which they prefer to their own.

* * *

Tidibaon, verb intransitive. Third person imperative: *odidibaân.*
Infinitive: *didibaâm.* To twist, to braid a certain number if times, or to
bend into a spiral. Word used when referred to hair being curled, etc.

Tidiba, verb. Third person imperative: *ôdidibawân.* Infinitive:
tidibawâ. Same meaning as word above but used when referring to
animals.

Pabidigan, intransitive verb. Third person: *opabidagaân.* Infinitive: *pabidigaân.* To fold something over flat, without forming a ring
or a cylinder.

* * *

Zibiug Nimmiidiwug, the dead that dance (northern lights)
Mayi Manito, evil spirit (there is only one according to the natives).
Manito, powerful spirit, favoring you or against you. He who rules.
Kitshi Manito, great spirit
Kizhe Manito, God that is good, the charitable spirit

They never mention the *Mayi Manito* nor the *Kizhe Manito* in
their harangues or prayers. They only talk of *Manito,* always *Manito.*
Naniboyou, a character of sacred memory, sometimes called *Minabo-
jou, Michabou, Missou, Shactac.* But the *Michabou* or *Missabai* is different from the *Niniboyou* or "great hare."

* * *

Kawinâ kidawidigemissinon? — do you not want to live with me? That is to say, do you want to marry me?

kigawidigemin — I shall live with you, *viz:* I shall marry, or, I want to marry you. Both sexes use the same expressions.

My brother-in-law	— *nitta*
Thy " " "	— *kitta*
His " " "	— *wittan*
Our " " "	— *kittanân*
Our " " "	— *nittanân*
Your " " "	— *kittawâ*
Their " " "	— *wittawân*
My sister-in-law	— *ninim*
Thy " " "	— *kinim*
His " " "	— *winimson*
Our " " "	— *kinimoonân*
Our " " "	— *ninimoonân*
Your " " "	— *kinimoowâ*
Their " " "	— *winnimoowân*

The words meaning: "to marry," "to get married," are the same as "to live together": *widige* — *widigen* — *widigem*, or let us say the verb is the root of the words used. Get married: *wiwin* (this is said to a boy), from *wiwôn* — wife. Get married: *ônabemin*, from *ônabemon* — her husband. (This is said to a girl.)

* * *

Anishmano — that's what it is
Shibayabemsigon — telescope
Piwabikû Sibiwisens — Little Iron River
Piwabikû Sibi — Iron River
Apawaika Sibi — Rush River
Mashkigi Minikani Sibi — Cranberry River
Shishkawekanig Sibi — Fish River (some kind of fish)
Shishkawekanig Sibiwisens — Little Fish River
Miskwi Minikan — Raspberry River
Wekwâ Kichi Gummi Sibi — St. Louis River, or Fond du Lac River
Wekwâ Kichi Gummi — Fond du Lac
Pakwai — rushes (cattails)
Dashôn — come here!

* * *

THE TOTEM

My totem — *nis todem*
Thine " *kidodem*
His " *ôdodemôn*
Our " *kidodeminân*
Our " *nidodeminân*
Your " *kidodedmiwâ*
Their " *ôdodemiwân*

Some Wild Rice Chippewa Indians, living on Snake River and Yellow River and on the Pâkégama informed me of the following details on totems:

He that is of the sturgeon totem says his closest relatives are the *Nibanabe* family. This is the name of a fish who is half man, half woman, living in the depths of Lake Superior without ever revealing itself to mankind.[1]

He that is of the bear totem says his closest totem parents are the bear totems of all the species upon earth, and also of a mysterious bear, an invisible one, dwelling in the abysses of the earth, called *Manito Pabidiganowe Mâkwâ*, the bear that has a spiraled tail like a shell.

* * *

ELEMENTARY CHARACTERS

They use this figurative language strictly for their needs as they travel or hunt or wage war in order to make known their whereabouts and the events they witnessed, to show where they came from, where they are heading, and what they plan to do, and to tell of the things they saw, etc. They mark all these things at the confluence of rivers, on lake shores, on portage trails, always in the most conspicuous places, along the paths traveled most by passersby who are carriers of these dispatches. The system consists in informing of one's position or where one may be overtaken.

Two rods, a few handfuls of grass, a piece of tree bark and a knife for engraving on the bark—those are the only things they need.

1. A rod planted straight up indicates the present. The objects placed before the rod pertain to things of the past; the objects on the

[1] Warren (*History of the Ojibways*, p. 44) gives the name of this clan as *Ne-baun-aub-ay*, which he defines as Merman.

other side placed in a given direction refer to the future. The direction to take one must read or derive from such indications imprinted on bark, on the ground, or on trees, etc. It is always indicated by clues such as marching animals or men or heads oriented in a certain way or the course of a river, etc.

2. A second rod is planted next to the vertical one. It is always at an angle with the vertical one. Its purpose is to show the route followed after leaving the place where the two rods are planted in the ground. Thus when a Chippewa finds two rods planted as follows at the confluence of two rivers, he will immediately conclude that those who passed there had ascended the river.

Although there is no indication as to where they came from or who they are or what they are going to do, his geographical knowledge of the region, his experience of the families that dwell in it, the customs of the nation, will allow him to infer many more things than those revealed by the two rods.

3. Indians count days by counting nights, add up the number of days traveled by adding up the number of times they pitched camp. The association of their notion of camps with the places on which they are pitched is the accurate method they use to determine time or the number of days from one date to another. They will say, "I have been gone from my family for a long time. I slept so many nights at such and such a village, and I camped so many times on my return." In order to register a certain number of nights at the rods mentioned, they gather up some hay and attach it to the rods, making as many rings as there are nights to express. Thus a Chippewa discovers two rods planted in the following fashion:

He will conclude: they slept three nights at camp A, the place they are headed for is oriented AB, and they are to camp twice before reaching their destination.

4. Should a child or a member of the party die while they camp, they will announce this by cutting a ring into the bark of the rod and blackening it with charcoal. The other nights at the same camp will be marked with hay as usual. One can see here, counting from the bottom up the marks on the vertical rod, that they camped four nights in A and that on the second night they were struck with grief. They left and shall return to the same place after camping five times.

5. If they have additional news to communicate besides these rudimentary signs, they use birch bark.

These signs represent a war party being mustered; it shall depart at the new moon; its chief is of the bear totem. Barks such as this one are posted everywhere by travelers who already know about the event. *Oshkabewis*, especially as they are fulfilling their mission, never forget to do so.

This means a white man took two nights to reach the camp and that he will spend one night there. It will take him two nights to go to the lodge. He will spend two nights there and will camp once on his way back to the same place.

Good news at the fort.

The bear and eelpout three nights ago left a son and a daughter in their lodge and took a son with them. They went to the two lakes where they are drying the meat of a deer killed by the husband.[2]

He that dwells at the two lakes is gone to fetch his canoe. The length of his trip is equal to the first quarter of the moon. He has already camped twice and must do so three more times before reaching the location of his canoe where he will spend a night.

[2] This was apparently an actual message copied by Nicollet. See p. 144. His reference to the eelpout totem is discussed in a footnote on the same page.

Nin — That is me. Friend.

Shagashkin — stoop down. Third person — *shagashki*. Infinitive — *shagashkin*, to stoop down in order to hide.

Pazigwin — stand up. Third person — *pazigni*. Infinitive: *pazigwim*, to stand up, to show oneself.

It took four men one night to reach the place where they rested for a night. They left at daybreak and will travel three nights to reach the fort where they will spend two nights.

He that is of the marten totem has killed a male deer.

Camped three nights. Left at dawn and will camp twice before reaching our destination.

Camped one night. Left at noon and shall return at the new moon.

6. When they wish to pass along information about the past, present, or future, on a number of persons, on their names, sex, whether they are traveling over land or on water, if they are on the warpath, or hunting, fishing, etc., they engrave all this on a piece of bark posted in an obvious place on the end of a stick planted in the ground. In these cases they inscribe the vertical and inclined rods on the bark and no longer use them on the ground as they did in the preceding cases. Here are now the conventional rules they observe:

The vertical rod, marked on the bark, indicates the present and the geographical site where the bark is placed. The inclined rod refers to the future or indicates the direction where the event will take place after having left the site. The side of the vertical rod opposite from the side of the inclined rod is used to mark the events that took place before reaching the place where the bark is posted. The nights, or camps, are indicated by little notches across the rods in imitation of the rings of straw tied around the rods when the latter are used instead of bark. Wherever notches are marked on a piece of bark, they indicate nights or camps. Since these marks are made with the tip of a blade or of some other hard utensil, they are colorless. Thus, should they wish to inform of their grief or of their happiness they color them either in black or in red.

To demonstrate what is said above, suppose we find a piece of bark with the following marks posted on the edge of a river:

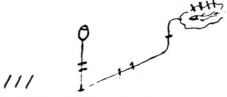

There is no indication here of the name or the number of persons involved. Whoever engraved the message, the fact the bark was posted along a river is an indication the people came over water. Further indications demonstrate they camped three times before reaching the place where they planted the bark; that they spent two nights at this place and left the next day at dawn. Furthermore the bark was planted in such a way that its flat surface pointed toward inland. On the bark we can see the inclined rod showing the route and the number of camps the people had in mind on their way to a lake where they will fish four days in a row. If instead of fish they had drawn a duck or an otter this would have meant they were going to hunt.

[7.] The osprey in front of the canoe, the eelpout in the rear camped there one night. They left at dawn with the intention of camping one night halfway to the lake where they will spend three days duck hunting.

At the new moon a man will go, or went, to the fort. He will return, or has already returned. This man is in mourning. The bark of both rods was blackened with charcoal or powder. The duration of his journey is indicated.

A white man married to a bear woman leaves their son in the lodge marked by the letter A. They reach a camp two nights later. They spend two nights there, leave at dawn, camp once more, and go to the first lake. They stay two nights there, then another three nights on a second lake, and camp thrice on their way back to their lodge.

Four men on the warpath will reach the two lakes at noon.

The osprey woman married to the bear man lost her son and buried him there.

A chief is buried there. He was asking for war.

1 camp — *kabêshiwin*
2 camps — *nizh kabêshiwinun*
3 camps — *niswi kabêshiwinun*
1 night — *ningodogoon*
2 nights — *nizhogoon*
3 nights — *nissogoon*

    8. They trace on the bark the number of canoes which form a

traveling party and mark the number of persons in each canoe. If the party is traveling overland, they mark the number of men, women and children it is composed of.

9. When they wish to indicate who the people are they draw their totem that can be an animal or some other object. Often, when they are making haste, they do not draw the persons but simply inscribe their totems.

The following signs:

First quarter   Full moon   Last quarter

The full moon sign is composed of the new and last quarter signs juxtaposed. By these signs they refer to the time or duration of the period expressed by the sign, not to the astronomical moment when the period of time starts.

These signs are used to indicate the period of time at which they arrived or left, but not the hour. They [the Chippewa] do not know the four periods of the lunar month we call new moon, first quarter, full moon and last quarter. They watch for the return of the moon, the new moon, and start then counting another month. But they do not take into consideration the exact time of the new moon. They are content with the observation of the moon's crescent to the west with its tips turned east. When it appears in this position they say the month is new.

When the bark on which they mark these signs is placed on the tip of the vertical rod, they are referring to the time at which they left camp. They never indicate the time or the hour at which they arrive. Their daily travels are always calculated in such a way as to arrive in time to pitch camp for the night.

If the bark showing one of these signs is attached to the inclined rod, this means they are referring to the time at which they will reach their destination. For example: [Nicollet seems to have omitted something here.] . . . they find everywhere in their country and which they always carry with them in their canoes since they invariably take rolls of bark to build a lodge or at least some kind of shelter when necessary.

Thus to mark the time of day, they draw the sun in the following manner:

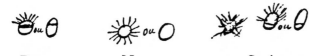

| Dawn | Noon | Setting sun |

The line crossing the disc is above the center for the rising sun, below for the setting sun. They then draw rays around the disc above the horizon. Sometimes they omit these. If they wish to be more precise regarding the time of day, they draw lines at distances from the center varying with the time of day. Examples:

9:00 A.M.   3:00 P.M.

But they seldom use the three divisions of the day indicated above.

 Rising sun. The top part of the disc (of the sun) appears above the horizon.

 Setting sun. The lower part of the disc hides below the horizon.

These signs mark the hour of departure or arrival.

Kikaigen — imperfect, third person, *kikaige*. Infinitive, *kikaigem*: to mark something, to inscribe a bark, or also to indicate or say where one is going, to communicate news, etc.

Kikaigon — a mark, an inscribed bark giving information. Plural: *kikaigonun*.

INDEX

Index

279

Portage Lake, 110, 235
Portages and portaging, Mississippi River routes, 26, 34, 47, 59, 60, 62n, 63n, 67, 69, 71, 72–74, 87, 104, 110, 122n, 124, 129, 131; described, 96–99; St. Croix River, 144-147; Brule River, 146, 147, 150, 151
Portier, Bishop Michael, 232
Prairie au Jeu de la Crosse, 40
Prairie du Chien, Wis., 11, 13, 27, 78, 215n
Prairie River, 129, 236, 242
Prairies, 253; described, 244–246
Pug Hole Lake, 71, 236

RAINY LAKE, 130, 236
Red Cedar Lake. See Cass Lake
Red Cedar Lake River. See Cedar Creek
Red Cedar River. See Goose Creek
Red River of the North, 101, 104, 236
Reed River. See Rush Creek
Remur, Simon Bruté de, 230
Renville, Joseph, trader, 38
Renville, Victor, death, 38n, 52
Rice Creek (Anoka County), 32, 34, 236
Rice Creek (Itasca County), 124, 236
Rice Lake, 124, 236
Rice River, 139, 236
Ripple River, 139, 236, 242
Rock Creek, 143, 236
Rock River. See Little Rock Creek
Rocky Creek, 41
Rocky Run, 151, 236
Rogers, Henry D., geology professor, 7
Rosati, Joseph, 227
Round Lake. See Upper Hay Lake
Roussain, Eustache, trader, 153
Royal Observatory (Paris), Nicollet's astronomy work, 1–3
Rum River, 242; name, 36, 236
Rush Creek, 143, 237
Rush Lake, 68, 237
Rush River, name, 237, 265

SAGATAGAN, Chippewa Indian, 41
St. Croix Falls, 32, 142
St. Croix Lake. See Lake St. Croix, Upper St. Croix Lake
St. Croix River, 237, 242; Nicollet's

journey, 26, 141–149; Chippewa chiefs and villages, 78n, 143, 145, 146; fish dams, 145, 146; sources, 147
St. Francis River, names, 37, 237
St. Louis, Mo., 23, 24, 25; Nicollet in, 6, 7, 9, 27, 59n; history, 7
St. Louis River, 26, 132, 237, 265
"St. Peter's," steamboat, 9
St. Peter's River. See Minnesota River
Sâkis River. See Sauk River
Sand River, 144, 237
Sandy Lake, 116, 134, 137, 249; Chippewa band, 45, 78, 82, 138; Nicollet at, 135–138; fur trade, 135, 152; name, 227
Sauk Indians, name, 38
Sauk River, 38, 39, 237, 242
Savanna Portage, 26
Savoy, France, Nicollet's birthplace, 1
Scalping, Chippewa customs, 168–174, 180; Sioux customs, 172; dance, 258
Schoolcraft, Henry R., explores Mississippi River, 5, 8, 13, 16, 18, 53n, 81n, 94, 96, 108n, 109, 110n, 121; Indian agent, 5, 12, 13, 15, 18; on St. Croix River, 144, 146n, 147
Schoolcraft Island, described, 100, 102
Schoolcraft Lake, 95n
Schoolcraft River, 94, 95n, 242; described, 107; names, 238
Shagobe. See Chagobay
Shagobai. See Chagobay
Shakopee, Sioux village, 32, 44
Shells, sacred, 203n, 205, 206
Sibley, Henry H., 19n; trader, 10, 15, 24, 25, 26; lake named for, 238
Sibley Lake, 60, 238
Siegfried Creek, 100n
Silver Creek, 37, 238
Sioux Indians, 21n, 163, 253, 254, 260; at Fort Snelling, 11, 12, 23, 24, 25; 1825 boundary, 11, 26, 78; warfare with Chippewa, 11, 31, 38, 44–46, 52, 78, 81n–83, 159, 173, 174, 178, 179, 180, 210, 252; rob Nicollet, 16; villages, 32, 44, 45, 173, 174, 210, 211n; scalping customs, 173; use of porcupine quills, 181; tattoos, 190; medicine ceremonies, 208n, 209–211; tribes, 210n
Sioux Portage, 144
Six Mile Brook, 119, 238
Six Mile Lake, 119